# M.C.C.

## The Autobiography
## of a Cricketer

# M.C.C.

## The Autobiography
## of a Cricketer

# COLIN
# COWDREY

HODDER AND STOUGHTON
LONDON SYDNEY AUCKLAND TORONTO

# Acknowledgments

FOR SOMEONE SO immersed in the game as I have been, when it came to putting my story down on paper I found it difficult to see the wood for the trees. I am grateful to Ian Woolridge, a rare journalist in the modern idiom, for gathering up the threads of my story and guiding me with a framework. In the closing overs I felt the need for a contemporary cricketer to look over my shoulder, and I am indebted to Tony Lewis for providing some finishing touches.

I count myself fortunate to have had the interest and support of my publishers, Hodder and Stoughton. The Attenborough family, Philip and Michael, together with their father John, have been the keenest possible followers of Kent cricket fortunes and have supported me all the way. I am delighted that they have undertaken the publication of this book.

It was typical of their painstaking care that they assigned Amanda Hamblin as my personal custodian of grammar and punctuation. This was an inspired stroke, and I thank her for her skill, not to mention her stamina.

Finally, I must acknowledge a great debt to Mary Ady, who has cheered and chivvied me, with infinite patience, and spent many hours typing the manuscript of this book.

# Illustrations

With Sir Alec Douglas Home
With Frank Woolley and Leslie Ames[8]

*Between pages 192 and 193*
Kent, after winning the county championship in 1970[2]
The Kent team toasted by Edward Heath[2]
Victory celebrations after the Benson and Hedges Cup Final[1]
With the Duchess of Kent and Asif Iqbal[6]
Knocked unconscious and bowled by Andy Roberts, Basingstoke, 1974[9]
Three uncomfortable moments in the second Test against Australia, Perth, 1974[9]
A warm gesture from Melbourne Cricket Club in 1975
Discussing golf with Brian Huggett[10]
Inspecting the wicket with Harry Secombe[11]
With my wife and sons after receiving the CBE[1]
Batting in Canterbury, Kent v. Somerset[9]
The England ladies' team putting me under pressure
Christopher Cowdrey making his first run at Lords[2]

## ACKNOWLEDGMENTS

[1] Press Association
[2] Central Press
[3] Sport & General
[4] Associated Press
[5] *Sydney Morning Herald/Sun/ Sun-Herald*
[6] Keystone Press
[7] *Kent Messenger*
[8] *Kentish Gazette*
[9] Patrick Eagar
[10] J. H. Benson
[11] G. Warmurst

## Lord Harris: Letter to *The Times* 2 February 1931

... "You do well to love it, for it is more free from anything sordid, anything dishonourable, than any game in the world. To play it keenly, honourably, generously, self-sacrificingly, is a moral lesson in itself, and the classroom is God's air and sunshine. Foster it, my brothers, so that it may attract all who can find the time to play it; protect it from anything that would sully it, so that it may be in favour with all men." ...

# Foreword

I WAS delighted when Colin asked me to write a foreword for his autobiography—apart from our long friendship and the fact that I am Christopher's godfather, I may well have been asked because in all our hours together at the crease I never once ran him out!

It was always a joy to bat with Colin, appreciating his wonderful sense of timing and the fact that he always seemed to be in the correct position to stroke the ball to the boundary. Not for him the power play—it was the full face of the bat with ease and grace. I am afraid I could never understand how any selectors could consider leaving Colin out of the side whatever duration of the game was involved— as for ever asking him to bat down the order after batsmen who weren't worthy of buckling his pads—I just could not comprehend it.

Colin's wonderful sense of timing, to which I have referred, made him in my humble opinion ideal to open the innings, and England prospered when he and Peter Richardson, and he and Geoff Pullar were so successful. However, he made it clear that he did not enjoy it and that was that.

Cricket and fortune have certainly inflicted many slings and arrows on Colin over the years, and watching intently from the sidelines, he has had my sincerest sympathy. If his untimely injury after the triumph in West Indies had not materialised then it is reasonable to assume that he would have been captain in Australia, which would certainly have been his just reward. However he has shown by his great love for cricket that he wanted to continue playing and has shown himself able to treat those Impostors— Triumph and Disaster—just the same.

I must mention briefly our memorable stand at Edgbaston in 1957 —in particular his steadying influence on me when I was charging down the wicket and trying to hit everyone into the car park. I recall that he calmed me down and said that occupation of the crease was the vital requirement!

I have heard from Colin's detractors that he was unable to make up his mind and if only he had been more ruthless in his approach then he would have achieved much more. Of one thing I am certain.

If this had been the case, he would not have had such a great and deserved affection as he now enjoys. As he says himself in his book, "the quiet way has always seemed to me to be the right way to carry one's talents".

Every possible good wish to you, Colin, for the future, and may I echo cricket's gratitude for what you have done.

PETER MAY

# I

The English summer of 1975 glowed with sunshine almost from start to finish; the ground was firm underfoot and the season generous for batsmen. It was not the time to talk of retirement, yet by June I knew, and duly announced, that it was the right moment to end my full-time playing career when September came around.

To arrive at that decision I had to interrogate myself many times. Was I getting enough cricket with Kent to continue? Sometimes I was low down the batting order, other times it was right to make way for younger players. Would I be able to emulate Jack Hobbs who scored a hundred hundreds after the age of forty? He was lithe and slim, played six days a week with a day's rest every Sunday. I was forty-three, as fit and keen as ever I had been, but I was not getting enough regular cricket to keep tuned. I wanted to play on for ever, but would it really be fun? There were no more peaks to scale in the international field. Yes, of course I would like to have got more runs in Australia for MCC during the previous winter, but I felt that I had justified the call. I would be finishing at the top.

What about my business prospects? That was a pertinent question. There had been so much talk of unemployment and crisis in the national economy, surely I must make my move before I was too old and it was too late. The same financial difficulties were bound to affect County Cricket. Were those letters truly representative of the majority, the ones which pleaded with me to stay on? Was I deceiving myself in thinking that the vista of first-class cricket ahead of me was alluring as it always had been?

Again, I shrank from the possibility of being asked to stand down. I had visions of Bryan Valentine, one of Kent's best captains and a close friend, being assigned to take me on to a golf course and drop the gentle hint that it was time to finish. He would not have enjoyed it either.

Understandably, all these imponderables spun around in my head. Yet when it happened, when I made the decision, there was no ache and no recrimination. I thought it would be much more difficult.

So I suppose it was a cool decision about a game which had driven me on over twenty-five years with feverish enthusiasm. But now that I have made the decision, how can I accept the consequences? Each year, driving home through the country lanes of Kent after the last match in September when the corn is down, my enthusiasm is rekindled for the next season. I have not lost that enthusiasm.

Just a few months before retiring I battled out five of the six Tests for England against Australia, facing the forbidding pace of Dennis Lillee and Jeff Thomson. In my final Test innings, Dennis Amiss went to Lillee first ball. I joined John Edrich in light which was barely fit for top-class cricket. Edrich played and missed many times, but for me everything was absolutely right on that day. My feet moved quickly into good positions. I avoided the dangerous balls, fenced off others—not a wrong move and England were safe for the morning. I will not forget the second ball from Max Walker the next morning which rose sharply to touch my batting glove and arrive safely in the gloves of Rod Marsh. Well, cricket is like that. Full of disappointments.

I also thought on that last drive home about the high spots ... an unforgettable 75 for Tonbridge at Lord's against Clifton when I was just thirteen years old. I had been terrified and overawed. I could not get home quickly enough away from the limelight. My first Test hundred at Melbourne on New Year's Eve, 1954. Could I ever again play better? Leading Kent to the County Championship and England to victory in West Indies; scoring a century in my hundredth Test; scoring a hundred hundreds.

At home, sometimes I sit in my armchair and see some of the triumphs glowing in the blazing log fire. Yet quite suddenly my eye is drawn to a rainy window pane, the trees swish back and forth in the cold winds, and I perceive the other side of the coin—the eternal courting of the English captaincy without ever taking MCC to

Australia; the agonies of a snapped Achilles' tendon, the poor reward of a Sunday match, which took me away from the England leadership and landed me once again in the team for Australia without the honour of leading MCC.

Also in this reflective mood I think of the life of Colin Cowdrey sometimes, almost as if it were not me at all. I have been a cricketer but so many waves have swept me into other crevices of life, bringing with them privilege, honours, hard work, pleasant people, bores occasionally and few truly private moments outside my own home. I am seen on my feet congratulating a pub for saving enough money for a guide dog to help someone without sight, and again, as President of a local branch of the Guide Dogs Association I am on the platform at morning assembly at Tonbridge Girls' Grammar School. They got enough money together to buy a dog. What a marvellous effort! It was quite something to be guest at Wandsworth Gaol one evening, showing a cricket film and answering questions, and be at the House of Commons the next night to talk to a group of Members concerned with sport about the changing cricket scene in this country. I owe it entirely to cricket that I should be invited to be the Voice of the Layman for ten minutes in Coventry Cathedral; the Prime Minister's guest at Chequers for dinner when he entertained a visiting Australian Prime Minister and to lunch with the Queen and Prince Philip at Buckingham Palace.

The Army are sending a car to pick me up to take me to speak at their cricket dinner ... What do I say to an association of architects? ... What can I say that can possibly be new to a Rotary Club? Yet there is peace, and good friends grow in a sporting community. Walking down the first fairway with my patriotic neighbour and true sportsman, Brian Huggett, is a great unburdening.

So many people have shown me kindness; I should mention just one. Every time I have visited Australia the Wesley Church in Melbourne have taken care of all my mail. On each of my tours I have spent hours there dictating, and they are happy to help. Our association began in unique circumstances. I arrived in Australia with Len Hutton's side in 1954, when I was brought a cable informing me that my father had died. Within hours I received another cable, this time from Dr. Irving Benson, the Minister, which read, "I speak for all true Australian sportsmen who share your sorrow today. We are at your elbow in Melbourne if we can help in any way."

These, and many other links, have made it a full life, extending way beyond the confines of the cricket field. There is one odd contradictory situation. How do I reconcile being a Patron of the Kent Alcoholics Anonymous with my new job on the board of the brewers, Whitbread Fremlins?

It is a full, busy life, though I am not the extrovert showman who happily wallows in the public eye. Indeed, I have always admired the unobtrusive touch. I shall never forget a game of golf I once played. My partner in a foursome, a tall, gentle man who introduced himself as Roger Wethered arrived at the tee. He puffed away on a pipe, wore a quiet country suit. There were others there with flashy trousers and huge sets of gleaming clubs. My partner carried a small bag containing a few irons and two woods. He stroked his way around that course quite effortlessly with an occasional word to me after I had landed him in bush or bunker. "Well played, Colin, so nearly a good one." He was fifty-five then, but had been one of our greatest golfers. That quiet style has always seemed to me to be the right way to carry one's talents.

In a way I see these as truly English qualities. I revere the manners and the customs which are rather scornfully written off these days as old-fashioned and typically English. In the first place I feel a strong devotion to this little island, the country that I was old enough to have played for on more than a hundred occasions and too young to have fought for once. I often drive along the Channel coast of Kent and find myself looking across to France, wondering how many Englishmen gave their lives on the other side, to preserve an England they would scarcely recognise now. I regret the lack of respect for established institutions, and the attitude which persuades third and fourth rate efforts to replace the best. The rising tide of vandalism is horrifying.

How clearly I recall the Tonbridge headmaster, Canon Lawrence Waddy calling me aside and saying: "Now then, Cowdrey, I am a busy man, but I want you to keep badgering me to play a game of rackets with you." He could not always manage it but I have a happy memory of him running towards the court from his study a quarter of a mile away, already changed, more excited than any schoolboy. Our matches would be played in earnest, but no matter what the score, he would look at his watch and say, "Sorry, I must be with visiting parents in a few minutes' time," and hare off to his study. His art was in finding time for everything and to take an interest in every-one, parent, pupil or school servant.

He was the sort of man who always has three books partly read at the same time and I once had the audacity to ask him how he could spend so much of his precious time on reading. The answer slayed me; an eternal lesson—"How can you create a new tomorrow unless you read today? A man who hasn't got time is not organised."

I have not been able to live up to that advice. I have never been as wide a reader as I would have liked. It has deprived me of much of that wisdom my headmaster possessed. I admired the way he always had time for people and I hope a little of that may have rubbed off on me. A day's cricket is full of chance meetings, and an overseas tour is positively crammed with odd conversations which means memorising names. Hurrying from the nets to pad up for an innings I would not wish to be interrupted by anyone who wanted to chat about "a friend of a friend of a friend" whom we might possibly have in common. But I have tried to find time if only to explain fully why I am so pushed for time. I would like to have been better at it.

Changing attitudes in society are naturally reflected in the cricket world, even in the game itself. The behaviour of players has changed in many ways. These days a touring side tries to dictate to the manager and captain on the matter of receptions attended or refused. At an official function there is always a temptation for us to huddle together to avoid the ear-bashings which are unquestionably in the air. Yet, how easy it is not to make the best of our unique oppor-tunities. I remember the late Duke of Norfolk asking Ted Dexter in Australia in 1961, before an official dinner, if the players had been briefed about the hosts who would be next to them at the table. "They ought to be," the Duke maintained. "Apart from the risk of being rude, just think, they may be wasting the opportunity to chat to a man who is a brilliant writer, a successful managing director or a double VC!"

The reader may therefore find it something of a contradiction to learn that I was a shy, nervous boy, with little apparent prospect of playing cricket at the top and travelling so much through the cricket countries.

Being brought up in England during wartime, without my parents who were in India, did nothing to harden my approach to adults.

I was always tucked up in some kind relative's spare room, either in Croydon, Bognor or up in Market Bosworth. I was forever expressing gratitude for their many kindnesses. I was eight when the first dog-fights were sighted just south of Croydon, and I remember those. I can also recall one of my first sights down at Bognor where I was moved for two years. I stood indoors, looking out to sea, and saw a British Spitfire gun down a Heinkel. The sight was unforgettable, as was the cutting out of the doodlebug's engine. My next haven was near to Market Bosworth, where I was to settle down on a Leicestershire farm during my holidays. Nothing could have been more isolated from the sporting life. I was just a farm boy, though uncle, a sage fellow who muttered wise old-fashioned sayings, adored cricket. He took me to see one day of first-class cricket at Leicester, where Kent were playing. Ewart Astill, the then Tonbridge coach, took me into the Kent dressing room. I laugh now to recall my first sight of Leslie Ames, the man who was to have such a bearing on my career for many years. He stood in the dressing room naked, except for his county cap which, through superstition apparently, he always put on first. However, it was the memory of the day's play that left its mark—like catching a glimpse of Everest while the sun shines through the cloud. Otherwise I trudged the farm and the country lanes, milked the cows, worked with a collection of Italian prisoners of war on the hayricks. I knew my birds, my hedgerows, and on a couple of occasions followed the hounds on foot.

So I think I have given a picture of my sheltered life. What I cannot explain is the speed with which I became a cricketer "to be watched", and never let out of sight. Of course, schools and schoolmasters play such an important role and I shall come back to that later. The fact is that within six months, from my thirteenth birthday at Christmas to July the following year, I had caught the eye of Alf Gover at his cricket school, had made a sharp impression on those who watched the progress of a little, rotund leg-spinner who batted a bit down the order, and struggled through a nervous cricket term among the senior boys in the XI to the unbelievable thrill of a long innings at Lord's. Thereafter my career took shape. I was in the Kent side when I was seventeen, the youngest player ever to receive a Kent cap; and was just twenty-one when I first played for England.

From this moment onwards I was enslaved. Cricket had entered my heart and soul. She was a mistress never to be taken for granted, she gave me her richest prizes and her cruellest lessons. There are innings I would love to play again and disappointments I would wish to avoid, but if I was given a choice as my last act on earth, it would be to walk to the wicket on the lovely St. Lawrence Ground at Canterbury in the sunshine, with the pavilion chattering and the small tents buzzing. I would then lean into a half-volley just outside the off-stump, praying that the old timing still lived in the wrists to send it speeding down the slope past cover's left hand to the old tree for four. The cover drive is the most beautiful stroke in batsmanship. Does that throw any light as to why I am a self-admitted lover of all things British and traditional? I don't know. It is certainly why I became a cricketer.

# 2

I was born into a family whose love for cricket amounted to an almost unbridled passion. To illustrate this I must go back to an evening around March 1938 when I was sailing back from India with my mother and father. They were going on leave and I was going to school. Precociousness was not exactly encouraged in seven-year-old boys in those days and I was already in bed in our cabin when they went up for their sun-downer cocktails with the other old India hands. The ship had just turned left at Port Said and was steaming westwards to a cool, green England and a Europe about to explode. I knew nothing of either and although my education was imminent, it was not to enlighten me about Hitler or Chamberlain, but about a still smaller, leaner man who, at that very moment, was overtaking us on the starboard side.

My father suddenly dashed into the cabin in a high state of excitement and called for me to come up on deck with him before it was too late. He hustled me along corridors and up companionways at such a speed that my heels barely touched the deck. At the rails he held me up in his arms for a better view of the s.s. *Strathmore* sliding into the gathering darkness. She was about three miles away, but I can remember the scene vividly, with her lights pin-pricking out her shape against the Mediterranean. What I can also recall most clearly is the change in my father's voice, for its tone, all at once, could hardly have been more reverent if he had been showing me the precise spot where Moses had delivered the tablets. He said: "Don Bradman is on board that ship. He's bringing the Australian team to try to beat England."

Sixteen years later, when I was on another liner travelling in the opposite direction with an England team to tour Australia, my father died. He had been the first major influence on my cricketing life.

The most valuable thing he ever did for my cricket was to use his ingenuity in overcoming the natural tendency of infant batsmen to slog every ball on the leg-side. He used to plant me with my back to the side netting of a tennis court and then bowl at me. Sometimes the challenge would be ten-to-win, at others twenty-to-win. But always those runs had to be gathered on the off-side. He never cared how exhaustingly he had to chase about the court in pursuit of the ball, so long as his four-year-old son was hitting into the covers or past mid-off, or even trying to cut. He also called on the assistance of a little mongrel dog called Patch who would have been a genius fielder in today's one-day cricket. Leg-side slogging brought no dividends except, perhaps, a grazed left elbow. Gradually my education widened and by the time I was twelve, I could play most of the shots. I could square-cut and late-cut and even on-drive, which is the most difficult shot for a youngster to play.

I do not think my father would have persisted with it had I not found it fun, or shown some real ability. This was no Mr. Worthington consciously drilling his son for the stage, although he was unconsciously preparing his only boy for the kind of life he would dearly have loved himself. He was a natural games player, excellent at tennis and good enough at golf to have had a low single-figure handicap had he played regularly. But his first love was always cricket into which he, too, was born. The Cowdreys were a sporty family and behind my grandfather's house at Sanderstead, in Surrey, there was a tiny ground on which an entire team of Cowdreys used to take on all-comers. We could even rustle up an aunt or a cousin who was handy with the scorebook as she was with her own housekeeping accounts.

It was from there that my father graduated to the Beddington Club, the Surrey Second Eleven and then Minor Counties cricket with Berkshire. But his father, in turn, was a shrewd judge and a realist and he could see the narrow but unbridgeable gap that separates even a good batsman from the front-rank county player. "You're not going to be quite good enough," he told my father, and put him in a bank. It must have been like caging a deer. My father went from the bank to teabroking in the City and then, in the jargon of the age, he went completely bolshy. He stomped off to India and buried himself on a tea estate, only returning on leave to marry the girl he had met four years earlier at Beddington Cricket Club. He then carried her off to India. My mother was to live there for the next twenty years and to this day I cannot say whether she liked it or not. She would never have admitted it if she hadn't, because she is a person with a very strong sense of duty.

It was there that I was born on Christmas Eve, 1932. The record books say my birth took place in Bangalore which, considering the size of India, is as near as makes no difference. Actually, it was a hundred miles to the north and several thousand feet higher up in the Nilgiri Hills. The district was called Ootacamund, which the Europeans inevitably contracted to "Ooty". I had barely eaten my first meal on earth before my father wrote off to two friends in England asking them to put my name down for MCC membership. Whether or not this gave him the idea of giving me the same initials, since I was soon to be christened Michael Colin Cowdrey, I shall never know. A number of journalists are convinced he did it deliberately but, strangely, I never once discussed it with him. He certainly had a good sense of humour, and he may well have been celebrating his relief that I was not a daughter.

He was a tiny man, about five feet seven tall, tubby, with a round face. He was rather like a compressed version of me. He also had very small hands, a characteristic I have inherited. His enthusiasm for sport never waned in the sun or the isolation, and for this I must thank him. I never went to school in India and from the time I could walk until the day we boarded the ship at Cochin to come home, there were few waking hours when I was not hitting or kicking or catching a ball of some dimension. There was a tennis court beside our bungalow and on the small lawn in front of it my father built a golf tee from which we used to play desperate Ryder Cup matches to a single green, with a hole and a flag, which he had cut out of the very edge of the jungle. I had had my own miniature clubs: a driver, an iron and a putter. The hole for him was a chip, but for me it was par five, demanding two full woods and perhaps a pitch-and-run as well before I could take my putter out. Golf featured largely in our lives before he went to work in the mornings. My mother even got one of the women on the estate to run me up a tiny outfit, including plus-fours, identical to the one in which Henry Cotton had won the 1937 Open Championship by two shots at Carnoustie. Presumably she got the idea from a picture in one of the magazines that were always about three months out of date by the time they arrived from England. The outfit must have been durable because I wore it at a fancy dress party on the ship back to England and won a prize.

When my father came home from work in the evenings the sporting syllabus turned to cricket on the tennis court. He was still a good player, for he had been chosen for the Europeans' Eleven against the MCC team that toured India, which included Arthur Gilligan and Maurice Tate. My father made 49. He was adamant that I should not idle away the hours while he was managing the 2,000-acre estate during the day. Like most of the European households we were not short of servants. There were half a dozen of them to look after the three of us and the duties of one of them, a lively teenager named Krishnan, virtually amounted to playing sport with me. If it was tedious for him to play cricket, soccer and golf with a five-year-old, he never showed it, and the friendship we forged then has survived the Raj, Independence and Partition. Thirty years later he was still writing to me letters that began "Dear Little Master ..." It was a great disappointment to me to miss meeting him again when MCC played in Bangalore in 1964, for I was flown out only for the later matches of the tour.

With Krishnan I could practise by day what my father taught me in the evenings. He was a methodical coach and I still have pictures of him adjusting my stance and correcting my grip at both cricket and golf. It was quite natural, therefore, for him to spend so much time with me; perhaps he was compensating for the long parting that was to change our relationship considerably.

It was an idyllic early boyhood, with love and security and sun and undivided attention. But apart from the sport I remember very little. There was the staggering view across the rolling tea estates from our home, perched several thousand feet up. I can recall the sudden torrential rain-storms and the grotesque ceremony that followed the only communal crisis I knew in India. A tiger, which had already savaged a number of cattle, suddenly killed a man. The villagers dropped everything to concentrate on the hunt. They dug a pit-fall and eventually trapped it alive. They then fenced in a small copse, drove the tiger into it and with much dancing and shouting speared it to death. My parents and I had to be guests of honour at this ritual execution and at its end I was presented with one of the tiger's whiskers. I still have it among the souvenirs of another sport whose alphabet I learned as the sun went down on British India.

I was too young to feel any nostalgia about leaving India. There was only intense excitement and impatience as we crossed off the days to the winding drive down to Cochin and the ship that was to carry us home. I might have been less excited and less happy had I known what was in store: the conventional education that awaited almost all the small sons of Europeans in India.

I had been to England before, at the age of one, but then returned to India with my parents when their six-month leave was over. This time I was to stay in England when they went back. I was to live with my maternal grandmother at Sutton, in Surrey, and attend a near-by preparatory school, Homefield, as a day boy. It was all neatly pre-ordained and efficiently organised. But then something happened that threw it out of gear. The Second World War started and trapped my parents in India. There was no way for them to get home, or for me to visit them. Instead of being parted from them for the normal period of four years, I did not see them again for seven. During this time, too, my grandmother died.

Before that painfully long parting we enjoyed one last summer together as a family. It was the year of Munich, mobilisation and martial music, but these things did not loom very large in our lives. The Australians were in England fighting for the Ashes and Donald Bradman, whom we had last seen disappearing into the Mediterranean night, duly scored centuries in the Trent Bridge, Lord's and Leeds Tests. Len Hutton had the last word by smashing Bradman's record with 364 at the Oval, but the series was drawn and Australia kept the Ashes. My father was totally absorbed by it all, breaking off only to play a little cricket himself. I used to watch the first few shots of his innings before going off to bat or bowl in some corner of the ground. My only other recollection of that summer which was to change my life and the world's history is my first flight, a ten-bob flip from Croydon Airport.

Then, one day, my parents were gone. They took me to school one morning and left me there. They never made any ceremony of saying goodbye but when I came out it was my grandmother who met me. She said nothing. When I eventually asked where my mother and father were she said, "Oh, they've gone to work." This was in September 1938, and I next saw them again in December 1945. It must have been a harrowing experience for my parents but they had prepared me well for the parting. I had been brought up in a non-moaning, unemotional atmosphere and I don't recall being sad or upset at what had happened. It probably never even occurred to me that other small boys were living at home in close family unity.

The reaction, oddly, did not come until seven years later when we were all united again. My parents finally got berths on a troopship back to England and landed at Liverpool just before the first post-war Christmas. I first spoke to them long-distance on the telephone and did not expect them even to talk as they did. They were strangers. When we met I could hardly believe how small they were, physically. My mother was short and my father tiny. So began a period of difficult re-adjustment. They were shy and I was shy and for the first time, around my thirteenth birthday, I was suddenly resentful at what I thought they had done to me. Thoughts which had never entered my head during their long absence began to pound at my brain and harden my attitude. "Where have they been while other kids have had their parents at home all the time? Why did they just go off and leave me?"

It lasted for perhaps two or three weeks but my father knew how to handle it and broke the barriers down. There was no cricket to watch so he took me off to watch professional soccer on Saturday afternoons. We watched Chelsea mostly, and at Stamford Bridge, engulfed in those huge, passionate crowds basking in the newly-won peace, the therapy worked. To those around us my father and I must have looked as close as Sorrell and Son.

I can only begin to speculate what turn my cricket career would have taken had the Cowdreys been together during those seven vital formative years. My father would clearly have encouraged and coached me but I doubt whether I would have spent hundreds, even thousands, of hours throwing a tennis ball against the brick wall of an uncle's house. I was the only child in the home and there was little else to do. As long as I had a ball I was self-sufficient, and the lonely catching routine in that little garden alongside a railway line could have done no harm in training eyes and sharpening reactions for future Test matches.

My father and I were to remain close friends until his death, but his cricket lessons were ended. He had taught me all he knew and my next mentor was in build, character and even prejudice, a very different man indeed.

# 3

Charles Walford was eminently Victorian. He was born at a time when Britannia ruled the waves and sent a gunboat to admonish those who raised a questioning eyebrow at her divine right to do so. Huge red tracts of the world map were administered by Englishmen whose fortitude and dedication to duty were only matched by their ritualistic mode of living. They really did dress for dinner when the temperatures were in the nineties and they did rise solemnly to toast our King and Queen, watched only by their native servants. Charles Walford, educator in the severe British tradition, taught many of those empire-builders how to read and write. He was also my first headmaster.

Forty years he rose at seven o'clock, took an ice-cold bath at ten minutes past and then appeared before his pupils to bully them into a run round the playing field before morning prayers. He was a great believer in both. He was a bachelor and an autocrat, six-foot-two tall, a ferocious taskmaster and a rigid disciplinarian who believed that child guidance was synonymous with corporal punishment. Summer and winter, weekdays and Sundays, he wore a Hawks tie. He had won a Rugger Blue at Cambridge but he was cricket mad. He recognised me as a talented cricketer and was sparing with his praise.

I first went to his school, Homefield, at the age of five and a half under circumstances guaranteed to alienate me from the other boys. I was not due to start there until the September of 1938 but as soon as we arrived back in Surrey from India, my father went to Walford with a special request for me to start during the summer term solely to join in the school cricket. The request was granted and I can still recall the perplexed looks of the pupils which clearly said: "We do all the work and he gets all the games." I cannot remember whether I distinguished myself as a cricketer or not that summer because we had not quite arrived at the point where scorebooks were kept or averages calculated. But Charles Walford's interest had been roused, and this was duly justified, perhaps, when I was applauded for scoring a century in the very first properly organised match in which I ever played. The word "applauded", I should add, is more significant than the word "century".

It was in the summer of 1940 and I was now a seven-year-old playing in an under-eleven game against another school. I must have concentrated mightily during the innings because all at once I became conscious of boys bubbling with excitement on the boundary. The words "seven more" floated across the ground to the wicket and it was only then that I realised I must be nearing my hundred. Dutifully, I made seven more runs and raised my bat with the panache of a youthful Denis Compton. All resentment of the cricketing privileges I had received two summers earlier was now forgotten. My school colleagues leaped off their seats and turned cartwheels until the respectable acres of Homefield looked like an animated Giles cartoon.

I was now very conscious that the form was to throw my wicket away in a last magnanimous gesture. This I did, racing down the wicket to let myself be stumped by a third of the pitch and running on to the applauding welcoming committee on the boundary. I had never been happier in my life. Nor, I think, have I ever been so downcast as I was a few minutes later when they re-counted my runs just to make sure it was true and discovered it wasn't. The "seven more" had been premature. The re-count established that I had made only 93. The master in charge of the match dismissed the small scorer and said nothing at all to the other boy who had tears streaming down his cheeks at the shattering disappointment of missing his century.

Walford was not there to see my innings. He was probably away with the Homefield first team. On his return, without telling me, he wrote off to the game's emeritus, Jack Hobbs, relating the story. Three weeks later I received the most carefully composed handwritten letter from the great man himself. "Dear Master Cowdrey", it began, "I take great pleasure in sending you this little bat which I have autographed. I shall be watching your career with great interest." He taught me a lesson which I have tried to remember to this day when writing to young cricketers. My headmaster, the stern and unbending Walford, was every bit as proud of the letter as I was. He read it out at the next school speech day before formally presenting it to me, together with the bat, on the platform. This rather set me off around the place. At the age of seven I was a cricket man.

From that moment Charles Walford took an intense personal interest in my career. There is no doubt that his methods and principles shaped the early development of my character. He was already over sixty when I first set eyes on him, but the memory of him even now evokes old-fashioned words like obedience, punctiliousness, truth, effort and conscientiousness. The idea that if a job was worth doing it was worth doing well was, for him, not a cliché but a concept. After morning prayers he taught classics, mathematics and scripture. After that he took sport, soccer in winter and cricket in summer. It all had to be good. He was ruthlessly tough and discipline was severe. His outlook was almost classically Spartan and he taught us to ignore the frills of life. As a boarder later I never thought about spending money on clothes or food. He also had an almost militaristic outlook which demanded subservience rather than obedience from his pupils. Bad manners were instantly punished. In fact, anyone putting a toe out of line was instantly punished. Beatings were frequent though I, personally, got few. I rarely put a toe out of line.

There was very much that was good about his ideas on education. He encouraged us to have enthusiasm for everything we did, and to read a great deal. He achieved his academic aims, for we were mostly good at our schoolwork. From the age of seven to ten I was always in the top three of my class and the only subjects at which I was a dunderhead were art and music.

Yet there was another side of Walford's style of education, and to this I probably have to attribute my outlook on many aspects of life today. The principles he taught were good but they have not left much room for manoeuvre in a rapidly changing world. Although I detest much of the shoddiness and work-shyness of modern Britain, there are other trends to which I would like to be able to adapt myself more easily. I find it difficult, for I am still trying to get rid of some of Walford's shackles. He was, I think, too tough, and although I admire the standards for which he stood, I would not like my own children to be subjected to such crushing discipline. The highest tribute I can pay to Charles Walford's curriculum is that what he drilled in apparently stays drilled for ever.

This applied to his methods of teaching cricket as well as everything else. I have said that by the time I was twelve I could play most of the shots of batsmanship, and this is true. What made it true were the evening sessions in Walford's nets, to which we were paraded like miniature guardsmen on the stroke of four o'clock on Mondays, Tuesdays, Thursdays and Fridays. His approach was every bit as ferocious as it was in the classroom. There was no warmth about it. He planted himself behind the nets to watch us bat for a while, and then came round to correct us. He might encourage the poorer players, who must have been frightened to death by it all, but it was the better players among us who got the full works. I was aware of the standard he expected from me, for immediately after my "century that wasn't" he had brought me into the school first team for one match against twelve-year-olds. I was out three times making 17 but Walford himself was umpiring and kept calling me back. When I was out for a fourth time he finally called, "That's enough." And then he said: "It's a hard game ahead. I wanted you to have a look at it. You've got a lot to do yet." I do not know whether he then regarded me as a potential England cricketer but he kept a close eye on me thereafter, and it was under his tyrannical tuition that I really learned to play. Not that I would ever have known the strides I was making from anything he said. One afternoon, when he was standing in his usual position behind the nets, I bowled a googly. Walford looked at me in astonishment. He said nothing so I did not bowl another. After ten minutes he could contain his curiosity no longer. "Cowdrey," he called, "did you bowl an off-spinner just now?" He knew damned well it was a googly but he just could not bring himself to ask me who had taught me. It was, in fact, the Sutton groundsman, Ken Harman.

It was not long after the ceremonial presentation of Jack Hobbs's autographed bat that my grandmother, then solely responsible for my welfare, decided that the war was getting too close on our doorstep for comfort. Sutton and Homefield seemed to be navigational landmarks for every Luftwaffe pilot heading for London. It was a ringside seat for watching Spitfires and Messerschmitts fight out the Battle of Britain and when Croydon was bombed my grandmother decided that merely making me sit away from the windows for fear of flying glass was insufficient precaution. It was decided that I should be evacuated to another preparatory school. Charles Walford could not hide his anger.

So to Bognor Regis I went and there I stayed for two years at a school radically more liberal in outlook than Homefield. The headmaster was a family man with children of my own age, and I was accepted and treated as one of them. There was a more balanced curriculum, and the atmosphere was more relaxed. We played cricket and football, but my cricket tended to stand still.

I was to stay there two years before returning to Sutton and almost at once my grandmother fell ill and she died in 1942. Although still not ten, I was used to the packing-case life, but this meant a vast upheaval. My base now became the home of my uncle John Taylor in Sutton; both he and my aunt, Mrs. W. Anns, were always so kind to me. I spent most of my holidays on the farm of another uncle at Market Bosworth, near Leicester, and I became a boarder during term time back at Charles Walford's school.

I cannot claim that he welcomed me back as the prodigal batsman. He isolated me somewhat, made rather miserable comments, and generally took it out on me, which I thought unfair since it had never been my idea to duck out of his school. The climax came when he finally condescended to stand behind the nets while I was batting. About every third shot I made he would click his tongue with disapproval and say: "What *have* they been doing to your cricket down at Bognor?" It was humiliating and it was a long time before he forgave me.

It is not my intention to make Homefield sound like Dotheboys Hall. I was probably happier at school sometimes than I would have been at home. At school I was living a full life, whereas at home, although there was always a welcoming atmosphere, I spent much of my time making my own fun. Walford placed idleness on a par with dirt and ill-manners. There was always something to do and something to remember, if nothing more than keeping off the holy ground of the cricket square even in the depths of December. So sacred was that turf and so small the Homefield playing field that our winter soccer and rugger coaching was confined to two narrow avenues on either edge of the ground. His soccer coaching deserves mention in passing: it was a unique combination of an Alf Ramsey training session and Trooping the Colour. Five forwards would assemble at one end of the field, advance on the command "Go", make a number of predetermined passes until receiving the orders "Centre" and "Shoot". Had we played it fast enough we might well have gunned down the Brazilians, the Italians or any other nation bereft of a long military history.

In the summer, when we were not playing cricket, Walford took us occasionally to watch it at Lord's. This in itself was a ritual, now that I can compare it with taking my own sons there some twenty-five years later. Within half an hour I am being held to ransom for ten pence for ice cream or lollies, or I have to go off to the dressing rooms for a particular autograph. At their age, under the unblinking eyes of Charles Walford, we were watching not a game but a performance of neo-religious significance. We were there to look and learn, to analyse and remember, and this required total silence.

# 4

It is interesting to look back now and attempt to analyse how Charles Walford, the paragon of Victorian standards, and an unavoidably nomadic childhood caused by my parents' absence, shaped my character. The one certainly made me law-abiding by nature, the other squashed any tendencies I might have had towards exhibitionism. Living in other people's homes meant that I could never get too boisterous. I did not even have the safety valve of being able to throw a fit of temper. I was conscious, always, of being in everyone's debt.

Most of the characteristics I developed have stayed with me ever since I have been able to recognise them in my cricket. I have never had a compelling urge to go to the wicket and bang the ball about for the sheer sake of giving an exhibition. Indeed, I have not been a good player when the going is easy, which may explain the fact that in my first fifteen years as a county player I never made a hundred against Leicestershire, Glamorgan or Derbyshire. Derbyshire, admittedly, have always had really good bowlers, but there was a period in the fifties and early sixties when the Leicestershire and Glamorgan attacks were thin.

The same outlook has haunted me on overseas tours, where the up-country matches are little more than exhibition games. Yet if someone had offered me £1,000 to turn on the kind of blazing hour's batting that Wally Hammond or Denis Compton could produce for the crowd's pleasure at the drop of a hat, I would hardly know how to set about it. I have tried to do it both intelligently and unintelligently. I have arrived at these games in good form and good humour, had a net and known enough about the opposition to realise that they simply couldn't bowl. Yet the end-product, the carefree showpiece, has almost invariably evaded me. The harder I have tried the more terrible I have been.

The first time I became really aware of this aspect of my cricket was on my first tour to Australia when we reached Rockhampton, a town high up on the coast of Queensland, whose immortal contribution to sport was to produce Rod Laver, the tennis player. Its contribution to cricket, that year, was less immortal. I had been playing pretty well in the previous weeks, the wicket was good and the opposition palpably weak. Peter May who, like Hammond and Compton, was a master at putting on exhibitions in these show-the-flag fixtures, batted beautifully for 70 or 80. I, too, played a series of terrific shots for about twelve minutes. Then I got out.

May was still in the dressing room when I arrived back. "You got out for your usual score on these occasions, I suppose?" he said. He then laughed and dropped the subject. But before the next up-country fixture he completed the remark. "Just try a bit today, will you?" he said. I asked him what he meant. "Well, you don't really put yourself out for these kind of games, do you?" It was the first time it had been brought home to me.

Even now, more than a hundred Test matches later, I cannot back myself to put up better performances in exhibition games and I cannot give a good reason why I have so consistently failed in them. I merely accept it as a characteristic, as another man might accept premature baldness, as something with which he has to live. Unless the match has provided a problem to solve, a theory to test, a hurdle to leap, a challenge worthy of battle, I have never been fully plugged in.

Most of my best innings have been fused by some problem or adversity. The problem may have been a personal one or a critical state of the match, the adversity may have been a patch of poor form or an injury. Whatever it was, these innings were usually the product of a highly tense state of mind at times when I have almost felt that I was fighting for my life.

There was my first knock for MCC overseas at Colombo when I went in half fearing that I would be unable to hit a single ball. I got 66 and the runs streaked from nowhere. There was my first Test hundred in Melbourne. There was my century in my hundredth

34

Test match at Birmingham when I was really badly injured. There was my Gillette Cup innings at Canterbury in 1968 which took us to the final. That was one of the greatest innings I have ever played but rarely, if ever, have I been in worse shape. I was hiding a variety of aches and pains and felt under considerable pressure. That morning I would have given anything to have turned my back on the ground and gone away to play a relaxing game of golf. But suddenly, after two or three shots, the ball was bulleting off the middle of the bat and I was launched into as fine a piece of batting as I have ever been able to produce. Almost all my Test hundreds, particularly, have some similar kind of story attached to them.

I have no explanation for this other than that it is the manifestation of a character shaped years ago by men like my father and Charles Walford. Occasionally it frightens me to have no control over it, particularly in more recent years when people have said: "You are the best player in England now. You should be 400 runs ahead of everyone else in the country and 15 runs clear of anyone in the averages." Sometimes, after a remark like that, I have tried to work for runs. This approach has lasted for three or four days. Playing cricket like that gives me no pleasure whatsoever. It would not give me a lot of satisfaction, for example, to build up a large total of 238 against, say, Sussex at Canterbury unless there was some real point to the exercise. A new bowler coming on when you are at 130 and suddenly whistling two or three past your ear for no apparent reason would create a fresh problem worthy of solution. Without such problems the innings, to my mind, would have degenerated into mere accumulation of runs.

This probably explains why I did not make more really big scores in a long career in the game. In the early years I tended to relax when I had made 50. It did not occur to me, in my first six or seven years, that centuries were targets worth achieving unless the team were badly in need of runs. I preferred to experiment and enjoyed taking risks.

I am not setting this up as the right approach nor suggesting that I was trying out the role of the gifted dilettante. There were amateurs at the time who played in a very different way. David Sheppard was one. He was wonderfully single-minded, always hungry for runs. Like Geoffrey Boycott, a decade later, he was a player of average talent who was determined to transform every last particle of his ability into runs. He would set his sights on ten, then fifty, then a hundred. Like Boycott, and certainly Donald Bradman, he would be ready to bat on for ever. There was a run-hungriness in Peter May, too. If Peter May was the more naturally gifted batsman of the two, make no mistake, Sheppard made himself a Test-class batsman who achieved his results the hard way.

I have often wondered whether I would have established a bigger run-scoring record had I been playing for cash in those early days. But I wasn't; I had everything that my simple needs required. The very fundamentals of Charles Walford's training had been to spurn the frills of living.

Sadly, I was to leave Homefield abruptly. My father, who was due to return to India from leave in the May of my final year at Homefield, wanted to see me settled in my new school before he left. This meant that Walford was to be deprived of his prize cricketer for one last summer. He was bitterly disappointed.

This decision to settle me in a public school in the summer term, instead of the autumn, was also to have far reaching effects on my life in cricket. Marlborough, in Wiltshire, was my father's preference but although he found it bleak and cold on the day he drove down there, it was not that which made him send me to Tonbridge, in Kent, instead. It was simply that Marlborough could not take me for the summer term; Tonbridge could. Since I had been born in India I had no qualifications so far for any English cricketing county. By going to Tonbridge I qualified for Kent. Had I gone to Marlborough I would probably have played for either Surrey or Leicestershire.

# 5

Every career has an ignition point somewhere and in my case it was not watching a giant batting but merely watching a giant walking out to bat. The giant was Hammond. Even now I could take you to almost the exact spot among the free seats at Lord's where I was sitting that sunny wartime afternoon, just another small boy in a prep-school blazer. I was waiting impatiently for a wicket to fall because the next man in was Hammond. When it happened I suddenly felt myself all alone in a private world of intense excitement. The retreating batsman disappeared from view and then came a gap in time when the whole ground was totally still. Gods, evidently, only appeared in their own good time. The first I saw of him was only his cream-coloured shirt, moving along behind the Long Room windows. And then, with the majesty of a man completely unaware of his supreme status in this world, he turned, came slowly down the pavilion steps and walked into the arena. He was not a cricketer walking out to bat but a god gracing the afternoon with his presence, and the effect on me was profound.

I would have died of fright had someone told me at that moment that I would be walking down those same steps myself within a couple of years, for at that point in my life I was honestly unaware that my talent for batting was anything much out of the ordinary. Praise had been more or less non-existent at Homefield. It was only in the three weeks between leaving there and starting at Tonbridge that I really realised I was any good at cricket. This came about when I went to Alf Gover's Cricket School and gradually became aware that I was causing something of a stir. People seemed to be taking an unusual interest in me and the two men who coached me, Leslie Todd and Andrew Sandham, were quite lavish with their praise and encouragement.

It was a pleasant sensation but it was also brief. I have no idea whether children of the television age are scared when they go to new schools but the small Master Cowdrey who presented himself at Tonbridge, founded 1553, was petrified. I felt completely out of my depth and was haunted by the fear that I would not be good at anything. My cricket reputation made life worse, for I had not been there twenty-four hours before I became involved in one of those embarrassing situations which make new boys at old-established schools only want to crawl away and hide.

I arrived on a Friday to settle in before starting work on the Monday. The Saturday was a free day and to pass the time I wandered down to the playing fields and lay on the grass behind the nets where all the potential first eleven cricketers were being carefully looked at by the cricket master and coach. The coach was Ewart Astill, formerly of Leicestershire and England and, remarkably enough, a member of the MCC team against whom my father had played in India many years earlier. I had met Astill briefly when my father had taken me down to get kitted out for Tonbridge, but what I did not know was that Alf Gover had recently written to him advising him to keep an eye on "that young Cowdrey". Astill took the advice all too literally for my comfort for he spotted me behind the nets and called me over. To my horror he said: "I'll just check with the cricket captain, but why not come and bowl for a while?" To my even greater horror the captain agreed.

I presume there could be worse moments, such as feeling your braces break at the altar, but I have yet to experience one. The first eleven men were resplendent in new flannels and boots and I was in my ordinary day clothes. All I could do was take my coat off and bowl. What came next was quite inevitable. A master in a neighbouring net, who had not heard the conversation between Astill and the captain of cricket, became apoplectic at the sight of a new boy, not even in flannels, with the audacity to join in one of the most serious rituals of the entire Tonbridge year. He gave me a look like a tracer bullet between the eyes and said: "What the hell are you doing here?" Astill, who was new to the school himself, tried to sort it out but the master was not to be pacified. I bowled a few discreet overs and faded from the scene.

This was a memorable start, but there was more to come for the small boy seeking only total anonymity until he had found his feet. On the Monday the lists of some thirty cricket teams were posted on the notice board. I could not find my name anywhere. This was hardly surprising since I had been looking in the wrong place. Alf Gover's letter had had such an effect that, at the age of thirteen, I had skipped all the junior teams and been drafted straight into the under-sixteen eleven. When I finally found it I could hear people talking about it. No one had seen me play and they could not make it out. I had a sudden urge to go round and explain that it was none of my doing, that I had been coached at Alf Gover's school and that a letter from him had brought it all about. But, of course, I did not. Instead I waited in a state of miserable apprehension for the game, where I confirmed all my latent genius by getting out first ball and taking no wickets.

The motto at Tonbridge is *Deus Dat Incrementum*, and whether or not that had anything to do with the fact that I was retained in the under-sixteen team for the following match, I do not know. But ten days later, against another school team this time, I improved considerably. My batting had matured to such an extent that I was out second ball but I did get four wickets with my leg-breaks. Indeed, it was the bowling, not the batting, that saw me survive. I was beginning to score tens and fifteens but I was continually bowling people out in matches and at the nets. After three weeks or so there was a trial to sort out the top twenty-two cricketers in the entire school. Twenty-one places went to seventeen- and eighteen-year-olds and the twenty-second place went to me. The trial was played on the first eleven ground and although, again, I scored only a few runs I bowled rather well. I took seventeen wickets in the match, nine in the first innings and eight in the second.

This, to desecrate a cliché, put the rabbit among the pigeons. Tonbridge's very next match was against the Free Foresters whose distinguished ranks were to include none other than Gubby Allen, the former England Test captain. The point at issue was whether a thirteen-year-old, a fag, a "novi" as they were known at Tonbridge, could be allowed to play in such exalted company. I have since learned that had the same question arisen at most other schools I would not have been allowed to play. At Tonbridge the case was put to the headmaster and after consultation with my housemaster, James McNeill, they decided to take a chance.

I had no idea that all this drama was in progress until McNeill sent for me. Our house was a small one of only twenty-three boys and McNeill, a former Welsh rugger trialist, was a sensible man. "We have," he said, "a slight problem on our hands." He did not talk down to me at all. He made it clear that my achievements on the cricket field were secondary to my general progress and if my playing in the cricket eleven caused any disharmony in his house he would step in and call a halt. In the meantime we should see how I got on— and he wished me luck.

But I played. Many among the large crowd, I suspect, had only turned up out of curiosity, and if some were secretly hoping that the prodigy would fail then I duly obliged. I batted at number ten and was out first ball, caught behind the wicket. The wicket-keeper, I think, would have liked to have dropped it, but that was not the way the match was being played. When I was out a large section of the crowd melted away, rather as though Bradman had just got out at Sydney. If such attention were flattering it did not inspire my bowling. I also failed to get a wicket. That day, for the first time in my life, I was really conscious that people were watching me. That evening, I had all the cares of the world on my young shoulders.

But someone, at least, had faith in me. The captain of cricket made no reference to my performance when he spoke to me afterwards. "I hope you enjoyed it. I'd like you to play against Malvern on Tuesday." It was in that game that I established myself. I went in last but made ten runs or so quite well. I also got four wickets. This confirmed me as a regular member of the side, despite the fact that I was just about half the height of anyone else in the team. There were no sensations, but I was taking more wickets than anyone and scoring the twenties and thirties and finally a 49 which saw me move up the batting order gradually from last man to number three. So we came to the end of July and the climax of the season: the traditional match against Clifton at Lord's.

It was during the week leading up to that match that I first experienced the sensation which I have already described, the deep-down desire to pull out, the temptation to find some injury that would provide me with an apparently honourable reason for being unavailable. This feeling has haunted me right through my years in the game. The most notable, I suppose, was on the England tour of West Indies in the winter of 1959–60. When we flew into Jamaica for the third Test we were already one up in the series but on the opening morning of the game I would have given anything not to have played. I was working desperately hard in the nets but only getting worse, and the knowledge that my whole future was now at stake made me literally sick and ill. But I played and the result, as it happened, was two innings as fine as anything I have achieved: 114 in the first innings and 97 in the second.

I recall this here only because it recaptures exactly my state of mind at the age of thirteen before my first appearance at Lord's. I would have given anything just to have gone there and watched. Again I felt sick and ill as I walked out to bat. All I could think about on my way to the wicket was how dearly my father, who was now back in India, would love me to score a single at Lord's. One run was the limit of my ambition but heaven alone knew where this single was going to come from.

It came from either the third or fourth ball I faced, I cannot remember which. There was a man at silly mid-off and I pushed it quite firmly past him out to deep extra-cover and took my single. I can still recall my thoughts. "I've run down twenty-two yards at Lord's. I've done it. Now I can get out." Then I looked over at the Tavern and along the boxes and remembered that afternoon when Wally Hammond walked out on the very square where I was batting now. My next thought was that maybe I could get five. That surely must be pretty good for a child of my age at Lord's. I got my five. Then I got ten, then fifteen and I finished up with 75. At the end of that innings I knew I was on my way in the game that, for me, had started on a tennis court high in the hills of Southern India.

Next day I caught the train at Paddington to go down to Cornwall for a holiday with an aunt. There were five of us in the compartment, a mother and a father with their two young children and myself. I watched them reading a certain story in the newspapers. It was to the effect that a young prodigy, almost as wide as he was tall, had scored a remarkable 75 the previous day on the most famous cricket ground in the world. It was a curious sensation.

# 6

Two experiences of great contrast lay in wait for me during that long summer vacation from Tonbridge. The first was a delight. From Cornwall I moved up to Leicestershire to stay with other relatives and thanks to the kindness of Ewart Astill, the Tonbridge coach whose home was in the Midlands, I was invited to play a few weekend games with the Leicester Ivanhoe Club, the leading club side in the area. Then came an even greater thrill when I played in Leslie Berry's benefit match on the Dog and Gun ground at Blaby. The fixture was Leicestershire versus the local village and the young Cowdrey was included in the county side. It must have been an incongruous sight: ten hardened county players plus one young minnow who barely came up to their waists. When we batted I went in quite early, made three or four runs and was then indulgently dropped in the gully. Somehow they contrived to keep me there for forty minutes or so which was a fascinating experience for, at the other end, Leslie Berry was thumping his way to a hundred. We walked into the pavilion together. It was a great moment for a boy who was the most junior in the school.

From this atmosphere of kindly paternalism I moved on to the very different scene of young ambitious boys battling it out on their own. Out of the blue I had received an invitation to play two matches for Surrey Young Amateurs against Middlesex and then Essex. Until that point in my life I had always played cricket with people I knew, but now I knew no one. I was on my own. There were no warm welcomes and no indulgent let-offs by the fielders. This second experience I did not enjoy at all. My bowling was hit all round the Oval and when I batted I immediately seemed to get mown down by some big fast and merciless bowler. If I had made some mark with my first appearance at Lord's, I certainly disappeared without trace the first time I played at the Oval. It was on this low-key note that I ended the season and the effect of it seemed to pursue me down the length of the following summer at Tonbridge. A great deal seemed expected of me there and although I played in the first eleven thoughout the season I failed to deliver the goods. I ended up scoring just about the same number of runs and taking exactly the same number of wickets that I had the previous year. I did not shine in the Lord's match, and although I had not played badly I had made no perceptible progress.

The winter that followed brought, almost by accident, a remedial process of confidence building. Apart from captaining the under-fifteen rugger side I also took up rackets, a game which could have all the universal appeal of squash if only there were more courts available. Tonbridge is one of the twenty or so schools with facilities. I enjoyed rackets, played it quite well and at the very point in my life when I badly needed success at something, I won the Schools' under-sixteen title at Queen's Club in London. This was probably an achievement of some significance because the confidence was apparent as soon as we started playing cricket again. My run output for the school, where I was then vice-captain, doubled from 250 to around 500 and I took more wickets. Then, towards the end of the summer, I ran into the real patch of form which was to begin my long association with the Kent County Cricket Club.

After my nightmare week with the Young Amateurs of Surrey two years earlier I was quite content when John (C. H.) Knott, the cricket master, told me that he had arranged for me to have three games with Kent Young Amateurs. The first two matches were on a perfect batting wicket at Canterbury. In the first, against a young Sussex side that included Jim Parks and Alan Oakman, I scored 157. In the second against Middlesex I got 87. The third and last game was against Surrey Young Amateurs back at the Oval, and perhaps the greatest satisfaction of all during those ten days was to make a good 79 there. By the end of it even my in-built caution could not blind me to the fact that the doors were opening. Kent did not let the autumn grass grow under their feet. Would I care to let them know what dates I would be available the following August? They wanted to play me in a few second eleven matches to, as they put it, "get me started".

When they did get me started, in the August of 1949, I had already had a good year with the school. By then I was sixteen and captain, did well with the ball and scored between 800 and 900 runs with three centuries. But from these sublime heights the next step was a big one, confirming yet again that the education of a cricketer is a very long process. My first second eleven match for Kent was at Norwich against Norfolk. Apart from one benign and somewhat elderly gentleman and myself the entire Kent team was professional. I found myself scared again and this time, too, there was good reason to feel out of my depth. For the first time I was up against bowlers who could maintain a really consistent length. Run-getting was suddenly very hard work. I struggled away for 35 and then got out through sheer impatience. Just to remind me of the Everest still to climb, one of the Edrich brothers then came in and hit 180 for Norfolk.

But it was the promised start. I also played against Wiltshire and Devon, and with this baptism behind me I could do little wrong when I played my final season for Tonbridge in 1950. I got several hundreds, plus another hundred for the Public Schools at Lord's, and doubtless my father, who was back from India on another spell of leave, was content that the considerable cost of my education was money well spent. I do not recall him asking too much about my schoolwork. He may well have been distracted, as I was, by the fact that I was about to make my first appearance in the real thing: county cricket.

The invitation came while we were both watching Kent play at the Oval. David Clark, the Kent captain, came up to my father and said: "I think we'll give him the last few games of the season. It's time to break him in." Those last few games were against Derbyshire at Derby, then a return match against them in Kent, against Nottinghamshire at Dover and then against West Indies at Canterbury.

Understandable misgivings accompanied me all the way up to Derby. Could anyone have stepped more naively into the county game? I knew from the newspapers that Gladwin and Jackson opened their bowling, but what did they bowl? And, for God's sake, which was Jackson and which was Gladwin?

I had only met my own captain, Leslie Ames, two or three times and certainly never played on the same side with him before. At the time he was recovering from all the celebrations and publicity given to him for scoring his hundred hundreds at Canterbury. When he walked to the wicket at Derby I settled myself down into a comfortable seat to concentrate on the Master. It was with some incredulity that I watched him suffer the agony of a pair in the match. Even more shattering to witness was the sight of our left-handed batsman, Peter Hearn, appearing on the top of the pavilion steps wagging an admonishing finger at our captain, with Ray Dovey's spectacles perched precariously on the end of his nose! I can think of one or two who would not have seen the joke at that moment. Leslie Ames was known to be difficult to live with on occasions in the few minutes after getting out for a small score, but happily, he took it all in very good part.

My first catch in first-class cricket was taken off Doug Wright, a miserable, high, swirling affair with a lot of spin on it. The batsman was Charles Elliott and in the same match their best spin bowler was Bert Rhodes. Over the years they have become two of the finest umpires the game has known and warm friends of mine. It was a proud moment when in my first year on the Council of the Sir Winston Churchill Memorial Trust Charlie Elliott won a Travelling Fellowship. I was equally proud when young Harold Rhodes, Bert's son, was chosen to play for England under my captaincy on several occasions.

When I went in to bat I played quite comfortably. The wicket was good, the early shine was off the ball and although the bowlers were clearly sharp they were not swinging it about as much as I had feared. I scored 15, playing natural shots, without any real problems at all. Then I hit one into the covers off Jackson and shouted "Yes" pretty confidently. It was a mistake. Not the run but the call. There was something that Jackson did not like about it. It plainly marked me in his book as a bit of a cheeky whipper-snapper. The next ball I got from him was a really vicious bouncer. It was the first bouncer I had ever faced and for just a few more naive seconds I stood there believing that it had suddenly jumped off the wicket. Then it dawned on me. Leslie Jackson and I were to play together in Test cricket and had many a chuckle about it. What a magnificent bowler he was, too.

I played a few more good shots and even picked Rhodes's leg-

45

breaks and googlies quite easily. Then I got out. I had batted quite well without much to show for it. I scored 104 runs in the seven innings I played in those four games and I was not dissatisfied. But I knew that I had now to leave behind for ever the schoolboy habit of playing myself in for five or ten minutes and then going for my shots. Oddly enough I had found the fielding a bigger strain than the batting. I had caught everything that came my way, including a couple of awkward skiers, but the responsibility was wearing on the nerves. If you dropped one at this level you could still be trying to get the same batsman five hours later. Whilst I was an outstanding fielder in school cricket, I was conscious that I had to apply myself to this aspect of my cricket and give consideration to being a specialist slip fielder.

All in all I had survived quite well, which makes this an appropriate moment, perhaps, to analyse why at every big new step in the game I had been "terrified" or "out of my depth" or "full of misgiving". This was fact, not coy modesty. I had felt that way at school, club, minor county and now first-class level. It had nothing at all to do with physical fear. Looking back now I recognise it for what it was, a fearful impatience to establish myself at each new standard and a nagging suspicion at the back of my brain that each step would be the last. I simply could not wait to move on for fear that *this* was my level. Soccer teams must feel the same when they reach the semi-final of the FA Cup. At least if you get beaten in the final you have played at Wembley. If you lose in the semi-final you have had all of the agony with none of the glory.

It will not have taken even the amateur psychologist a moment to recognise this raw ambition. Right from the start I had set my heart on playing for England. My whole life was a narrow corridor surrounded by cricket. Nothing intruded on that world. My life was Spartan and my needs were few. I did not smoke, drank little, had no hankering for new clothes and "pop" records. If someone was actually concerned enough about me to ask what career I was contemplating I would usually answer "schoolmastering" without giving it a moment's thought. It seemed to satisfy them and it left me in peace.

# 7

I sat a scholarship for Oxford and missed it, but I won a Heath Harrison Exhibition worth £60 a year, and a place at Brasenose College to read geography. Before going up to Oxford I had had, at my father's suggestion, a summer completely free to play cricket for Kent. After a tough start I eventually found my feet. I scored my first hundred, made a thousand runs and was awarded my county cap.

There were two particular landmarks, a hundred against Oxford University and a hundred for the Gentlemen against the Players at Scarborough, pitted against some good bowlers, including Alec Bedser. This was to hold even more significance as Len Hutton was playing for the Players.

It was an apprehensive young undergraduate who got out of the train at Oxford with a couple of suitcases, a bicycle, a squash racket and a pair of football boots. It was a lonely experience walking in; I knew not a soul. I might have been Tom Brown. I found the first two winter terms tough going, for unlike Cambridge, where there is an important examination every summer term, Oxford presents one stiff hurdle in March, after two terms. This Preliminary Examination, as it is called, has to be passed or you are out of the race. There is no redress. I had anticipated playing some rugby football, but was soon the College's scheming inside right, trained to the minute for two enjoyable matches each week. I played College squash, too, and in February I was first string in the University Rackets pair against Cambridge. But the threat of the examination ahead temporarily took the fun out of life. I have to admit that most of my colleagues amid the dreaming spires were earnest, ambitious young men who put in more hours at books than I had expected. Once I had settled I found Oxford a calm, happy place. I loved wandering around the colleges absorbing it all. I was fascinated by the Union debates, regretting that I had not sufficient confidence or skill to speak myself. My eyes were opened to a whole new range of people, ideas and attitudes. Like the wise owl, the more I thought the less I spoke. Everyone else seemed to have opinions to offer and targets to scorn.

The spring and the summer were heavenly to me. Though these are memories in a long career which tumbles together, even confuses me for a moment, cricket at Oxford will always be perfectly embalmed in my mind. When I recall the opportunity afforded the young Kent cricketer in that first summer of 1952, I can still feel the anticipation. My exam was passed and behind me, and the new term presented a golden vista. Warm days in the sun, net practices which were never a chore, good wickets, good fellowship—a simple, uncomplicated life.

Whilst students pedalled endlessly to lectures I was drawn to the Parks and those tall trees, many-hued, a handsome, colourful audience for our endeavours, which were too often plain in the particular period I played there. Bookworms nestled in the grass around the boundary, vagrants paused to investigate, girls from language schools swished by, choral scholars passed on the longest possible route to choir stalls, old men dozed in deck chairs, young nannies tamed restless infants—all sought, and found, peace in the Parks.

I am sure county players enjoyed their visits. I have known none who did not. One old campaigner was heard to say, "Different sort'a game, int' Parks." But he was happy. The masters relaxed in these matches and often played better for it. The undergraduates always fielded like demons and this gave pleasure.

We used to lean heavily upon a professional coach, Laurie Fishlock in my first year; and then Lofty Herman, a man of real humour, came to live in Oxford and became part of Oxford University cricket for a number of years. I am a great believer in having a senior adviser and father-figure near at hand. At Fenner's they have been lucky enough to have Cyril Coote, who has found time to guide the players and tend the ground. At Oxford, Norman Morris is a much loved character in the same vein.

When H. R. H. Ranjitsinhji arrived from India for the summer term at Cambridge at the turn of the century there were twenty

48

professionals employed by the University Cricket Club, and on most fine days the fifteen immaculate net strips were all in action. On coming down Ranjit selected four of those professionals to travel with him everywhere he went with Sussex. Cyril Coote's father was one of those so chosen. His only job was to bowl to his master for an hour a day for the princely sum of twelve gold sovereigns a week. I referred this to the Cricketers' Association recently and they reckoned it was mighty good remuneration.

At the time of writing I am President of OUCC, a three-year term of office which, happily, brings me back more often. Things are just the same. It is an encouragement to them to hear that in my three years at Oxford I was never on the winning side. The only change is in the itinerary, where they are lucky enough to participate as a combined Oxford and Cambridge eleven in the One-Day Benson and Hedges Tournament. With the help of Arthur Milton they recorded victories against both Northamptonshire and Worcestershire in 1975, and the Oxford President became very excited. How he would love to be on the precipice of Oxford pleasures again! Yes, it was a delightful routine: breakfast, nets, the match, a beer or two, dinner at Vincents and few cares. Vincents Club was the haven for University sportsmen, a warm comfortable place, with its deep leather armchairs, polished wood, tankards of ale, and laughter. Meals were so reasonably priced that you could take in a visiting county player as a guest and do him proud with a good dinner for under a pound. What an evening of celebration it was when Roger Bannister, skilfully paced by Chris Chataway, broke the four minute mile along the track at Iffley Road!

I am indebted to my three years at Oxford for so many things, but in truth I was, even in that environment, a disciple of cricket. The summer term held more for me than any other. Lectures were the pursuit of the winter season. Alan Ross captures the torn loyalty of one who loved cricket, yet was committed to join those rushing shoulder to shoulder to lecture rooms.

> When perhaps the Australians were playing
> On a May morning—he might cross
> As lacking sensibility, swaying
> Down the Broad between family saloons, those
> Who, with heads like his own humming

Black tunes of Baudelaire, money-box cantos
Clinking from Pound, did not also hanker
As they rode, gowns lateral, for the drumming
Music of the Parks, his magnetic anchor.

The Parks, perhaps like a favourite golf course, or stretch of river, has a natural beauty. With each fresh visit one should stop to marvel that it remains unchanged.

# 8

It never crossed my mind during that last summer term at Oxford that I would be on my way to Australia, as a member of the 1954–55 MCC touring team. And the reason for my inclusion, unquestionably, was the century I made for the Gentlemen against the Players at Scarborough in the presence of Len Hutton, now knighted and living quietly in Surrey, who quite probably, to this day, does not fully comprehend the considerable influence he exerted on my life.

Apart from Sir Donald Bradman, whose mystique had become apparent to my infant brain back in the Mediterranean on that homeward trip from India, Len Hutton was the first cricketer to become an identifiable hero. The reason was the same for me as for many of my generation: Hutton's record-breaking 364 in the Oval Test match of 1938. That was my first summer home from India and I had never heard a radio cricket commentary before. My father was going up to the Test match daily, but at home we were listening for what seemed three solid days as the young Yorkshireman, then only twenty-two years and two months old, first made his hundred, then went on to his two hundred and then began drawing nearer and nearer to Bradman's record of 334. The commentator was Howard Marshall and even his measured tones vibrated slightly with emotion as Hutton smashed the record and added another thirty runs for good measure before he was finally out, caught by Hassett off O'Reilly.

It was inevitable, therefore, that I should be Hutton every time I went in to bat in the garden thereafter. I was not actually to see him in the flesh until some years later when my uncle, John Taylor, took me to a wartime match at Lord's merely to watch him batting. I was interested in no one else. He almost ruined my day. I could not believe that such a master could get out for anything less than 50 and so I was almost in tears when, after some fifty minutes' immaculate batting he was dismissed for nineteen. The occasion was saved by walking round the back of the pavilion during the lunch interval. My uncle suddenly nudged me and there, not ten yards away and coming towards us in their scarlet and gold braided MCC blazers, were the two Olympian figures of Hutton and Hammond. They split up to pass me. They could do little else, for I froze and stood stock still, gazing up at their faces in awe. The blue blazer, the gold braid, the George and Dragon became firmly printed on my mind.

I saw Hutton again, briefly, playing in one of the 1947 Tests against South Africa, but the first time I was able to settle down and study him fully was just before I began my own first-class career. I went to the Oval to watch him against West Indies and there, on a testing rain-affected wicket, he scored 202 not out. No apprentice could have watched it without falling completely under the spell of the sorcerer. In that year he was at the height of his powers and his innings was an exercise of such technical brilliance that it was as close as one could come to witnessing cricket perfection.

The following year, just before going up to Oxford, I was playing against him in three successive matches towards the end of the season. The first was for Kent against Yorkshire at Canterbury. Hutton got 120-odd which was more than half of the Yorkshire total. The next was for MCC against Yorkshire at Scarborough. Hutton scored a century in each innings. The third was for Gents v. Players, the match in which I got a century myself. Hutton made 99 that time before hitting a shot to me at cover. I picked up the ball, threw it and ran him out. It had little to do with my sharp fielding. He was having some sort of a misunderstanding with Johnny Wardle and Wardle sent him back when he was fully committed to run. Had it not been for that run-out I would have seen Hutton make four hundreds in a row. In the Canterbury innings, certainly, he had played and missed occasionally at Doug Wright, who could always make the ball bounce off a quick wicket. But in the Scarborough innings he had not made a false stroke. I was fielding in the deep in those days, and and so I had time to watch and analyse this fabulous automaton throughout three innings. He was always in balance. When he played forward his head, his left knee and front toe were always in perfect, text-book position. Nothing seemed more certain than that he would go on making hundreds. There was no logical reason why he should ever get out again. I became a total disciple of the way he played. My temperament was adjusted to his method as opposed, say, to the methods of Ted Dexter and Graeme Pollock in later years.

I had also had the opportunity of getting to know him personally. Between the first and second of those three matches I had travelled from Canterbury to Scarborough in Godfrey Evans's car, a Bentley inevitably. Len Hutton was the other passenger. I had to keep pinching myself to believe that I was keeping such company. I asked a few questions but I never felt more than a schoolboy who had stowed away on the back seat.

Throughout the journey I was aware of the significance of this meeting with Len Hutton and the freak opportunity that the Scarborough Festival offered me. This had been my first full season in top-class cricket and mid-way my confidence had been badly shaken. I'd had a lean spell, culminating in the traditional Whitsun match at Southampton when I was out for nought and one against Shackleton and Cannings. I had offered to stand down from the Kent side but Tom Crawford, acting captain at the time and always a warm supporter of mine, insisted that I persevere. His firm, decisive hand gave me confidence and I played well under him. The following week I scored a hundred for the Free Foresters against Oxford. I finished the season on a good note with 71 against the South African touring side and was awarded my county cap by David Clark. I was now an established county cricketer, conscious of how much more was still needed to live in the Test arena.

I think it was at Scarborough where Hutton first began to watch me closely. In my anxiety to do well against Tom Pritchard and Alec Bedser in front of 20,000 spectators I must have been getting lower and lower in my stance at the wicket. Several times as he passed in the field between overs Hutton said, "Stand up higher and play straight." That evening he sought me out to elaborate on what he had had to say. I have no doubt that it was that innings and my response to those discussions that helped to win the place to Australia under Hutton's captaincy.

To put the record completely straight, Len Hutton has told me since that he never pushed for me to go to Australia. Rather, it was the influence of several others expressing their faith in my technique and temperament which swayed him into taking the gamble. Tyson was a gamble with so little experience behind him and I was the same.

I did not play in the final match of the Scarborough Festival and as I was leaving the Grand Hotel to return home I had an encounter with another Yorkshireman, Brian Sellars. I said, "Goodbye, Mr. Sellars," to which he replied, "Judging by the shot you got out to I'm not surprised that you are not playing in the last match up here."

I was thunderstruck. What I did not know at that shattering moment, was that this was Sellars' manner with everyone. I was going out of the door when his voice boomed again. "Hey, coom back, coom back. Listen, lad, I want to tell you something. If you're not playing for England and on that boat to Australia there'll only be one person to blame. You'll be to blame. It'll be your fault and nobody else's." I was many miles down the A.1. before I realised this was a back-handed compliment. However, he was right about the boat, but I did not play for England until I reached Australia. The years 1953 and 1954, as Oxford captain, were such disappointing seasons with long, lean spells. The only phases to remember with pride were a hundred in a University match and two good fifties against the Australians at Lord's in 1953. For the most part my cricket seemed to stand still, whilst in the agonies and struggle of personal failures my personality might have been broadening.

The University match of 1954 behind me I settled into the daily routine of a county cricketer with Kent. It was then that the news of my selection for Australia came as a bolt from the blue. After the Surrey match, standing in the car park at Blackheath, I heard the news headlines on a stranger's car radio that there were a number of shocks in the MCC party to tour Australia in the coming winter.

For one thing there was no Jim Laker. For another there was no Tony Lock. Finally, there was no Willie Watson. The great Yorkshire left-hander had been left out and an untried youngster, yet to play for England at home, had been given the place. Me.

There were certain other distractions going on at the time because the match we had just finished at Blackheath had been against Surrey, in those days a fixture watched by ten thousand every day and fought out with all the chivalry and mercy of, say, Culloden. To reach the car park I had had to pass through the Surrey dressing room and the atmosphere in there could have been cut into cubes and sold as solid fuel. They had already heard; I knew nothing about it. Laker had lost his place to Jim McConnon and Lock's place had gone to Johnny Wardle. The news of my inclusion came a few minutes later, in the main body of the news bulletin. By then I had stowed my cricket bag in the boot of my car and was listening for the remaining names of the touring side out of sheer academic interest.

I was still recovering when some Surrey players appeared. I was out of the ground and off to Northampton before anyone could challenge me! Most national newspapers were at pains to point out that a selection committee comprising Harry Altham, Gubby Allen, Walter Robins and Wilf Wooller was inclined to have an old school tie ring about it. Other papers pointedly ignored my selection. I have to confess that I would not have picked myself had I been a selector, for I was twenty-one and had not scored a championship hundred, was quite untried at Test level and had never toured before. At the time I was thoroughly embarrassed and did not relish the thought of having to justify my selection in the eyes of both the public and the cricket profession.

The pressure was on. The very next morning we were playing against Northants and it seemed to me that every newsreel camera and Long Tom in the country was on the ground. It was the perfect spot, apparently, for pictures since Frank Tyson and Keith Andrew, both of Northants, had also been selected for Australia the previous day. With a bit of luck they might get a shot of Tyson knocking Cowdrey's middle stump flying. They were lucky. Tyson did bowl Cowdrey but not before I had countered his exceptional speed for an hour and eighteen runs. I had survived my first test.

There was still one Test match to play against Pakistan that season before the tour party left. Today, undoubtedly, a player in my position would have been drafted into the team to blood him for what lay ahead. I was made twelfth man. All the nerves and misgivings which had marked my arrival at every other step in the game came flooding back again. When I arrived at the Oval for net practice the day before the Test began, I was desperately shy and could not find anything to say to anyone.

I got there about two hours earlier than anyone else and felt thoroughly uncomfortable and out of my depth. Although I had played against most of them, Godfrey Evans was the only man I knew well. It was even worse when the match began. I relaxed when England were batting but when they were in the field I was a bundle of nerves. If someone should come off I was the one who had to go on. This I had to do for a spell of 20 minutes, and when the ball came to me I was the "novi" back at Tonbridge again.

Happily for my constitution I did not have to endure it for the whole of the match. Over the weekend my injections for the tour flared up and gave me a splendidly nasty temperature. The doctor sent me to bed for the day. The next morning I rushed to the Oval, packed up my kit and fled from the ground in huge relief. It was a strange performance. Half of me wanted to play, half of me just could not face up to it. Yet this was the future I had planned. I was angry with myself for being so stupid.

# 9

Today, before an England cricket team sets off on an overseas expedition, there is an elaborate prelude of conferences, net practices and photo-calls for the press. In 1954 it was all more nonchalant and haphazard. We assembled in London the night before we sailed, attended a dinner at which the MCC President addressed us as though we were just off to Agincourt instead of Adelaide, spent the night in an hotel and then caught the boat-train down to Tilbury the following morning. Today, too, jet travel has cut three months off the length of the Australasian tours. The 1954–55 tour to Australia and New Zealand lasted seven and a half months, so the farewells were all the more poignant. My parents had driven down to the docks to attend a large formal lunch given by the shipping company on board and to say goodbye.

Len Hutton, as captain, was much in demand that morning and yet he still found time to move in among the crowd of reporters and relatives to find my father, draw him aside and talk to him earnestly for some twenty minutes. The tone of it, I gathered later, was that there was no need for my parents to worry. "I'll look after him," Hutton reassured him again and again, which suggested he knew a good deal more about how I was feeling than I gave him credit for at the time. My father was immensely impressed by Hutton's thoughtfulness and concern and indeed, looking back now, there was something almost uncanny about the care he took to put my father's mind at rest. I was never to see my father again. Three weeks later he was dead.

I must confess I gave my captain precious little chance to "look after me" during the early days of the voyage out. The feeling of being an intruder among great players still prevailed and somehow seemed to lock my tongue whenever I was in their company. I was sharing a cabin with Peter May, who was later to become my closest cricket friend, but I found myself rather dodging the star names, Hutton included. He played it wisely and coolly and in due course our relationship became natural and relaxed. The turning point was Colombo where we stopped to play a one-day match against Ceylon.

It is not easy to play cricket after a long spell at sea because the ground seems to be swaying gently beneath your feet as you stand there. It certainly seemed to be swaying under our early batsmen because in no time at all we were something like 30 for four. Hutton himself was not playing and he sat there surveying the whole proceedings with a set expression as though this was an awful omen for what lay ahead in Australia. I went in at the fall of the fourth wicket and as I walked out into that Turkish-bath heat, before a huge crowd clamouring for another quick wicket, I honestly felt that it would be an act of God if I even made contact with the ball. In fact, from the outset the ball kept hitting the middle of my bat. I made 66 not out and I felt ten feet tall.

Hutton was visibly impressed and our relationship began to warm. On the rest of the passage down to Fremantle we were joining in deck games together and we talked a great deal. He seemed to recognise that, in spite of myself, I had what he called "match temperament" which was clearly going to be badly needed in the campaign just starting. He used the word "rough" a great deal. The Australians were going to play it "rough". I had to get used to a "rough" reception when I went in to bat. "You'll find the language can fly in the Test arena. Be prepared. You're a young player with quite a reputation. You'll find that they're going to let you have it to try to rough you up a bit." This did not worry me. By the end of the voyage I was less ill at ease and seemed to be fitting into the party.

I was dressing for the landfall dinner on the ship when the cable arrived that made Hutton take me under his wing for the rest of the tour. It was curiously worded. It was sent by John Taylor and read: "Congratulations on your Colombo innings. Happy landings tomorrow. Regret father not too well. All at home." I knew, instinctively. It did not ring true. The next morning we landed and were driven through many of the glorious beauty spots outside Perth before we were taken to the Palace Hotel. There, on top of the pile of mail awaiting me, was another telegram. It informed me that my father had died.

Peter May was with me and after discussing what I should do we concluded that there was nothing to be gained by my going back to England. I went to my room, unpacked and stayed there on my own for the rest of the afternoon. When I went down to dinner Len Hutton said nothing. It was only after the meal, when I was having coffee in the lounge, that he came round the back of my chair, put his hand on my shoulder and said, "I'm sorry." There were tears in his eyes. Then he walked away. I knew then that it had taken him a long time to work out how to react. He never mentioned my father again but from that moment he made certain that I was occupied every minute of the day. The following Sunday, when MCC played a golf match against a local club, Cowdrey, the junior of the party, was partnering Hutton.

This was Hutton's method of approaching every problem: most of his actions were premeditated rather than spontaneous. He was a mass of contradictions and this was never better illustrated than by the way he began and ended that tour as a public speaker. At the initial landfall press conference in Australia he dazzled the toughest and most cynical journalists with a performance that would have outshone Danny Kaye or Bob Hope. By New Zealand, Hutton was distinguishing himself at a Government House reception in Auckland by repeatedly calling the Governor "Sir Norroughly Willie". This was unfortunate, since his name was actually Sir Willoughby Norrie.

Perhaps the strain of the tour had drained him emotionally, and by the end it was evident that he was exhausted physically and mentally. His wife, Dorothy, joined him in the New Year and was clearly a great comfort to him. He was, by nature, anything but a gregarious man. He could be ill at ease with strangers and was slow to trust them, but his striking blue eyes and open smile are the evidence of a warm Yorkshire heart. His streak of isolationism, however, may have made him the great captain he was.

None of these characteristics of Hutton was apparent at that initial press conference in Australia. It was held on board ship before we landed, and was attended by some sixty or seventy reporters, many of whom had flown across from the Eastern States to greet him and grill him. These conferences are always ordeals for visiting captains but Hutton's performance was brilliant. He had clearly worked out the role he intended to play and sitting there, tanned, superbly fit, lightweight suit immaculate, he played it so superbly that his character dominated the whole room. I was intrigued by these affairs and out of curiosity I crept in and sat down at the back. I was the only England player, apart from Hutton, present.

Two factors were very much in his favour. He had won the respect of the Australian critics on his last tour by the mastery of his batsmanship. Now he was back not only as captain, but also as the first professional ever to captain England. This, since Australians tended to look at the English class system with eyes narrowed by distrust, got him off the mark with a boundary before he opened his mouth.

The Australian press, I suspect, were expecting a lot of bravado, even bombast. They received the opposite. When they phrased a question to bring a head-on collision Hutton sat there, smiling slightly, turning the words over and over in his mind. Sometimes the pauses lasted fully thirty seconds and they became so long that twice at least Geoffrey Howard, the England team manager, glanced round to see if the captain had fallen asleep. When the answer came it would be shrewd, pointed and dryly witty. After about a dozen answers Hutton had them rolling in the gangways.

It was all underplayed. "Noo, we 'aven't got mooch boolin'. Got a chap called Tyson but you won't 'ave 'eard of him because he's 'ardly ever played." "Ah, yes, Lock and Laker. Aye, good boolers, but we 'ad to leave them behind." (No explanation.) "Batsmen? Well we 'aven't got any batsmen, really. We've got these youngsters, May and Cowdrey, but we haven't really got any batsmen." Then, wearily: "What it comes to is that we're startin' out all over again. We're 'ere to learn a lot from you."

They asked him what he thought of Australia's new ball attack. Another long, long pause as he groped to try to remember their names. "Oo, aye. Lindwall and that other feller." Pause again. "Don't think they like me very much. Didn't really know whether I ought to have coom back out 'ere again."

Question: "What do you think of Arthur Morris now?" Answer, after an immense silence: "'Ave they got any sight screens yet down the bottom end at Brisbane?" Long silence. "Saw Arthur Morris make 196 once when the sight screens had blown down." Then he would lean forward, almost confidentially, to one of the reporters and say, "Remember that, Bill, the day the sight screens blew down?" and then he would retreat into some extensive reverie of his own, while the entire Australian press contingent sat transfixed by the performance in total, respectful silence.

It was a brilliant achievement. He took the wind out of their sails with almost every reply. He had the whole room poised, waiting for his next answer, and when the answer came it told them nothing at all. When the question was tough he glanced it neatly down to fine-leg and they actually applauded the way he did it.

During the next two or three days he made quite a number of speeches and each time he used the same tactics, the slow, deliberately hesitant, almost fumbling approach, with instant success. His idea, I suspect, was to play the part of the humble, unsophisticated cricket professional. It probably required a good deal of nervous energy that he could not spare when the Test series got under way.

I worked hard and played well in the nets at Perth whilst we acclimatised before the matches started. It paid dividends. I got 48 not out in the two-day up-country match at Bunbury and then went straight into the opening major game against Western Australia. Here for the first time I batted with Hutton at the other end. He had already scored about 70 when I joined him and my concern this time was for him and not for me. I was petrified at the thought of running him out, which seemed a distinct possibility as he never called. He simply stroked the ball away and then ambled up and down. To me it was like flying for the first time with one of those RAF aerobatic teams. If you took your eye off your leader, either you were dead, which was bad, or he was dead, which was infinitely worse. I had no inkling of his intentions. I had to be ready in case he wanted to pinch a quick third run to keep the strike. At other times he hit the ball into the covers and stood there watching it. I did not know whether to watch him or watch the ball. Then he would suddenly look down the wicket at me with an expression which said, "Why aren't you running". There was no time at all to worry about my own batting. My entire concentration was focussed on not running him out.

We put on 127 for the fourth wicket. I scored 41 and Hutton went on to make 145 before he retired with a pulled muscle. But it was the partnership which forged our relationship for the tour. He treated me almost as if he had been appointed my guardian. Once, half way through an over from a left-arm fast bowler coming over the wicket, he held up play for what seemed an eternity, called me into the middle of the pitch and asked what guard I was taking. I said "Leg-stump". He said "Um" and walked slowly back. Two overs later he called me down again. "I think you've got to take centre. Move over and play down this bloke's line." Occasionally, after that, he would say "Good shot", as we passed for a run.

For his most junior player, meanwhile, there were few problems. I was enjoying the tour and had little anxiety about the Tests. For a while, at least, there were not going to be any Tests. I missed a couple of games, then failed to make any impression at all in Adelaide as we moved across Australia towards the start of the series. Then, against New South Wales, in Sydney, it happened. Although I had yet to score a century in the County Championship in England I now made two centuries in a match against probably the most powerful of the Australian State sides: 110 in the first innings, 103 in the second.

It was a very significant game for me for more than the obvious reasons. In the first innings I went in number six, after MCC had lost four wickets for 38, and put on 163 in a stand with Hutton. In the second innings I opened. Someone was ill, I think, but whatever the reason Hutton suddenly asked, "When did you last go in first?" I told him I could not recollect ever having done so. "Well, you're seeing the ball pretty well," he said, "have a go." I could not argue against his reasoning but I did not relish the prospect. When we batted again, Reg Simpson, who should have been England's opening partner with Hutton, batted badly. I got my second century and I think from that moment Hutton saw me as a certainty for the first Test in Brisbane, possibly as his opening partner. It did not work out that way. In the remaining game before the Tests, against Queensland, I opened again. I got four in the first innings and nought in the second.

I have two other particular recollections from the match against New South Wales. The first was of my demise as a bowler. Earlier, in some up-country game, I had been given a bowl, taken a wicket with my first ball and ended up with something around five for 30. My leg-breaks had impressed the local batsmen but, more to the point, they had impressed Hutton as well, because when we were taking some terrible punishment from the New South Wales batsmen in Sydney a week or so later he suddenly threw the ball to me again. It was my misfortune to bowl to Alan Davidson. He, too, was clearly impressed with me because he hit me clean over the stand out of that enormous ground and when I sneak a look at *Wisden* now to discover what happened later I find that I was removed from the attack shortly afterwards with an analysis reading: no maidens, thirty-eight runs and no wickets. I did not bowl again.

The other memory is of batting with Hutton on a turning wicket. It was so slow that even Davidson was bowling spinners and Hutton fancied his chances. He asked me to take Richie Benaud at my end while he stayed facing Davidson. His performance after that deserved an Oscar. If the duel had gone on for twenty years Davidson could never have got Hutton out. But Hutton's imitation of a great batsman in trouble was classic. He tied himself into all imaginable knots and then, sportsman that he was, he would nod a little "Well bowled" to Davidson down the wicket. He kept Davidson on for most of the morning, rationing himself with great restraint to only a boundary every so often.

As we walked off he said: "How are you then?" I said, "It's hard work." His reply was a classic Huttonism. "Aye, and what's more you're not getting paid for it, are you?"

A week later we witnessed the nearest thing to a Test captain in a coma. The match against Queensland was the last before the first Test and it was played on a Brisbane pitch alongside the Test wicket. Hutton did not play in the State game. Instead he took a chair out to the front of the pavilion and watched every ball bowled in the game without uttering a single word. They even brought drinks out to him, left them by his chair and departed without daring to interrupt his concentration. Like those old fourteenth-century generals plotting their campaign through the night, he was absorbing every factor, planning every move in the battle for which we had come across the world.

My own failure as an opening batsman did not help him, but his main strategy concerned something more fundamental. What to do if we won the toss? Hutton missed nothing. He duly noted the early dampness, the small amount of grass, and the way Lindwall and Archer moved the ball around to the discomfort of the batsmen during the first day and a half. It was during this period, clearly, that he decided to take the gamble of sending Australia in if he got the chance. He convinced himself that his bowlers, Tyson, Statham and Bedser, would blast deep into the Australian batting on the opening morning and thus create the breach through which England could storm to victory. He picked his side to that end.

On the morning of the Test, Hutton duly won the toss and sent Australia in. We went into the field on that Friday morning and were still fielding the following Monday lunchtime because Arthur Morris hit 153, Neil Harvey 162 and Australia eventually declared their first innings at 601 for eight. They then bowled England out for 190 and 257 to win by an innings and 154 runs with more than a day to spare. My own scores in my first Test appearance were 40 in the first innings and 10 in the second.

Hutton was unapproachable. He communicated with no one. I suspect that even when he went out to toss that first morning, on a wicket with neither grass nor moisture, he was tortured by the fact that he was making a ghastly mistake. But he had planned his moves throughout the preceding days and would not go back on them. His self-torture afterwards was pitiable to watch. The party's spirits were at zero, we were one down in the series and the whipping boys of every Australian cartoonist. Now we had to fly miles up the Queensland coast to Rockhampton for a two-day exhibition game. We flew in an ancient plane and it was one of the bumpiest trips of my life. Hutton, in the seat next to me, was yellow-green. He was a bad traveller by air anyway, but his complexion seemed to owe just as much to what had happened on the ground back in Brisbane.

He found two ways of getting the nightmare out of his system. The first was in the Rockhampton match where after the first day's play the wicket was in such an appalling condition that the local organisers asked Hutton if they could patch it up again. This was not only against the rules but against everything that Hutton stood for. But he said, "Why, of course, we're only here playing friendly cricket anyway." The pitch was duly repaired. On the second day, however, the local country eleven put up a tremendous fight. Hundreds of spectators poured into the ground in the final hour to see if their team could hold out against the might of MCC, which would have been the biggest thing they could imagine short of an oil-strike. With two balls of the last over left, the locals still had two wickets standing. It was at this point that Hutton walked off the field, found the official to whom he had given permission to repair the pitch and said: "This is only friendly cricket, anyway, so I'm sure you'd like us to forget about the playing hours and finish the match

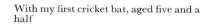

With my first cricket bat, aged five and a half

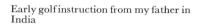

Early golf instruction from my father in India

Charles Walford, late headmaster of Homefield

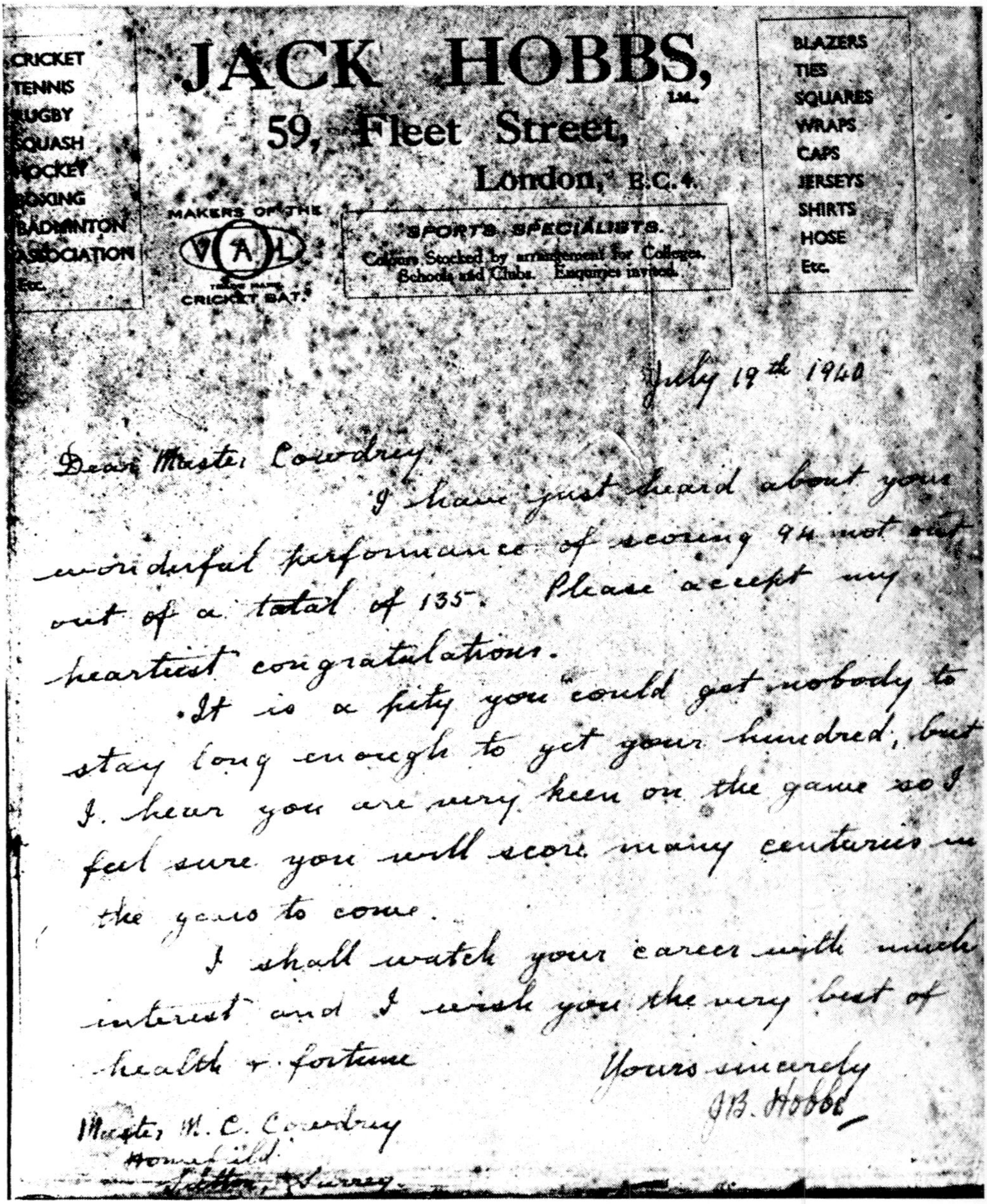

**JACK HOBBS,** Ltd.
59, Fleet Street,
London, E.C. 4.

CRICKET
TENNIS
RUGBY
SQUASH
HOCKEY
BOXING
BADMINTON
ASSOCIATION
Etc.

MAKERS OF THE
V A L
TRADE MARK
CRICKET BAT.

"SPORTS SPECIALISTS."
Colours Stocked by arrangement for Colleges,
Schools and Clubs. Enquiries invited.

BLAZERS
TIES
SQUARES
WRAPS
CAPS
JERSEYS
SHIRTS
HOSE
Etc.

July 19th 1940

Dear Master Cowdrey,

I have just heard about your wonderful performance of scoring 94 not out out of a total of 135. Please accept my heartiest congratulations.

It is a pity you could get nobody to stay long enough to get your hundred, but I hear you are very keen on the game so I feel sure you will score many centuries in the games to come.

I shall watch your career with much interest and I wish you the very best of health & fortune

Yours sincerely
JB. Hobbs

Master M. C. Cowdrey
Homefield
Sutton, Surrey.

*A letter to remember.*

Letter from Jack Hobbs to Master Colin Cowdrey

Captain of cricket at Tonbridge School

Still a schoolboy, but about to start my
first innings for Kent at Canterbury,
against West Indies in 1950

Batting for Kent v. Surrey at Blackheath,
July 1955; Peter May is at slip

Peter May leads his team out at Lords
against India in 1959. This was my last
Test match with Godfrey Evans

After my wedding to Penelope Chiesman in 1956; Peter May was best man, David Sheppard
assisted at the service

Two great cricketers who had such an influence on my career: Sir Donald Bradman welcomes Sir Len Hutton to Adelaide, on the arrival of the MCC touring team in 1954

Sir Donald mastering the game of golf with characteristic determination

MCC at Perth, Western Australia, on our 1962–3 tour

Arriving back from that tour, which I vice-captained, with our tour manager, His Grace the late Duke of Norfolk

On the way to my highest score of 307, at Adelaide on Christmas Eve 1962, backed up by Tom Graveney. It was my birthday

It was Tom Graveney again who saw me through my century in my 100th Test, this time at Edgbaston v. Australia in 1968

Walking out to bat with a broken arm for the last two balls v. West Indies at Lords, 1963

Diving full length to catch Charlie Griffith off Derek Shackleton at Lords, 1963

anyway." There was little the official could say. MCC duly won the match in their own good time and Rockhampton's civic pride at holding "England" to a draw had to be contained until they could be granted another fixture years, decades perhaps, in the future.

Hutton's other memorable performance after that disastrous Test involved an English pressman, E. W. Swanton, of the *Daily Telegraph*. It was inevitable that the British critics, generally, should have hammered Hutton for his decision to send Australia in at Brisbane and Swanton's criticism, when the air-mail editions of the British papers arrived, made particularly strong reading. It was being discussed by a number of players in a hotel foyer when, by some mischievous fate, the two men of the moment walked in. Hutton came in at one door and Swanton, with the dynamite edition of the *Telegraph* neatly folded under his arm, entered by another. One of the senior England players chose this moment to call out: "Oh, by the way, Len, have you seen what the *Telegraph* said?"

The declaration of World War Three could have hardly had a more dramatic effect. No one moved and the silence was total until Hutton eventually said, "No. I haven't."

Slowly he walked across the foyer and removed the newspaper from under Swanton's arm. Even more slowly he unfolded it and turned the pages until he found what he was looking for. He absorbed what he was reading in his own good time, then re-folded the paper and handed it back. "Yes," he said with a twinkle. "Yes, I've seen the *Telegraph*." The general opinion was that he had been consulting his share prices in the stock-market columns. Len was smiling again.

# 10

Alec Bedser's figures, one wicket for 131 runs in Australia's only innings, were unusual for him, but he was not alone. Tyson's solitary wicket had cost him 160 runs and Brian Statham's two were bought for 123. Bedser had also been handicapped by the fact that he was recovering from shingles and was physically under par. Looking back it is clear that he should never have played.

Despite the disparity in the figures, Hutton now decided that Tyson was his key weapon. He would go after the Australians with sheer, blind speed, which is a reasonably accurate description of Tyson's bowling at that stage of the tour: immensely fast but still lacking in skill. He was operating off his long run, which later he was wise enough to cut down. It took him eleven minutes to bowl an eight ball over and at times he was wildly inaccurate. But even the most scornful Australian critics could not fault his physical stamina and tenacity. At Brisbane he had toiled on and on, giving everything to every delivery, in tropical conditions. It may well have been the critics' reactions that spurred him to his later successes, but certainly as we approached Sydney and the second Test, Tyson was Hutton's man. He got himself fitter than ever. Harold Dalton, the Essex physiotherapist travelling with us, was set loose on him as though he were being tuned up for a world heavyweight title fight. His diet was studied and on match days he would eat special concoctions of mixed up raw eggs.

All this was contributing to the eclipse of Alec Bedser and the end of a truly great career. Ironically, it was drizzling slightly on the morning of the Sydney Test and the wicket was both moist and grassy. The conditions could not have been more perfect for Bedser, one of the twelve players selected. It was a desperately difficult decision. Edrich, Evans, May, Bailey and Compton all looked at the pitch and each one would have had views. There is a shortage of time on the morning of a Test match and Hutton had a real problem. One minute his heart said Tyson, his brain said Bedser, then his instinct said Bedser, his reason said Tyson, and the clock was moving round swiftly to the moment when he and Arthur Morris would toss. The clock moved so quickly, indeed, that as the two captains went out we still did not know who was in the England team nor, I suspect, did Hutton himself. He made a last second snap decision on the wicket, exchanged teams and then Morris tossed. He won it for Australia and put England into bat. This meant that Hutton had fifteen minutes to inform his players, get himself padded up and compose himself, walk out to take guard and shape up to the first ball. Under those multiple pressures he was guilty of an understandable but tragic omission. It was not just that he dropped Alec Bedser but he failed to tell him personally. The first Bedser knew about it, so I understand, was when the manager pinned the team list to the dressing room door, a list that did not include Bedser's name.

Today the impact would not have been so great. There is now more of a squad philosophy about team selection. No player, however experienced, however established, is sacrosanct. But in those days the star system was at its height. Dropping a celebrity player, which Bedser unquestionably was, required immense tact and careful public relations. In Bedser's case Hutton showed neither. I understand his dilemma completely. On his batting days he retired into a world of his own. He neither spoke to anyone nor appeared to hear them if they spoke to him. That morning he was in a trance as he returned from the toss, but the damage was done. Bedser was deeply hurt; this was the end of his great career overseas.

England won a thrilling, low-scoring match by 38 runs. Tyson's selection was completely vindicated when he took ten for 130. The mental pressures of that Test, however, left Hutton exhausted. The result could have swung either way, even in the final hour when Australia's last man, Bill Johnston, joined Neil Harvey at the wicket with 77 runs still needed.

Australia had wanted only 151 to win with eight wickets standing when the fifth day began, but in his second over Tyson yorked both

Burke and Hole. By lunch, with Australia 118 for five it seemed to be England's day. Harvey, however, kept so much of the strike when the last man joined him that it looked just possible that he could win the game on his own. Australia's target came down from 77, to 67, then 57 and 47. When it had reached the thirties we were going berserk until Johnston suddenly lashed out and slicked a huge deflection for Godfrey Evans to take a superb running catch down the legside. England won, and squared the series, one-all. Harvey's innings of 92 not out was the best I saw him play.

During the second Test, I saw Hutton apply the sort of psychological pressure to a batsman that on the boat he had warned me to expect from the Australians. Hutton's target was Richie Benaud. Carefully filed away in his mind was the memory of Benaud in trouble against Tyson's bowling. Benaud came in apparently to face the bowling of Johnny Wardle, a hope which Hutton actively encouraged with an expression of bland absent-mindedness. He actually let Wardle take the ball, set his field and turn to run in before he called out: "Oh, hold on a minute, hold on." Then followed an extraordinary act of pretending not to know where Tyson was fielding. He peered everywhere before finally looking down to third man, where he knew damned well that Tyson would be, and then went into an elaborate rigmarole of calling him up from the distant boundary, taking the ball from Wardle and handing it to Tyson with a long, whispered conversation. The build-up was nerve-racking. Benaud watched and waited anxiously, a tactic which he used from time to time in his days as captain. Hutton used variations on that theme against Benaud practically every time he came into bat throughout the entire series. Whoever was bowling at the time, Tyson would be summoned up to take over, even if he were on his knees with exhaustion. The tactic did not work at Sydney but on three other occasions it was Tyson who got Benaud out. It conjured up the picture of Jardine's similar use of Larwood against Bradman twenty-two years earlier on these same grounds.

As I have said, the second Test match took its toll of Hutton's nervous resources, and its curious sequel, again illustrating the wildly contradictory facets of Hutton's character, is still vividly remembered by every member of that touring party. There was little time to relax before the third Test at Melbourne and, indeed, apart from a day watching a Davis Cup tie, Hutton did not relax at all. The outcome was that at breakfast on the morning of the game, Hutton was still in his room, downcast and sick. It was rumoured that he was not going to play. I don't know what was said, because, as the junior member of the party, I was not present. Happily, he let himself be cajoled into playing and everything came right for him.

But it only heightened the tension of an already very tense situation. The series was wide open again, Tyson was making the critics eat their words and more than 60,000 spectators turned out for each day of the Test. England made a disastrous start. We were soon 29 for three, then 41 for four. Our final total was 191 of which I scored 102. This kept us in the game and Hutton was very generous to me and, indeed, clearly moved by my innings. In the end Australia needed 240 to win and everyone agreed that the only people who could now win the match for England, on a turning wicket, were Appleyard and Wardle. In the event Australia were bundled out for 111 and the hero was Tyson. He took seven for 27. In five weeks, therefore, England had swung from one down to one up in the series.

The Melbourne Test provided a curious insight into Hutton. He had himself caused a crisis by not wanting to play, yet his captaincy was magnificent. He was accused of keeping a brake on the game with a slow over rate but no captain, before or since, could have handled his bowling better or set his fields more effectively. I was conscious throughout the match that he was manipulating everything as though playing a very tight and ruthless game of chess, which contrasted so strangely with his performance in those tense hours before the Test got under way. My own view was that this kind of mental stress was more likely to occur in a person with less experience of leadership. Here was a man used to withstanding fearsome pressures as a batsman; now the cares of captaincy exposed a chink in the armour. It is interesting to recall that Len Hutton came to the England captaincy in 1952, at the age of thirty-six, never having captained any cricket team before. I could not help thinking at the time that a man more used to the pressures and vicissitudes of captaincy, a man with a longer experience and a more conventional training in leadership, for example, might have averted the whole crisis over Bedser. Hutton had been confronted with a huge dilemma.

This may read like a harsh judgment of a great cricketer. It is not meant to be. His kindness and consideration to me on that tour went far beyond anything he had promised my father at Tilbury.

In the fourth Test at Adelaide, England won the series that had started so bleakly. Here, to my amazement, I found myself the pace-setter in a big partnership with Denis Compton. The wicket was slow, the Australians were bowling defensively, and runs were hard to come by if you were out of form. Compton was out of touch and as we fought our way onwards, there were outbreaks of barracking and slow-handclapping. This unnerved me into playing shots that I had never previously ventured in Test cricket. It may have been that I suddenly had a reputation to live up to, or that I was somewhat prematurely launching into an innings of which I was not yet really capable at the highest level of cricket. Whatever my reasoning, which I cannot recall, I was taking chances and trying to enliven the afternoon's play. If the crowd had not got on our backs, I would not have been playing that way at all.

This was soon made very clear to me by one of the most unusual hold-ups in a Test match. I looked round, at the end of an over, to see Vic Wilson, the twelfth man, calmly walking out to the middle. He was wearing his blazer. As I had not signalled to the dressing room for anything, nor was it the drinks interval, I could only assume that Compton had indicated that he wanted some fresh batting gloves. Wilson, however, kept walking straight to my end. I was mystified. I was still mystified when Wilson reached into his blazer pocket, produced two bananas and gave them to me. I said: "What the hell are these for?" Wilson replied: "Well, the skipper thought you might be hungry. He watched you play a couple of wild shots just now. It rather suggests he is keen for you to stay out here batting a little longer. Get your head down."

The crowd and the Australian players must have been intrigued by it all. From that moment I batted properly and scored 79.

If I had been learning some new aspect of Hutton's character in every Test match, I now began to widen my education with every innings. When the Australians batted I was struck in the face, fielding close to Arthur Morris, and had my nose broken. By the time England batted again, needing only 94 to win the match, the series and the Ashes, my eyes were black and almost closed. Peter May asked Hutton which batsman he wanted to send in in my place. Hutton looked at me as though I had just returned fresh, bronzed and supremely fit from a surfing holiday and answered "No one." I batted in my usual place.

In fact seven of us had to bat in our usual places, despite the small target we needed to win. Bill Edrich, Hutton and I were all out in the space of twenty deliveries from Keith Miller. We lost our first wicket at 3, our second at 10, our third at 18. When the fourth wicket fell at 49 Hutton delivered an immortal line. Though the next man in was right at his shoulder he could not restrain himself. "The booggers," he said, "have done us." The comment could have been better timed. Poor Denis Compton walked to the wicket with the captain's despair ringing in his ears. Fortunately, he stood firm and won the day. All of us, Len and Denis too, had a good laugh about it afterwards.

The fifth and final Test was a formality. The worst rainfalls known in New South Wales for fifty years caused millions of pounds' worth of damage in the Hunter Valley and, in Sydney, prevented the Australians from getting at us. Had the match started on time I would not have played. A combination of shock from the broken nose and a chill put me in hospital for five days. On what should have been the second day of the Test, I got up. On what should have been the third day I left hospital, weak at the knees. Back at the hotel I met Hutton. "Good," he said, "you're playing." The game finally got under way the following morning and my contribution to England's only innings in a draw was a duck. Hutton had little time for doctors' opinions.

In contrast, he had a good deal of time for successful businessmen, even when they came from such fertile cricketing soil as Philadelphia, USA, as did Henry Sayen. Henry, to put it mildly, was well heeled. He had also developed a wild enthusiasm for cricket the previous year when, on a casual visit to Lord's, he had met Hutton. He had been invited by Hutton to meet the lads in the England dressing room and perhaps stay awhile to learn a little more about the game. Hutton was at his most genial, explaining the fundamentals and even the lesser known tricks of the trade with a rare patience. Henry's enthusiasm soon extended to handing out substantial financial bonuses to the players for special performances. Hutton did not actively discourage it and we gave him a warm welcome in Australia.

I was probably too young to have formed any serious assessment of Hutton at the time. I had great respect for him as I also had for Bill Edrich who, despite having an indifferent tour himself, was exceptionally kind to me. Looking back now, with greater experience, I think Hutton must be rated as a complete cricketer and probably one of the four or five greatest batsmen of all time. He has to be judged against the background of his times and that background, in the cricketing sense, was tough. In his prime he had to make his runs against Lindwall and Miller in their primes, which was more demanding even than facing Hall and Griffith in the early 1960s. His greatest years were between 1947 and 1952. From 1953 onwards he was slightly past his best so that, when I played with him, you could not have said that he was a better batsman than, say, Peter May or Ted Dexter on their best days. Yet his supreme technical ability, his immense concentration, his fine cricket brain assure his place among the masters as long as the game is played.

# I I

The significance of that first Australian tour for me was that I had earned my keep. If there was a spare chair at a dining table already occupied by the much-photographed Messrs Compton, Bailey and Edrich, I no longer felt an intruder if I joined them. I knew that I fitted in on merit. My selection had been justified and, above all, the cross of "privilege" had been lifted from my shoulders. I was no longer "Tonbridge and Oxford". This became literally true when I came back to England and decided that to return to Oxford for my planned final year would be a mutual waste of time.

All I wanted to do was to play cricket. This, however, was not possible. Having relinquished a University place I was now in line for National Service. It would be hypocritical to pretend that I relished the prospect. At best it would mean a huge disruption of my cricket career; at worst it would mean a posting to some far-flung garrison from which it was unlikely that the RAF would fly me home to play for England. Nevertheless I must emphasise that I had resigned myself to the inevitable because what happened next, my discharge from the RAF after two weeks' instead of two years' service, was not due to any high level string pulling on my part.

It must have looked pretty suspicious to the public because on the day I reported to Cardington, Bedfordshire, I had a tan like a Red Indian. I had just come from an arduous seven and a half month tour of Australia and New Zealand where the grounds, generally, had been as hard as concrete. This was not overlooked by the medical officer when he noticed a reference on my reporting documents to a "long history of foot trouble". Understandably, perhaps, he said: "There can't be much the matter with your feet," but there he was wrong. The problem was an hereditary disability of stiff, rigid toes.

73

At school, while playing soccer, they had caused me a great deal of pain and I had been in hospital for more than two months after having an operation on them. The danger now was whether a prolonged period of square bashing in ammunition boots would cause permanent damage and thus make the RAF liable to pay me a disability pension for the rest of my days. The matter was referred to an Air Ministry specialist in London who examined me for twenty minutes and then discharged me from the RAF on the spot.

This might have been passed over quietly had I not gone straight from Kingsway to Lord's and run into instant good form. Playing for MCC against Oxford I scored 47 and 101. I then linked up with Kent, made 139 for them against Northants in my first match and took 48 and 44 off Surrey in the next game. In my third match against Essex immediately after that I hit 115 not out in the first innings and 103 not out in the second.

The press came down on me like a ton of bricks. In Parliament the late Sir Gerald Nabarro's moustache bristled with indignation as he virtually accused me of dodging the column. Happily, when I wrote to him explaining all the facts he had overlooked, he had the grace to apologise. But the damage was done. The letters poured in. I am still getting three or four letters a year on the subject, even now. One non-admirer has pursued me relentlessly. He never signs his name nor puts an address on his letter, but the postmark is always from some Kent coastal town. Twice, sometimes three times a year, he writes brief messages like: "This fickle world applauds you, but you get no applause from me. I served at the front ...", etc. The only time he leaves me alone is when I am having a bad time, which appears to satisfy him greatly.

When I was chosen for the third Test against South Africa in that summer of 1955, and was badly knocked about by Heine and Adcock, my mail increased again. Mostly the letters came from parents who had lost sons in the war or had lost them in accidents during National Service. One said: "It serves you right. If there was any justice you should have an injury for the next two years." I wrote back to them all and, in many cases, received friendly and understanding replies.

If it is any consolation to these correspondents, the fear of permanently crippling myself by damaging those controversial toes has lived with me ever since. I do not, for example, join in knock-about games of football, even with my children. The only time I broke that rule was on a subsequent tour of Australia when, fortified by Christmas morning champagne, I joined in a kick-about on the beach at Adelaide. My toes swelled up like balloons and I had to have injections for a week to get me fit for the coming Test match.

Equally, that third Test match appearance against South Africa in 1955 did not fuse off a glorious new chapter in my career. I had coped with Lindwall and Miller in Australia but Heine and Adcock, huge, hostile men who brought the ball down from a colossal height, were different propositions altogether. I played them unintelligently. My success in Australia had come from playing forward, and obstinately I believed I could play the same way against these two gigantic South Africans. I cannot now understand how I could have been so stupid. There are certain bowlers to whom you must be prepared to get on the back foot right away, but at that time I had not learned the lesson. I played forward regardless, and for my pains received the worst going-over I have ever experienced in a Test match. I came away from Manchester with so many bruises that I was not completely fit again until the winter.

By an unpleasant coincidence those injuries were responsible for doubts being raised for a second time that summer of dodging the column. After the fourth Test at Leeds the series against South Africa stood at two-all with everything to play for at the Oval. I had not played at Leeds, but a few days before the Oval match the selectors rang me to enquire about my fitness. I told them frankly that I did not think I would be a lot of use to them. If I got struck on one of my old injuries early in an innings I would probably be out of action for the rest of the match. It was an outlook which I believe Sir Alf Ramsey, in another era in another sport, would have understood and appreciated. The press were not on my side and the publicity seemed to leave the England selectors baffled. They asked me to turn up for a special fitness test at Lord's and two of them, Gubby Allen, and my own Kent secretary, Leslie Ames, together with five of the MCC ground staff boys, bowled to me at the nets. With respect to them all, this was like sparring against a keen young amateur boxer before climbing into the ring with Mohammed Ali. I batted against their medium pace without a lot of pain in my hands, but I could not stand any jarring from a short pitched delivery. Wisely, I pulled out, but these are the most difficult decisions one ever has to make for fear of being misunderstood.

# 12

In the autumn of 1955 with no cricket in prospect for the winter, the awful thought occurred that I must look to making a living outside cricket. I had never envisaged myself standing behind the drapery counter of a large store in Lewisham, confusing lady customers over the respective merits of Witney and Hong Kong blankets. This somewhat dramatic turn of events had been brought about by an earlier meeting with a well-known patron of Kent cricket, Stuart Chiesman. He became the next man to have a considerable influence on my life. Kent had been anxious that I should have some kind of winter employment and so I had been officially introduced to him in the hope that he might be able to help. His family owned a small group of department stores in Kent and he suggested that when I had finished at Oxford I might take a took at the world of commerce for a period of six months.

At nine o'clock on a September morning in 1955, I was plunged into the deep end of business. I arrived just in time for the white sales, at a time when the single word "Sale" in a store window attracted bigger queues than you would now see fighting to get a Cup Final ticket. Hordes of women rushed in, firing questions in all directions as if these were the last sheets and blankets ever to come on to the world market. Thankfully, the man in charge of the drapery department was a cricket fanatic but even he, in rare moments when he had time for lucid thought, must have rated me as something less than God's gift to the bazaar business. By the next sales I had been transferred to the toy department where I turned my hand to anything, even vice-captain to Father Christmas in his lunch hour.

By the end of that winter, I had at least advanced to the position where I understood the difference between profit and loss, but there was also one reason why I knew that this kind of work was never really for me: the store was open on Saturdays. The idea of working on a Saturday afternoon, when Charlton were playing Arsenal just down the road, was too much. The thought that anyone should *want* to go shopping instead of going to a football match was beyond my comprehension. I actually raised the suggestion that it made far more sense to close the shop from three o'clock until five, if Charlton were at home, and then open again between five and eight, but no one agreed. The store stayed open. I missed my football.

My ties with the Chiesman family, however, were to become somewhat closer over the next few years. On the occasion when I first met Stuart Chiesman at Canterbury, I also met one of his two daughters, Penny. In September 1956 Penny and I were married. The service was conducted by the Bishop of Rochester, Dr. Christopher Chevasse, who was a double Oxford Blue at athletics and rowing. David Sheppard also officiated and Peter May was best man.

Apart from being a member of the Chiesman family I was also now a fully-established England cricketer. Although I had my limitations in the blanket and toy departments, I did have some value to the firm in a different way. My name was beginning to have a certain commercial value. I was useful when it came to entertaining visiting firemen, or chatting up contacts when I accompanied buyers to factories. And it did the firm no harm when my photograph appeared in the newspapers in some connection with the Chiesman business.

The only problem it did not solve was the agony of Saturday afternoons. My role in the business was not specific. I had to decide for myself what I could do to benefit the commercial interests of Chiesman's and my own common sense told me that this meant attending the store at its busiest time, namely Saturdays. This was the day when all the directors themselves worked particularly hard. Stuart Chiesman and his brother Russell were always there shortly after nine, and they never left much before six. If I had said "May I go and watch Charlton?" I am sure he would have agreed. But I had my own conscience to live with, and I watched soccer on only two afternoons during that winter.

My father-in-law's methods of working and living would have

destroyed many people's misconceptions about the way company chairmen conduct themselves. I learned a great deal from his example. He worked extremely hard. There was no carpet on his office floor. His office door was always open. Whereas everyone else had an hour for lunch, he had forty minutes. He rarely drank at lunch time. He was tough on himself and expected a lot from his staff. He took a deep interest in the welfare of all of them, yet he had no time for fools. His own relaxation came during the summer when he spent a lot of time on the Kent cricket grounds, but even then on Saturdays he would call in at one of his stores before the start of play and might leave around tea time to hear the day's progress. This was the way he conducted his life until the day he died at seventy-three.

I have vivid recollections of my last meeting with him because, as in the case of my own father, it was on the eve of leaving for an overseas tour, this time in February 1969. England were flying out to Pakistan and after picking up Derek Underwood, who lived close to my home, something made me drive to the Lewisham store to say goodbye to him. It was not a thing I normally did. He was a man who was always in an immense hurry during business hours and could often be quite curt if interrupted. On this occasion he was very relaxed, chatted happily away about cricket to Underwood and myself and even strolled down the stairs to the car park with us to shake hands. He was the picture of health and was, in fact, about to go off on a fortnight's holiday in Barbados. Yet, oddly, I had an uneasy feeling that I might never see him again. As the plane left London Airport, I knew it.

During the last Test in Pakistan I received the news that he was dead. He had only been ill for four days. I flew home immediately. In many ways he had been a second father to me and our friendship was close. Soon after his death the family business was taken over. Although I had not been able to give much time to it over the last five years, I still saw it as holding a future for myself. Now I was totally committed to cricket.

# 13

MCC, the Marylebone Cricket Club, comprising more than 15,000 members, means different things to different people. To the cartoonist it gives a picture of the Long Room full of elderly members in even more antiquated dress, with moustaches and bushy eyebrows and accents of their own. Cricketers like myself, who have had the fun of playing under their umbrella in so many parts of the world, will always feel a debt of gratitude. To visitors from overseas MCC means the Lord's cricket ground, an aura of mystique and grandeur.

It is extraordinary how, from this little site which Thomas Lord purchased and built as a cricket ground in 1774, a club has been created which has taken the game of cricket to so many corners of the globe over the years. To think that the MCC tour to West Indies, which I had the honour of captaining in 1968, was the first time we had gone to the Caribbean on a profit-sharing basis, after expenses had been paid. Previously, the cost of sending the England side fell upon MCC.

The position of Treasurer is all-embracing. There has never been a chairman of MCC and the high honour of President is held only for a year at a time. The general in the field, historically, is the Treasurer and he is in close liaison with the Secretary. Together they hold the reins, keeping watch over the day-to-day affairs and an eye to long-term planning as well. Lord Harris of Kent before the war, H. S. Altham post-war and G. O. Allen these last ten years have each in their different ways made an enormous impact on the development of the game.

79

I count myself fortunate that in my years as a senior cricketer S. C. Griffith should have been secretary of MCC. Under him were fifty-six people, in the various offices, the printers of the score cards, the groundsman and his staff, numerous gatemen, the staff of the tennis and the squash courts and, of course, the cricket coaches. They were all responsible to him and he, in turn, was responsible for the service that his large family provided. He was successful, in my view, in the same way as Leslie Deakins at Edgbaston, Geoffrey Howard at the Oval, John Nash at Headingley, Jack Wood at Old Trafford— they all managed to create a family spirit.

Billy Griffith is a rare person. An outstanding cricketer and rugby footballer in his own right, his career was cut short, like so many of his vintage, by the war. In this he distinguished himself too, as a Colonel in the Glider Regiment, flying the first glider (taking the General and his staff) into Normandy an hour or so before the main invasion forces landed on the beaches. He was awarded the DFC.

After the war he was both captain and secretary of Sussex for a while before coming to Lord's as assistant secretary to Ronny Aird. It was in these years that he built up a special relationship with all the cricket countries, apart from his demanding work for cricket at home. Cricketers loved him and respected him; and most important of all, they trusted him implicitly.

As his reign at Lord's came to an end he saw the formation of the Cricket Council and the Test and County Cricket Board. With these developments came the splitting up of the role that he once held and, in consequence, the reducing of MCC's part in the future development of the game.

These changes have had to come, I suppose. The Cricket Council is eligible to receive Government money, whereas MCC as a private club could not do so. The TCCB is an independent body incorporating the voice of each one of the counties and they are responsible for our county cricket and Test matches at home. Donald Carr is at the helm here, whilst Jack Bailey, secretary to the Cricket Council, is also secretary to MCC, now the private club which has had to stand aside a little in the modernisation. Happily, MCC is still responsible for the laws of the game, and plays host in England when the International Cricket Conference meets annually. But somehow I am a little sad about the changes. I view it all with some misgiving, and wonder whether the commercial conglomerate into which it appears to be developing can ever have quite the same family touch again.

Let me say at once that there has been a splendid reappraisal of the financial structure of county cricket. Without it we could not be surviving as well as we are. How long can we maintain it as a fully professional game? Can it attract good players by its present pay structure? Can it survive as an inherent part of the English way of life? The questions are obvious and the solutions are becoming increasingly difficult to find.

Certainly my own career has spanned the greatest upheaval the county game has known. It is now unrecognisable from the game played back in the early 1950s.

There have been domestic developments in county cricket which the public have never been aware of; but there are others obvious to everyone. On a sunny Saturday in the immediate post-war years there would have been 20,000 to watch Lancashire play Kent at Old Trafford. Today if you get 10,000 it is regarded as a huge commercial success. There are many reasons for this, some social and many technical. But the single most important change has been the decline of the personality player and the rise of the professional attitude. The county players themselves wanted this. It is a product of the times, a tangent from trade unionism. There are individualists still, Clive Lloyd being the prime example, but they have to conform. The team is all.

This outlook has produced a startling change in the very structure of a county cricket match. When the 20,000 turned up at Old Trafford to see Kent just after the war they had come to see Godfrey Evans and Doug Wright. Evans's first agile deed would be greeted with a roar. Cyril Washbrook's first square-cut would produce a tumult. Then came sophisticated, knowing applause when, after only fifty minutes, Doug Wright was brought into the attack. Today a captain would be classed as mentally unstable if he called up a leg-spinner so early in the game. In those days the crowd merely settled down to watch the giants duel. People were less concerned with Lancashire beating Kent or Kent beating Lancashire. It was not so much the result as the personalities which caught the imagination.

It would all be repeated again in the next match, say Middlesex versus Kent at Lord's. The traditional prelude was some lovely, crisp batting by Robertson and Brown while the crowd settled themselves and waited for Edrich and Compton. At lunch Compton was probably already there, twenty not out, and for that forty minute interval the whole ground was bathed in a warm expectancy of afternoon glory. The world was wonderful and, again, few were concerned with whether Middlesex was going to beat Kent. The Middlesex lunch score was probably 130 for two. Today if any team had taken 130 off us by lunch I would walk off a worried man. Then it was almost a matter of self-congratulation that you had kept them *down* to 130.

None of this should be regarded as wistful nostalgia on my part for the dear, departed days of the imperious amateur. But it was the existence of the amateur which allowed the star system to prevail.

In the twenties, there were a handful of outstanding amateurs: Gilligan, Allen, Jardine, Chapman, Wyatt, Duleepsinhji. There were even more outstanding professionals: Hobbs, Sutcliffe, Rhodes, Hammond, Larwood, Tate. By the immediate post-war years the trend had developed to the point where county cricketers could be classified into one of four distinct categories. First there was the star-bracket professional, better than any amateur in the country: Hutton, Compton, Washbrook, Bedser, Evans. Second, then, was the really gifted England-class amateur who was just above the general level of professionals: Trevor Bailey, Norman Yardley, Freddie Brown. Third, a few full-time amateurs alongside about a hundred county professionals. There was a host of part-time players who really typified the county game at the time: the gifted amateur cricketer, maybe a schoolmaster who could only play in August like M. M. Walford of Somerset, J. R. Thompson of Warwickshire, R. Sale and J. D. Eggar of Derbyshire, who enjoyed the game and could get a holiday place in his county side. He could come in fresh, and his contribution could be stimulating. The junior professional simply had to stand down to make room for him and this was generally accepted. This pattern has not been in evidence in recent years; such a player would probably be happier to have a match or two with the second eleven to prove his mettle before assuming a regular place in the county eleven.

It is not difficult to see, therefore, why the stars shone so brightly on most summer days. The ability gulf between class one and class four was so vast that the Huttons and Comptons stood out like immortals. Talking to men like Arthur Fagg, John Langridge and Harold Gimblett, seasoned opening batsmen and superb players, it was clear that the balance of county bowling was thin. Each county would have one great bowler, and a couple of good ones—Yorkshire excepted, of course. The batsmen would usually be tested in the first hour of the morning when confronted by the opposing team's one top-class professional bowler. There might be duel with a good leg-spinner during the afternoon before the ball got too soft, but the rest of the bowling would have been what we used to call "help yourself". This is one of the reasons why there was such fast scoring mid-afternoon and nos. 5, 6, 7, 8 in the batting order could score so heavily.

The county with its sights unwaveringly set on winning the County Championship was probably stricter on its selection of amateurs during the holiday weeks towards the end of the season. But, of course, the priorities then were very different. Even as recently as when I took over the captaincy of Kent in 1955, this was one of the first things made clear to me. At the very start of the season I was presented with a small book which listed the addresses and phone numbers of all the players and notes about the amateurs' availability. I was then expected to keep in touch with them, ask them which games they would be prepared to play in and book their places in teams to represent Kent the following July and August. This could lead to some incongruous situations. In the thirties Percy Chapman would have had six names in the book for Canterbury Week, already booked in April. That meant there were places for only five professionals from the county staff. Let me say at once the amateurs were really fine players and worthy of their places in the Kent side. It was just so hard on the pros, a man like Bill Ashdown, for instance, who had to wait many years before he played in his first Canterbury Week. It made balanced team selection quite impossible and from the outset Leslie Ames and I altered the pattern, without offending anyone. In any case, the few amateurs that we had were not of the same calibre. The team was chosen match by match, the bowlers to fit the conditions. If that may sound glib I can only recall a sigh sadly at the number of times we played Douglas Wright on a grassy damp wicket in Essex, or elsewhere, when he had no chance of making an impact. These days a rest on wickets which were unsuited to him would have set him up to help us win the next match. The amateur-professional distinction in cricket was officially abolished in 1962 but, in fact, there had been a gradual breaking down after the war.

83

At Test level Peter May and I were the last genuine amateurs, in that neither of us received any money for playing and our expense allowance did not cover our costs. Moreover, we were not really accorded any privilege, and quite right too. We appeared on the first day of pre-season training, played in the county or Test sides right through to September, and played in the fund-raising benefit matches on Sundays.

It was this change in outlook which altered the traditional character of county cricket. With it went, too, much of the glamour of the individuals, the real personalities. It is not that there are no longer any stars in the county game. It is rather that there has been such a levelling up in talent and such an all-round improvement in standards that the stars no longer stand out so prominently. Instead of four categories of county player there are now only two: the top class cricketer and the rank-and-file professional who is not very far behind him in ability. Gone are the top-grade amateurs because they are now top-grade professionals. Gone from the game completely are the fancy-hat amateurs for whom the pros had to stand down. Playing standards have risen; there must be a great number of overseas players to compare with the all-time greats. I long to see a few more English batsmen rule the roost.

Gone too, for the same reason, is another class of old-time county cricketer, the veteran pro, sage and full of humour. He was probably symbolised by the ageing Patsy Hendren, ample girth made to look more ample by two sweaters, fielding down at deep third man with the big professional cap pulled well down over his forehead. Every county seemed to have two or three of them and crowds were always sympathetically warm to them, remembering all the pleasure that these men had given them in the past. They, too, are victims of an era of efficiency which demanded a man down there whose sprinting is going to turn twos into ones. I cannot envisage a forty-two-year-old veteran being flown out to Australia as a reserve again! The emphasis on the one-day competition cricket forces change.

The irony, of course, is that it is this very levelling up in county standards that has contributed so much to the game's critical financial plight. There is no doubt that the cricket watched by the big crowds just after the war gave a false impression. They saw a run-harvest which delighted them. But I doubt if one in a hundred understood that what they were really watching was total batsman-domination of mediocre bowling. There was not a single genuinely fast England bowler in the County Championship immediately after the war. The nearest to measure to that description was Pritchard, the New Zealander who played for Warwickshire. Tearaway Trevor Bailey might have been the fastest English bowler, but on his own admission he was no Trueman or Statham for pace. So the batsmen continued to take huge scores off unbalanced attacks. True, most sides had a quality spinner, but the lack of balance made for weakness. As long as the runs flowed the spectators did not spend too much time making a critical analysis of the field placing. Nor did one frequently read the critics tempering their eulogies of Denis Compton's second century in a match by pointing out that the opposition bowling after the initial burst, or apart from one good spinner, was often there to be plundered. Then, two or three sides stood out as real champions. Today, there is little to choose between the top twelve.

That is why the star system has gone. That is why John Edrich and Geoffrey Boycott, fine players though they are, do not receive the ovations on their way to the wicket that Hutton and Washbrook, Compton or Bill Edrich, received before them. Today runs have to be fought for against strategic field settings and against seam bowling attacks, about which I shall have a good deal more to say in a moment. At this point, though, I think it important to point out that cricket has not suffered alone in the collapse of the personality cult. Soccer, surely, has become an even more regimented game, with its marshalled defences and destructive strategy. For every George Best there are now ten club defences who would be lined up before the firing squad if they conceded more than one goal per game. Like cricket, star performers were soccer's big selling line in those frenetic post-war years. The whole game was basically a stage for the Matthewses, the Lawtons, the Mannions, the Carters, the Swifts. Soccer, as a game, has come to terms with the modern developments by accentuating competitiveness to the borders of hysteria. This is possible over ninety minutes. It is not possible over three days.

The other inescapable comparison between the two games concerns the prosperity and attitudes of the professionals who play them. Soccer has undergone its own industrial revolution and emerged highly paid and highly successful. Today, the old disciplines are being challenged, coinciding with hooliganism on the terraces. Cricket has its own Cricketers' Association which, because of lack of finances in the game, does not have the negotiating strength of soccer's Players' Union. But in terms of attitude its strength is such that, as a county captain, I would have to tread warily if I were going to make demands or take action which I knew would cross swords with the views of the Cricketers' Association.

The modern player is very conscious of his rights, though admittedly this not so much reflects the ambitions of the Cricketers' Association as a trend throughout the country. But it can lead to awkward, unpleasant and unnecessary tensions. An example occurred in 1970 when a number of Kent players appeared for breakfast in the dining room of the Grand Hotel, Leicester, wearing sweaters instead of jackets and ties. It was the last morning of the match and that evening we were driving off to another game. Sweaters were probably more suitable for the evening drive but the fact remained that this was breakfast and I had always requested my players at least to wear a blazer, if not actually a suit, when they appeared officially for a Kent match. No one in the hotel complained but the fact remained that Kent County Cricket Club looked more like a coach party than a professional cricket team with a long tradition. I felt that we had a responsibility to the club and to cricket to look the part, both on and off the field. Twenty years earlier the captain would have informed the senior professional that he had better see to it swiftly that the players were properly dressed, a course of action which the players would have accepted without complaint. In 1970 I played it quietly. I knew that if I created a scene I would probably have had to live with the resentment of the players for the next two matches and it was the cricket that was important. I was perhaps weak for not intervening but in these emancipated times a captain has to wear kid gloves if he is to get the best out of his players on the field. Certainly a captain of the older school, like Tom Graveney, would not have stood for it. Today, of course, the same standards are not expected. Casual dress is accepted at meal times in hotels and it would not be an issue.

Management has always been an art, but it can be a chore unless those who are led are prepared to be led. In today's England, it seems, we are not so gracious at conceding a point, either as manager or as player. It appears to be a sign of weakness to be generous even about another man's ability. The highest accolade that anyone now seems capable of sparing another man is "Not bad" or "Pretty good".

The technical development that has changed the face of county cricket is the discovery of "seam" bowling, a word which in its present sense was not even in the glossary of cricketing terms when I started playing for Kent. Here is the classic instance of new conditions producing a new art. It did not come about by accident. Its development can be traced through the changing wickets during the post-war years. The period from 1946 until 1953 was the era of the good brown wickets on which bat dominated ball to the point where the scoreboards looked like huge, crude computers. This worried the counties themselves. For the first time there was a feeling that the spectators wanted to see more finished matches. The edict went out to prepare more sporting wickets. This significantly changed the game. The spinners came back, and for the next seven years men like Lock and Laker, bowling on under-prepared wickets, were rarely out of the headlines. Now the counties had a new worry. The pendulum had swung too far in the opposite direction. It was after their next edict that seam bowling really took hold.

"The under-preparing of wickets is not quite the answer", they agreed. "They are breaking up a little too early. What they need is more grass on them." In that one decision the whole character of cricket changed. The seam bowler took the game away from the leg-spinner and now it is rare to find a county with fewer than three, even four, seamers in its team.

The effectiveness of seam bowling is closely allied to the fact that grassier outfields, as well as pitches, protect the skin of the ball for much longer periods. In Australia bowlers used to find it almost impossible to swing the ball after eight eight-ball overs because the shine had been worn off. Now the shine stays on indefinitely. In England in 1975 I played in more than one game where there was still a deep shine on the ball after sixty overs. If you now operate with a spinner at one end and a seamer at the other, the seamer is liable to become volubly neurotic if he does not see the spinner polishing up the ball on his trousers or shirt between deliveries to keep it in "condition". Wilfred Rhodes or Doug Wright or Bill O'Reilly, indeed, most of the great spinners, would have resisted. Today the condition of the ball is preciously guarded by all bowlers, fast and slow.

The first time I consciously came in contact with seam bowling was late in the 1950s. I was by then an established Test as well as county player but I did not understand what was happening. We were playing against Middlesex on the traditionally high-scoring wicket at Gravesend. There was nothing out of the ordinary when Middlesex batted first and declared at 363 for seven. Yet when we were left to play out the closing twenty minutes of the day batting suddenly became a nightmare. The pitch did not appear to have changed at all yet the bat must have been beaten a dozen times. The ball seemed to be flying all ways and wobbling unpredictably. In the end Kent were beaten heavily. I still could not understand it. The explanation came from John Warr: "We bowled better than you did," he said. "Or rather, we bowled *differently*. Your men were trying to pitch it up and get it to swing early on. Why didn't they try to keep the shine on the ball? On a wicket like this I don't attempt to bowl flat out at all. I ease back, polish up the ball and get it to seam about." What I was hearing for the first time was the description of the most significant technical development in post-war cricket.

Its significance must not be under-rated because it has affected every part of the game. From the batting aspect it has deprived spectators of some of the violent spectacle. Whereas men like Frank Woolley stroked their way to high scores, today's cricketers are more circumspect. They accept that the odds are frequently loaded against them so they get their heads down and battle it out. Nor has it really encouraged the fast bowlers, which was one of the original intentions. They may bowl themselves to exhaustion only to find that the skilful medium-paced seamer has reaped far more impressive rewards with half the effort. This can perhaps be most vividly illustrated by the fact that in three separate Test matches I have been confronted by England bowlers who did not take the second new ball. On each occasion they thought they would be more effective with the old one, which remained heavily polished on one side. Indeed, I have actually taken a new ball in a Test for the benefit of the spinners who wanted a hard ball instead of one softened up during eighty-five overs.

I honestly believe that at certain times it is now actually easier to play in Test cricket than in county cricket. By unshakable tradition fast bowlers picked for Test matches are genuinely *fast*. Thus over a period of five years Trueman and Statham were automatically selected for Test matches at Lord's when they were not necessarily the bowlers best suited to the conditions. Lord's during those years was a seamer's paradise and had England picked Jackson of Derbyshire, while he was still playing, plus Shackleton of Hampshire and Cartwright of Warwickshire, we would have been more successful. Against those three men I would not have backed a visiting Test team, whatever its reputation, to make above 200 in an innings more than once in twenty attempts. The trouble was that we never had the courage to come to terms with the power of seam bowling.

Among the counties, I must confess that Kent was very slow to catch on, too. It took a long time for us to accept the utilitarian principles of seam bowling. Douglas Wright would never have been asked to bowl defensively. He played automatically and always bowled in attacking vein; on a good day he might take six for 70. Now, if he were in my team, there would be certain days when he would not bowl at all and certain matches when he would not even be selected, for the simple reason that a bowler like John Shepherd or Alan Dixon would be more effective on some occasions. Wright's six for 100 might lose the match whereas Shepherd, in the conditions made for him, might take six for 40 and win it.

It is easy to be cynical about the changing philosophies which have given rein to the seamer. The ideal cricket wicket that equates skill with entertainment and provides a fair duel between bowler and batsman is extremely difficult to produce. We have seen practically every type in England since the war. The worst of all was probably the true, brown but totally bounceless surface which ended Frank Tyson's career prematurely at Northampton. Jeff Thomson has had a taste of these wickets, too, in England. One hundred per cent effort on the bowler's part achieves only sixty per cent return. It is so dispiriting. All over the world wickets seem to be slower.

Wickets are going to be a real headache to cricket administrators in the years ahead. There is much more know-how today, yet less expertise. The scientists are uncovering new techniques every day in their soil research, turf analysis, in the growing of grass and the use of fertilisers. The scientists fail us in one respect: they cannot do anything to supply men who are born to be groundsmen. Like many experts on the land, groundsmanship is a trade forged by an instinctive love for what one is doing. Rolling is a chore and few grounds get the heavy rolling, hours and hours of it in the early spring, that used to be administered.

Let me say at once that there are still a number of magnificent groundsmen on our main grounds, but they are gold dust. We need many, many more and the difficulty is that the financial rewards are not particularly inviting. I doubt if they ever will be. However, there is one priceless compensation. I cannot think of a happier or more fulfilling vocation than to have your own house on a lovely ground and be a vital cog in a friendly club.

# 14

It should surprise no one that cricket is not self-supporting. It never has been. Before the war it survived with the help of patronage from wealthy and influential benefactors. A county membership was usually small. The expenditure was much lower because many of its players were amateur. For example, Bryan Valentine, who captained Kent, received £250 in expenses and it might have cost him £1,000 out of his own pocket each season.

Since the war the counties have tried many fund-raising ideas but only one, Warwickshire, has succeeded in remaining on a firm financial footing. For the rest a sudden surge in running costs co-incided with a crisis in the national economy. Overnight, patronage of the old style was out. Whereas you could once rely on donations of perhaps £100 you were now lucky if you could get £10.

Our own experiences in Kent illustrate the common plight. We had a rough time in the 1950s, losing as much as £12,000 in the year before I became captain. We then staged a recovery until, in 1969, a single bad year of poor results and soaring overheads meant that we were losing money again. In 1970 the county committee gambled. They allowed me a full and comprehensive staff in the hope that we could get results to keep the attendances up. They knew when they took the decision that anything short of winning the County Championship would mean another financial loss. And I, as captain, knew that anything short of winning would mean that my playing staff would be cut and that I would have no complaints about it.

The gamble, as it happened, paid off in the most remarkable

fashion. In due course I shall indulge myself in the full story of how Kent stormed every bastion in sight during the second half of that astonishing summer to come from the foot of the table to win the title. Yet thrilling and gratifying though it was, it brought only temporary relief from the pressing problems of finance. To be honest, we could not afford the champagne we drank and shared with our friends that September evening in our dressing room at the Oval.

Success, even of that magnitude, is less of a solution than a delaying action against the day when the whole game grinds to a halt, as it surely would have done by now had a massive infusion of sponsorship not been found.

I do not pretend to have a panacea but I am certain that the timid approaches of cutting the programme or paring the overheads of a county club to the bone is not the answer. The trite argument that "We play too much cricket" was exposed as nonsense during the early stages of the 1975 Championship. After playing two matches, Kent did not have another game for ten days. Not a drop of rain fell during those ten days, the sun shone continuously, yet not a ball was bowled nor a run scored. How can you have a professional game and not play it? It is ludicrous. If cricketers complain that they get tired, what of it? So do miners, commercial travellers and surgeons. Similarly, trimming expenses and playing staff to the minimum has no future. I applauded Essex for their shoestring achievements in 1969 when they virtually managed on twelve players. They contributed only one player, Keith Fletcher, to two of the six Test matches. What standard would they have been if they had had to release as many as Yorkshire or Kent or, indeed, suffered a crop of injuries? They were quick to realise that to be a viable county side they must have a larger circle of players to call on. This they have done, and today Essex are one of the best-managed counties.

We all realised that if the game was to survive it had to be offered to a sponsor as a going concern, poor perhaps, but patently honest, vitally dedicated to giving its backer value for money. Despite all this we can never again expect to see mid-week queues at the county turnstiles. Even so, county cricket still has millions of adherents who follow the game through the newspaper reports and scorecards at their breakfast tables. Any sponsor who doubts this should contact the Fleet Street sports editor who once rashly decided he would save space by reducing a number of county scores to the bare minimum of total and top scorers. He was so deluged by complaints and threats to give up the paper that he immediately revised his opinions about the imminent mortality of cricket.

The counties, therefore, have much to offer a sponsor in terms of constant publicity, provided they maintain their standards. They must advertise cricket's strengths and stop wallowing in self-pity and nostalgic back-glances at the cloudless days when the coming of Compton and Edrich was guaranteed to put hundreds if not thousands on the attendances. As I have tried to show, the overall standards of the game have risen and produced a competitiveness equal to anything you will meet in the cut-throat atmospheres of big business board rooms. This reflects today's outlook and as long as it maintains this attitude, I cannot see how potential sponsors can have doubts about publicity returns.

Naturally they want their pound of flesh. In addition to national newspaper, television and radio publicity they want their trade names, brand signs and privileges at the county grounds. Those who sighed and complained that this would disfigure the pastoral beauty of the Canterbury or Worcester grounds soon accepted it.

It was not a question of cricket selling its soul. Motor-racing, horse-racing, above all golf, have maintained the happiest of mutually beneficial relationships with major sponsors for years. Golf, particularly, has lost no face in the process. It has a strong professional body not only to represent the interests of its players but to control them as well. This, if sponsorship is to be successful in county cricket, must become the role of the Cricketers' Association in conjunction with the Test and County Cricket Board. Such a relationship between professional and administrative bodies, for example, would have avoided the self-immolatory publicity that cricket suffered in the summer of 1969 when Tom Graveney was banned from the remaining Test matches following his decision to play in a Sunday game during the course of a Test. I am not, here, presuming to suggest who was at fault in that case. But a close liaison between an enterprising body of administrators and a strong professional association would have made such a situation impossible, and I am sure that this would have found a happier solution to Boycott's dilemma in 1975. As in golf, cricket would have established a code of conduct, agreed to the mutual advantage of both the game and its players, which would have prevented such a crisis even looming on the distant horizon.

The Cricketers' Association, indeed, could be the key to the whole crisis in the game. If a sponsor can be found to lift the burden of players' salaries off the backs of the counties, say by underwriting the wages of twelve capped players, six second eleven players and two apprentices, the county treasurers would begin to see daylight. A wage scale common to all counties could then be administered by the Cricketers' Association itself in direct consultation with sponsors and the Test and County Cricket Board. It would not only improve the pay structure within the game but also end the wage differentials which exist between one county and another today and which, inevitably, are a cause of irritation in a small profession of only just over 300 members. Indeed, I have known a case of an international from a weak and poor county receiving almost a thousand pounds less than his counterpart in a more successful county.

Cricketers, of course, have never been highly paid and inflation has not helped. When I first came into the game, top Kent players like Godfrey Evans and Arthur Fagg were probably paid a basic salary of around £500 plus £5 per match and seasonal bonuses of something like £100. Thus a county cricketer of experience was earning about £750 in a season compared with a schoolmaster's £500 in a year. A non-capped player would probably earn £600 and a second eleven player £350. For the small galaxy of real stars there were other sources of income: Test match fees, winter tours abroad with the England team and, in some cases, advertisement and endorsement fees. Denis Compton's neatly-groomed hairstyle did not appear on massive hoardings all over the country for nothing. At a reasonably intelligent guess, therefore, it would be possible to put an England player's income in the early fifties at something between £2,000 and £2,500.

Money, at that stage in my life, meant little to me but even looking back now I cannot say that the pay scale was calamitous. In relation to other jobs and even other sports, it was good. It was on a par with professional soccer, for example, which until the early sixties operated a pegged maximum wage system. It is only since then that cricketers' pay has failed to keep pace with the national trend. A capped player with the average county side can now expect a basic salary of not less than £2,500 plus bonuses which could bring his income up to over £3,000 in a successful year. One argument which suggests they are not so badly off as they appear is that the county player who does not make an overseas touring team is then free to do whatever he pleases in the six out-of-season months to earn more money. In practice this is not quite so simple as it sounds. With unemployment as it is, firms are increasingly disinclined to take on part-time employees during the winter. Whatever the pros and cons of cricket's interminable money talk, those salaries bear no relation to the money coming in through the turnstile. Yet they are not good salaries compared with the money coming into the game as a whole.

That, unhappily, is no incentive to the talented young player who is considering a career in county cricket. It is a curious paradox that the young potential recruit today is in precisely the same take-it-or-leave-it position as the amateur of twenty years ago. As an illustration I can quote the case of Graham Johnson, who became fully established in Kent's championship-winning programme in 1970 and is such a fine cricketer today. He won his way to a grammar school, then London University and a degree in economics. Immediately there were more lucrative fields at his feet than the professional cricket field, so he was confronted with the old-time amateur dilemma of either making money or indulging himself in something he passionately wanted to do. In Johnson's case we were fortunate enough to find a compromise by introducing him to a firm who were prepared to release him for cricket. Even so it is likely that he will soon have to decide on one job or the other as a full-time career within two or three years. In my opinion he still has the talent to make an England cricketer, which would probably settle the argument. But if he doesn't, which does he choose?

This is no isolated instance. In the past when youngsters came to the county nets for trials they were not accorded a red-carpet welcome. They were probably set to bowl for three hours and then told to come back the following week on the off-chance that they might be allowed to bat. Today's aspiring county cricketer does not take kindly to such off-hand treatment. He is better educated, more businesslike, more smartly dressed and visibly in a hurry. He wants a trial, he wants to know the current rate for the job and he needs to know the answer quickly.

This constant plea for money should not be misinterpreted. It is not the cry of a game so down on its luck that it is left with the begging bowl as its last resort. County cricket's own efforts to combat the crisis have been both strenuous and imaginative. It cannot be called reactionary or unreceptive to new ideas. In recent years it has promoted a near-revolutionary form of one-day cricket, flung open its gates to a whole task force of talented overseas players and introduced a points-scoring system in the County Championship which has forced every captain to take a new and more aggressive tactical approach to the game.

The Sunday game is unashamedly a money-raising project. Forty overs is too short for top-class cricket and while it brings a great deal of excitement, the players do not really enjoy it at heart. If the same idea had been put forward to the leading players of the 1950's they would have been convinced that the administrators had taken leave of their senses. Now, as then, the talented player sees it as a slight affront to his professionalism and this is understandable when a batsman cannot afford to play himself in, cannot afford to play back a maiden and knows that a swiftly slogged 40, full of luck and mis-hits, has a greater intrinsic value than a properly constructed innings. The whole tactical emphasis has swung from the taking of wickets to the "dot" ball, the delivery off which the batsman cannot score. Defensive fields with no slip are often set, and although you do see spin bowlers in action not many of them are actually spinning.

Like many players, I have come to play it cheerfully because of its undoubted public appeal and, therefore, its commercial value. In that frame of mind there is a certain stimulation about it, rather like downing a large gin and tonic too quickly. It has also had one beneficial effect: it has liberated a number of batsmen who were blockers by nature. But there is little to be said for it from the technical point of view. It is a game, but the game is not cricket. I am opposed to the introduction of any more one-day cricket because of the long-term effect on the development of the three-day game and Test cricket. Cricket at that level is not an "instant" affair, and the one-day philosophy is no preparation for it. It cannot produce leg-spinners and indeed makes it hard for any spinners who must be allowed a long bowl somewhere if they are to learn their trade. Young batsmen, equally, must be given time to build the big innings of 100 or 200. Neither can hope to get the opportunity in the frenetic atmosphere of the Sunday afternoon game. While recognising the commercial necessity, therefore, I am convinced that cricket must be cautious about going further down the aisle towards a shot-gun marriage it may live to regret.

The second major recent development, the lifting of restrictions to allow a whole galaxy of star overseas players into the county game, has been a resounding success. There was certainly a period during the 1970 season when I might have been a little less effusive about it, for in three successive matches we were beaten by Glamorgan, Lancashire and Warwickshire. Glamorgan's victory was achieved almost single-handed by Bryan Davis from Trinidad, Lancashire's was entirely due to a remarkable innings by Clive Lloyd of Guyana, and Warwickshire's match-winner was Rohan Kanhai, also of Guyana and West Indies.

There are many others who have contributed enormously to raising still higher the standards of county cricket. This is very gratifying to those who championed the cause for their admission; for there is no doubt that, at the time, they were playing with fire. There was the danger of widespread resentment among the English county staffs and also the alarming possibility of the whole pay-structure of cricket being wrecked by free-for-all bidding to sign men like Gary Sobers and Clive Lloyd. Kent deliberately avoided this by signing Asif, from Pakistan, and John Shepherd, one of the younger West Indian players, who were both prepared to fall in with our existing scales of pay.

It was obvious, though, that a county with the resources of Warwickshire could have wrecked the venture before it got off the ground. They could have offered £12,000 as opposed to £1,200 to lure any player they wished and it is greatly to their credit that they resisted the temptation. A number of the big-name overseas players do receive more money than other members of their team but by and large their impact has been such that this has caused few problems.

Cricket has moved handsomely with the times and is to be congratulated on its fight for survival. The argument that we play too much cricket is a dangerous fallacy. True, some indidivudals could be highlighted as being subject to too much continuous international cricket. I think of some of the leading West Indian players who by the end of 1975 could look back over two years in which they might have been asked to play more than twenty Test matches.

But for our domestic cricket I shall always fight any move to reduce the amount of cricket played. It is such a short season and we cannot always expect long, hot, dry summers. Apart from the Test matches, the Prudential One-Day Tests, with careful planning, have a place. The Gillette Cup and the Benson and Hedges tournaments are proven successes. The John Player Sunday League has been a distinct success from the point of view of the television package and the crowd atmosphere as the excitement builds through July and August. Most cricketers have reservations about the restriction of bowlers' run-ups and would like to see the game lengthened. Can you play a truly satisfactory top-class game in so few overs? Every five years the Prudential World Cup will be a welcome addition but I hope this will not be staged more frequently.

Finally, we must do all in our power to preserve the traditional County Championship, costly as it may be. At the moment it consists of twenty three-day matches and some would like it to be sixteen four-day matches, with no restrictions. The statutory declaration after a hundred overs means, in practice, that the fielding captain can always fall back on defence. There is not enough incentive to take wickets. In a four-day match the side fielding first on a good wicket will risk more to buy wickets, attack and keep close fielders up for longer periods.

On balance I go along with the four-day match, but the wickets must be the best we can produce, and fully covered, and dare we hope the captain would be more inclined to include the leg-spinner in his armoury?

# 15

The next figure to loom large in the continuing story of my cricket career was a small dynamic man known as Robbie to his closest associates, Walter to those who were never quite admitted to that magic circle and R.W.V. of Middlesex and England to the public at large. Apart from shaking hands and exchanging a few formal greetings I did not get to know Walter Robins until the late 1950's on a minor overseas tour. MCC were playing Dublin at the end of the summer, and because a player had dropped out at the last minute I was brought into the side unexpectedly.

Robins was captain. Now in his fifties he fielded at mid-off, bowled a few erratic but highly entertaining overs of leg-breaks, batted number eleven, wore his MCC cap and never stopped talking about himself and the cricket and cricketers of his era. He was the unforgettable character of an entertaining weekend: witty, dominant, charming, magnetic. By the time we had returned to London I had fallen under his spell.

A few months later I was talking to Peter May. He suddenly tackled me: "Have you heard the rumour that Robbie is going to be made manager for the West Indies tour?" I hadn't. But I reacted immediately. I said: "Well, I've only really met him once, in Ireland. He was tremendous fun. It could be a very good appointment." Peter was relieved and encouraged by my comment.

There was a good deal of background to this brief exchange. In the winter of 1958–59 I had toured Australia for the second time. Peter May was captain, I was vice-captain, and the expedition, from every point of view, was a terrible disappointment. We lost the Test series

4–0 and in the frustration and recrimination that accompany a beating of that magnitude no real sense of pride in a team could possibly survive. My own appointment as vice-captain, as I look back, was a mistake. Trevor Bailey, vice-captain under Hutton in 1953–54, had already been superseded by Peter May as captain. Now he was superseded by me as vice-captain as well. Although I was clearly being blooded as a Test captain of the future and felt duly honoured, I was uncomfortable about it. Had anything happened to Peter May, Trevor Bailey would have been the best person to lead this galaxy of stars in a Test match. Not that Trevor was difficult from my point of view, quite the opposite. He has always been a good friend to me. He was an individualist with a mind of his own and there were some other independent minds in the party: Tyson, Trueman, Loader, Lock, Laker, Wardle and Evans. If we had been a winning side all would have been well.

The press soon exploited the situation by publishing a photograph of Peter May and his wife, Virginia, sun-bathing beside a swimming pool. "Wives on tour" suddenly became a hot issue for debate and the photograph was used to explain, quite unfairly, why May was aloof from his team. In fact, no captain took more care to look after his team than Peter May and he was justifiably hurt.

After the immense status he had built up for himself over several years, both as a batsman and as a winning captain he was infuriated at the innuendo that the presence of Virginia should be linked with our failures on the field.

On paper, this was a magnificent England side, full of experienced, mature players. It might have been the best England team to travel abroad, perhaps a little light in batting, but we did not win a Test match. Peter May returned home a very disappointed man. This was the first major setback in an illustrious career.

With England, as with Surrey, his authority had never been questioned. He was a big man, of great integrity, and was deservedly given a free hand. He had struck up an ideal relationship with the then chairman, G. O. Allen, a wise man. Under Gubby Allen, Peter May became fully captain of England as perhaps only Don Bradman had been captain of a Test team since the war. They had worked happily together and it had been a thoroughly successful partnership.

If you lose, the balloon goes up and everything becomes disseminated. In the inquest which followed that calamitous tour there seemed to emerge a line of thought which was to have a profound effect upon English cricket for the next decade. It was held to be high time that the players were brought down to size. Our defeat in Australia was explained away by an excess of player power. In future there should be less room for personality cult and a tighter enforcement of discipline. The new style demanded a strong, dynamic manager as figure-head. It was to this end that Walter Robins was appointed as manager of MCC to West Indies. He had a clearly defined role and it was to collect and create a new young England side with a fresh approach to the game.

He set about his task with relish as soon as the banana boat *Camito* had weighed anchor at Avonmouth. Already the clear-out had begun. The team was unrecognisable from Australia: no Tyson, Loader, Laker, Lock, Wardle, Evans or Graveney. May was captain but it was soon clear that a good deal of his energy was to be spent standing up to a will as strong as his own. The first clash came at dinner before we had approached Land's End.

Among the new players in the party was the Lancashire leg-spinner Tommy Greenhough and we were still on the soup when Robins launched into a powerful peroration on how he expected Greenhough to be used on the tour. Peter May was nonplussed at his aggressive approach. He took a deep breath and all he could say was, "Waiter, may I have a little more toast, please?" Robins would not be shaken from his theme. Peter May listened and then proceeded to commend the excellence of the soup. Robins continued to harry us day after day, throughout the voyage, and with typical courtesy but no lack of firmness, Peter May would not be drawn.

After a week or two we learned to live with the extraordinary histrionics of our manager, and to smile with him. We shall never know how the Robins-May partnership would have worked out, for tragedy was to strike.

During the second Test match in Trinidad, the scene of our great victory after the bottle-throwing riot, May began to be troubled by an internal wound that would not heal. Each day, morning and evening, he would slip away quietly to hospital to have it dressed. By the end of the third Test match in Jamaica the doctors expressed concern because it had not improved and he was advised to be treated in London. He stayed on to watch us draw the fourth Test match, and with much sadness left for England. We were one up in the series, a situation which confounded most of the critics. With good reason they had given this raw and newly re-grouped England team little chance against an immensely powerful and flamboyant West Indies team playing on their own ground before their own volatile supporters. It was quite a responsibility for me taking over the captaincy for the last two Test matches and I had no intention of gambling away the chips Peter May had fought so courageously to win.

I was now to see Robins at even closer range and became still more confused at the contradictions in his character. He was a magnificent raconteur, especially in reminiscing about his own cricket era. He was splendid company on the golf course. To the press he was charming, persuasive, understanding and cooperative. Some of the journalists still maintain that he was the best MCC manager they encountered. They were never without a story nor the latest inside information.

Like Peter May, I found a close manager-captain relationship difficult, and once Peter May had returned home I was distinctly vulnerable. The team enjoyed listening to him telling the story but were puzzled by his determination to administer military style discipline.

As we prepared for the final Test in Port of Spain an overseas telephone call brought us the news that Brian Statham's son was seriously ill. It was a desperate moment and we rushed him to the airport for the plane just leaving for London. To be deprived of May and Statham was asking a lot, but there was no doubt that the team united and were in the most determined frame of mind to give everything they had.

I led the way with an innings of 119, one of my best. Robins appeared to be quite pleased with our approach. By the end of the fourth day, however, we were in trouble, only 200 runs and six wickets down. It was a bad night to live through as defeat stared us in the face.

Mike Smith and Jim Parks fought it out bravely, and then tore the opposition apart in a seventh wicket partnership which eventually established a new English record of 197. We were out of trouble but there was no time to bowl the West Indies out and win the match. There was no point in risking all with a quixotic declaration. Soon after lunch the game was dead and a draw had clinched the series. It had been a good cricket match with several swings in fortune.

For some reason Walter Robins was not on the ground on that last morning to watch our magnificent show of batting. His bustling arrival by taxi and public dressing down of his captain in the dressing room only served to spoil what I thought had been a successful day for English cricket.

At the end of the match we were joint hosts at a happy party for our many West Indian friends. It is to my regret that apart from a few formal greetings over the next few years he had little time for me.

Significantly, and on the strength of our victory in the West Indies, Robins was soon to become chairman of the England selectors. Although I led England to victory in the series against South Africa the following summer, Dexter was the next England captain to tour Australia.

# 16

That West Indies tour was memorable for other reasons and I had to build in a new batting technique to survive against the tremendous pace and wildness of their new-ball bowlers, Wesley Hall and Chester Watson. I had to bear the brunt of them, for on the passage out I had been persuaded, much against my inclination, to open the innings. This was not a new request. It had frequently been in Len Hutton's mind in Australia because he believed my method was right for it. I played very straight and had a limited backlift against the fast bowlers early on. The theory fell down because I was temperamentally unsuited to open. I always have been and always shall be.

Had I been really professional in outlook, I would have resisted all the appeals to open in West Indies. I could have argued that not only would Wally Hammond have scornfully rejected any such suggestion thirty years earlier, but that he would not have been asked in the first place. Equally I might have suggested that either Ken Barrington or Ted Dexter did the job. But I could see the problem all too clearly. We were desperately short of openers, we badly needed an experienced old hand to go in with Geoff Pullar and I was, in any case, one of the best players of fast bowling in the party. So I agreed. I cannot pretend, though, that it was not hard to live with when I was soon watching Barrington and Dexter making brilliant hundreds on the placid afternoon wickets which had been so brutish in the early morning.

This was precisely what happened in the very first Test match in Barbados. I shall take the memories of the opening morning of that game to the grave. There was a good deal of early moisture under the pitch and Watson and Hall let us have it flat out with the new ball. Watson's first delivery was mercifully a fraction wide, for it pitched, flew past Pullar and went on climbing. Gerry Alexander, the wicket-keeper, was standing yards back but he still had to fling himself up like a goal-keeper to claw the ball out of the sky. That ball was an introduction to what we might expect and the two new-ball bowlers did not disappoint the crowd. One moment we were ducking under bouncers, the next we were fending off some brutal delivery out of our ribs. Their speed was horrifying and although they bowled quite a few wide, the utter wildness of their attack added an element of shock. Batting against them was an unforgettable experience. When I was out, caught at slip off Watson just before lunch, I had scored 30. By early afternoon, with the pitch dried out and the shine off the ball, it became a different sort of contest. Barrington batted well and scored 128, and Dexter played a great innings of 136 not out.

The pattern of the second Test in Trinidad was almost identical. I failed in both innings while Barrington made 121, Dexter 77 and Mike Smith 108 in the first. To add to my problems Hall had struck me full-pitch on the bridge of the left foot. I thought it was broken. More seriously, I was beginning to wonder whether I had reached the end of the road. I had played an enormous amount of cricket but I could see nothing in my armoury to counter the staggering pace of Hall and Watson. It was like nothing I had known before. It bore no relation to facing Lindwall, who was fast and swung the ball but who based his whole art on a disciplined length. Here were two men who attacked you with explosive violence. They were trying to frighten you out. If anything, the Trinidad wicket made them seem faster than ever.

If I were to survive at all I had to re-model my entire approach to batting. I asked myself, "How did Hutton play this type of bowling?" and then began to analyse the problem as he would have done. Had the West Indians known the plan that evolved in my mind they would have fallen about laughing. Grim experience had proved to me that I did not have time to move in the crease. I did not even have time to lift the bat. So I decided not to move at all. I would merely stand there with my feet spread and the bat right by my toe. If I did not move at all they would not hit the wicket.

This theory, of course, had two distinct drawbacks. Firstly it severely restricted stroke-making and secondly it was inevitable that I would have to take a great deal of physical punishment. Having accepted that, it was only a question of who cracked first, for I reasoned that not even Hall and Watson could sustain that fearsome pace for more than an hour. If my plan survived that long I could yet emerge the winner.

There were fourteen days between the second Test in Trinidad and the third at Sabina Park, Jamaica. I spent some of them working out what I had to do next, and used the rest to prepare for one of the most significant Tests of my career. I went to Harold Dalton, the team masseur, and got him to sew into my vest a thick layer of Dunlopillo padding which stretched from my neck to my waist. This caused great hilarity in the England dressing room but it undoubtedly gave me a new-found confidence when I tried it out in the nets. Without it I could not have withstood what came next.

I have already described, in a different context in an earlier chapter, my mental state as I went into that Test. It was not good. But by the time it was over a great deal of steam had been taken out of the situation. I scored 114 in the first innings and 97 in the second. I would not claim that the first innings was a particularly good one, as it took me almost seven hours. But neither would I pretend that it was not immensely satisfying. I took ball after ball, blow after blow on that improvised body-shield but was able to stand firm. The effect of knowing that my theory was watertight was remarkable. The second innings was the best I have ever played. From the firm foundations of real confidence I was able to get after the bowling and repay Hall, particularly, for some of the anguish he had caused me. I had one glorious hour against him. At one point he pitched one up and I hit it back past mid-on for four. Instinctively I knew what was coming next and I was not mistaken. It was the fastest bouncer I have ever faced. But the absolute certainty of what kind of a ball it would be gave me the initiative. I hit it first bounce into the crowd. Hall then changed ends but this, at last, was to be my day. I hooked him twice in a row and reduced him to the kind of despair which, but a fortnight earlier, had been exclusively mine.

At 97 I went to run a ball from Scarlett down past third man for four. Instead I got a top edge and was caught at the wicket. Many people wrote of my dismay at failing, by a single shot, to take two centuries in a single Test off such an attack. Admittedly I was a little disappointed but that emotion was soon drowned by the relief that, finally, I had batted really well.

The Jamaica Test match provided one of the other two indelible memories I have of that extraordinary expedition. Tension ran high throughout the game and it was by no means lessened when, at one point, Peter May refused to allow the injured Rohan Kanhai to have a runner. May, as few realised at the time, was ill and had in fact made a mistake. I was of little help to him since it was not until afterwards that I learned the rules to prevent a batsman having a runner. It is merely an accepted courtesy on the part of the batting captain when he informs the fielding captain that one of his batsmen will use one.

May's reasoning at the time was that he was under the impression that Kanhai had come into the match injured, as opposed to being injured during the game. He concluded, therefore, that West Indies were taking advantage of a situation of their own making and insisted that Kanhai's efforts should be all his own work.

Naturally, the confusion and antagonism that followed were manna from the gods for the press. It had all the ingredients for a front-page story, in the pursuit of which the reporters left their vantage point and rushed round to the pavilion like greyhounds. Unfortunately, the dust they raised in their haste was so considerable that Walter Robins, our highly press-conscious manager, had seen them coming. He instructed the twelfth man to inform them that he could not be found and locked himself in the dressing room lavatory. He remained there until the close of play when he could finally discuss the incident with Peter May and decide what should, or should not, be announced to the British public.

My other recollection is of the tension and rivalries that exist between the Caribbean islands themselves. This could be reduced at times to such a parochial level that in the Barbados Test Frank Worrell, himself a Barbadian by birth, received an extremely mixed reception when he walked out to bat. The applause from the pavilion was soon lost beneath the storm of booing that followed him all the way to the wicket from every other part of the ground. In my innocence I was bemused. Worrell was one of the idolised "Three W's" who had done more than any statesman or writer or artist to put the tiny speck of Barbados on the world map. He had already played thirty-six Test matches for West Indies in the preceding dozen years. It was not until that evening that it was explained to me. Worrell had gone off to live and work in Jamaica. He had then gone off to live and study in England. The fact that he had come home again with a University degree did not count. Somehow he was not one of them any more. The world had taken him away from them.

There was only one way he could win back their esteem on that Saturday. He could only do it by giving them something to feast on and this he proceeded to do. If I remember correctly he was something like 170 not out that evening and left the field to a tremendous ovation from the same throats that had been reviling him only a few hours earlier. Worrell was deeply moved and close to tears by the time he reached the dressing room.

# 17

The actual process of cricket touring changed radically during my years as a Test player. On my first tour you walked up a gangplank and waved farewell to your family for more than seven months. There was an element of pioneering about it. You had to be prepared for discomfort in some outback town or newly-developed island, and you took as much toothpaste as Sir Francis Chichester probably stowed away for his entire round-the-world adventure. Again, with everything geared to sea travel, you took more bats and more pairs of pads than you needed. A dinner jacket was *de rigueur*. There was considerable socialising both on the ship and throughout the tour.

Times have changed. Jet travel and the pruning of itineraries have reduced the most arduous tour to a little over five months. There is no longer any virtue in overloading yourself with reserve supplies of equipment. A telephone call one way and an airliner the other can bring a new bat, a fresh cap or even a reinforcement player from Lord's to the furthermost cricket outpost in the world in under thirty hours. This happened to me when I was flown to Perth in 1974. Dinner jackets are no longer required. We are still guests at Government Houses, High Commissions, civic receptions and private parties, but today these are less formal.

Instead of travelling first-class by sea a team now travels tourist-class by air. Their heavy equipment, however, is still sent ahead by sea. For a full tour now I would take four bats, one pair of pads, four pairs of batting gloves, two pairs of studded boots, two pairs of rubber-soled boots, six pairs of flannels, six cricket shirts, one long-sleeved sweater, one sleeveless pullover, an MCC tour blazer and three caps. If you think three caps is excessive it is because they get so wet with perspiration.

Each tour has its own distinctive characteristics. Australia produces the hardest cricket of all, the toughest Tests of all. If you win a Test match you know you have been through the mangle. There is no light relief. The State teams are strong and cannot be patronised.

Even the country teams in the outback are straining to make their names at your expense. You are hard pressed to beat anyone, anywhere.

This attitude reflects Australia itself: tough, arid, aggressive, friendly and highly individualistic. The Australian cult of individualism is nowhere more vividly demonstrated than on its cricket grounds. We play forward and they play back. We throw side-armed so they throw over-arm. We stand in a tight unit in the slips and they spread out in an arc. They move differently in the field and wear different shaped caps differently. You could never mistake an Australian wicket-keeper for an Englishman.

Everywhere you know what to expect. The crowds are "at you", yet not unpleasantly so. The players, equally, strive for psychological advantage by exerting constant mental pressure. There is a logical explanation for this. Unlike English cricket, which has so many variable factors, Australian cricket is a constant. It has few variables to exploit and so, almost as a substitute, its players are always creating pressures for the batsman. Its bowlers pound in, not jog. Its close fielders radiate aggression. Behind you there is a constant stream of chat. "Well bowled" ... "Bad luck" ... "Well bowled." What might be unacceptable at the Oval is understandable in Australia. If a batsman gets in on those wickets he might well be there for the day. The application of early pressure is all part of the game. Everything is heightened to such a degree that when you take an Australian Test wicket you feel as though you have scored against Brazil. I like it. It is a mental as well as a physical contest.

Probably I am more romantically receptive to the Australian atmosphere than younger English cricketers because of the very length of the love affair. It did not start with Hutton's tour. It started long before as I shivered in the early-morning darkness of a Tonbridge dormitory, head low over a crackling radio that brought the Test commentaries from Adelaide or Sydney. Alan McGilvray's crisp metallic voice would report that Wright was now bowling to Bradman, words soon lost in a breaking wave of static or applause as the ball crashed into the pickets. Always pickets, never fences. Always sundries, never extras. Then came the more modulated tones of Arthur Gilligan telling us that earlier in the day, temperatures had been well into the hundreds but now the long shadows were beginning to creep over the ground. Clichés perhaps, but still words to fire the soul. I couldn't imagine a hundred degrees of heat. These were words and pictures from another planet. Australia.

Inevitably the quickening ways of the world have destroyed a little of the romance. When I first toured there English cricketers were still links with the Old Country. In some RSL Club up-country we would hear long speeches with repeated references to Winston Churchill and our battles side by side in the Western Desert. Today that up-country town seems to have been sprinkled with Europeans who have no interest in cricket. The sense of isolation has gone. Hundreds of spectators now follow us out from England. We receive the English newspapers within thirty-six hours. We can even sit down in a Melbourne motel on a Sunday evening and tune in the television to yesterday's match between Chelsea and Manchester United. Live pictures are transmitted via the Satellite.

Television, too, has minimised the significance of the many minor matches that MCC touring teams used to play in the remote interior towns. Once this was missionary work, spreading the gospel of cricket to areas where they would not see a Test player from one harvest till the next. Today they simply flick a switch and watch a Test match on the screen. Already the process of reducing these journeys into the interior has begun. Two-day matches in these areas were always rather meaningless since they rarely produced a result. Most people are in favour of eliminating even the one-day ones for if they cannot attract better crowds, they have no significance or value. Personally, I still think there is a value for us and them, in a one-day jaunt, flying there and back in a day from the big City.

Yet, for all the changes, much survives. The haul from Brisbane to Perth is still as far as from London. This is the flight between first and second Test and a day's rest is needed to recover fully. The sun still shimmers and the heat still dances visibly over the stark, white grounds. Melbourne's massively-tiered arena still makes the incoming batsman feel like a dwarf. As you come over the hill from the city and drive down to the Sydney Cricket Ground, with its green domes and turrets, you can still feel the same tingle that was evoked years ago by those crackling voices across 11,000 miles of airspace. Perhaps not everyone feels it, but Australia will ever be thus for me.

The lasting impressions of a West Indies tour, in contrast, are made not so much by the cricket or cricketers as by the crowds and the unique atmosphere. They are exuberant, noisy, passionate, intensely partisan, highly critical, but knowledgeable and warmly generous to good cricket played by either side. I love them when they see the funny side of something. There have, of course, been some historic eruptions: bottles hurled in Port of Spain, Trinidad, and tear gas turned on the crowd in Kingston, Jamaica. It would be wrong to attach too much significance to these events, for their causes have usually had nothing to do with cricket but a great deal to do with local politics. The average cricket fan probably lives a humdrum existence in a small dwelling house on the outskirts of a town. His little spending money will probably go on a few rums and a ticket to the ground when the cricketers come. He knows them all by sight, he knows their records, their favourite shots and their fallibilities. He will have strong views about John Edrich's late-cut and know precisely what the state of the wicket was on the final day of the Test back in Jamaica.

The West Indian fan has neither inhibition nor embarrassment about stopping you in the street and engaging you instantly in highly technical cricket discussion. "But Mr. Cowdrey, when Mr. Snow bowled Mr. Sobers, where did the ball *pitch*? Why did he play *back*?" It probably happened on an island 600 miles away the week before last but his facts will be right and his opinions intelligent. He will then expound where he would bowl to Sobers and although he might be wrong, it would take till midnight to shake his argument.

Occasionally they will even demonstrate. Such a moment came during England's 1968 tour of West Indies when, on a rest day, the Kent contingent in the party lunched with Tom Crawford, who had just arrived by sea, at a beach hotel along the lovely west coast of Barbados. As one of the waiters passed, Tom said: "That lad keeps telling me what a great bowler he is." The waiter heard the remark. His eyes lit up. Before we knew what was happening, he had persuaded us to clear the tables back to the wall while he demonstrated his fast leg-cutter and his demon inswinger with bread rolls down the centre of the dining room. The exhibition caused a forty-minute delay between the soup and the main course and I have never seen an aspiring cricketer take a trial more seriously. We invited him to join us in the nets the following day, two days before the Test match began. He duly walked the five miles into Bridgetown next morning. He was wearing a green sweat shirt and a pair of trousers which appeared to be doing service for the third generation of his family. But he had his cricket boots slung over his shoulder and he nearly burst his lungs bowling flat out to us for an hour and a half. He bowled quite well and a few of us rewarded him with a wicket, a moment which his grandchildren will probably hear about in due course. Tom Crawford was to hear about it at breakfast, lunch and dinner but he loved it, just as we had done.

West Indies is, of course, the travel-brochure tour with small, heavenly beaches, palms as slim and elegant as mannequins and golf courses where the fairways are fringed with bougainvillaea. It has a more prosaic importance for the professional cricketer. Unlike Australia or South Africa, where there is constant, frenetic travel, a Caribbean cricket tour is more relaxed. You can settle down on a single island for a fortnight, even three weeks, at a stretch. The pace of everything except the bowling is slower.

Cricket there, however, has a communal intensity as nowhere else in the world. At a party in Jamaica a surgeon once told me that he dreaded the coming of the cricketers. "It's so distracting," he said, "having to operate with all those transistors tuned in to the Test match." Then there was the night in Trinidad after Gary Sobers had declared and England had beaten West Indies. The lights went out early all over Port of Spain. It was like a city in mourning, and when we finally caught up with Sobers he was having a few drinks at the bar of a club. He was sitting alone.

If West Indies is the exotic tour, South Africa is safari by Rolls-Royce. There is no nation which so lionises its own national sportsmen or so lavishly entertains its cricketing guests. In a later chapter I shall have more to say about South Africa in the context of the D'Oliveira affair but, for the moment, this is not the place to discuss the pressures and implications of its apartheid policy. Inevitably my recollections are dated because of the cancellation of England's last scheduled tour. But my memories of my only visit there are of the staggering natural beauty of the Garden Route and the coastline of the Cape, and of the overwhelming hospitality that was lavished on us everywhere we went. It was the only tour on the whole international cricket circuit where an England player need never be booked into a hotel. He would be welcomed into a succession of luxurious private homes from the moment he landed until the moment he left.

It was this open-handed welcome that created the only playing problem I can recollect. If we were not actually killed by kindness we were certainly reduced to something well short of the fitness that a Test team must maintain. In the end this was quite noticeable in the cricket we played. Our standards dropped alarmingly. It was not fatal at the time for in 1956 South Africa did not have the cricketing resources to expose our indulgence. Of their Currie Cup teams then, Transvaal were powerful and Natal quite good. The others were barely above English minor county standard. Such judgments would certainly not apply today, although I am concerned that if they do not come back into the international scene soon their standard of cricket must deteriorate.

I treasure two fond memories of South Africa. One is of a fascinating evening sitting next to "Sailor" Malan, the wartime fighter ace, during a dinner given by Harry Oppenheimer in the diamond town of Kimberley. The other may solve for many the mystery of how a golf ball was fielded at mid-on in the middle of a Test match in the huge Wanderers ground in Johannesburg. It was kept fairly quiet at the time because the South Africans never really appreciated that a cricketer who was not actually involved in the Test might well not want to sit around watching it for five days. In this case Alan Oakman of Sussex had been injured and was short of exercise, so had been given permission to go and play golf instead. There was a course running right alongside the cricket ground and it was from there that Oakman imparted such a colossal slice on one of his tee-shots that the ball flew straight through the towering tiers of open-work seats and came hurtling on to the field of play. It was miraculous that it did not maim a spectator, for there was a huge crowd packed into the ground that day. This thought never occurred to Oakman, whose only anxiety was to get his ball back during the lunch interval.

New Zealand, like South Africa, provides a red-carpet welcome to English cricket teams and I have always been conscious while playing there that we treat them rather shabbily. We tend to regard a Test series with them rather as a family-visiting chore that has to be done just because we happen to be in the neighbourhood. Almost invariably English teams visit New Zealand after a long and exhausting tour of Australia and since players are tired and understandably anxious to see their families again in England we have frequently played jaded and uninspired cricket there.

Admittedly cricket has come a poor second to Big Brother rugby football in New Zealand but, nevertheless, it still has a passionately keen, if small, following and is seen by the whole country as an activity which will help maintain its links with Britain. Of all the countries we visit, New Zealand is the most fervently pro-British and this makes me more than ever uneasy at our off-handedness. It is not easy to re-adjust to New Zealand's bounceless wickets after five months in Australia. It is a pity that MCC could not reverse the traditional order and play a Test series in New Zealand first. The grounds are too wet and muddy until after Christmas. But we must be prepared to send an "A" side or even the full England team there for a much longer visit. Maybe it could be combined with a tour of Pakistan, six weeks to each country. To make this possible it would be essential for New Zealand to guarantee that it would be financially viable, but such is their enthusiasm for cricket that I suspect this problem would soon be overcome.

The most fundamentally changed cricket tour of them all is that to India and/or Pakistan. The and/or is obligatory because in the days before Partition there was only India. Although I was born there I know nothing of Raj cricket from personal experience, only from hearsay. But the hearsay is pure Kipling. Until the mid-thirties, I gather, even packing priorities were somewhat different. The bats, the pads, the gloves came last. First came your white dinner jacket, then your black dinner jacket, then your tails. Fourth was your topee, fifth your sports jacket and sixth your rifle. After that, if you had room, you might cram in some cricket equipment. If there was no room it hardly mattered. You could borrow the lot from some nawab or maharaja who was already providing you with so many bearers that you had one to carry each cuff-link. You stayed in palaces, not hotels. Test matches were things you played between tiger hunts and they were always played in the European club atmosphere. It was, without question, the most luxurious cricket ever played in all history and, as far as visiting English teams were concerned, it ended when Douglas Jardine's side beat C. K. Nayudu's Indians two-nil with one drawn in the campaign of 1933–34. The next time a full England tour party returned was eighteen years later and by then, of course, things had changed.

When England teams first went back after the war there were no European homes to accommodate them, and in many big centres modern hotels were either non-existent or in such an early state of development that your promised room was likely to be a large cube of air held together only by girders. By 1970 conditions had improved out of all recognition, but I fear that the intervening years had their effects on visiting English players. There was good reason for this. When I was flown out to India as a replacement for Mickey Stewart in 1964, I arrived to find a party of sixteen men reduced to only four fully fit players. Stewart was seriously ill and had to be flown home; four others were in hospital. The others were actually engaged in a Test match although they were so sick that a journalist travelling with the England party was alerted to go on to the field in place of the next man who collapsed. They were all suffering from stomach disorders of varying degrees of severity and the explanation was simply that their European-trained digestive systems could not settle easily to the changes of water and food.

So we evolved a strange diet for professional sportsmen: hard-boiled eggs, bananas and whisky that had mercifully been put at our disposal by the British High Commission. We even brushed our teeth with soda water to avoid contact with the hemlock that came out of the tap.

Today living conditions have changed both in India and Pakistan where there are now air-conditioned hotels with hygienic cuisines to equal most in the world. This is potentially the most fertile cricketing soil on earth and, happily, MCC are due to visit India for an official tour in 1976–77 for twelve weeks. Every day during a Test match in India you can guarantee a full-house audience of 40,000 rising to 60,000. It would be 160,000 if they could find room to accommodate them. Pakistan, meanwhile, has the potential for putting out the best team in the world in the foreseeable future. It has the latent talent but badly needs another good fast bowler, a strong captain and a team spirit which is unimpaired by the geographical division of the country itself. A firm, united administration could make Pakistan a powerful force in the game.

Sadly, most of the anecdotes told by English cricketers about recent tours to India and Pakistan return to the same theme of rigorous living and alimentary disorders. So may I make it clear at this point that I quite appreciate the fact that many Indian and Pakistani players find it equally impossible to face the food that we serve up for them on our English grounds. Indeed the Cowdrey kitchen is at their disposal if they find the curry uneatable when they visit Kent. Until we reach this level of mutual frankness I am afraid that the misunderstandings will continue.

It would be pointless for me to pretend that an Indian tour was just like a sightseeing visit to the Taj Mahal when, for example, Mr. E. M. Wellings of the London *Evening News* has already regaled his readers with a perfectly accurate account of how rats ran all over his bed during the Kanpur Test of 1964. There was also world-wide distribution of photographs of bored spectators setting fire to the main stand during the Calcutta Test on the same tour, and it may be recalled that a few years later we actually had to abandon a Test match in Pakistan and return to London because there was no point in staying any longer. My own favourite recollection is far less sinister. It concerns the Kamala Retreat, a former palace where we were once housed in India. One of its more startling amenities was a swimming pool so huge that it would have made the normal Olympic-sized pool look like a fish-bowl. It was also equipped with a wave-machine, apparently installed by an enterprising prince who had acquired a passion for surf-bathing during one of his world tours. At what expense he had installed this toy some seven hundred miles inland in India was beyond the comprehension of the tax-conditioned British mind. Not that we cared much as we stripped for an exhilarating swim in those glorious, crashing breakers. Our anticipation was matched only by our dismay at the state of the water that was breaking. The pool, I fear, had not been cleaned out for at least a decade. Dead animals and rotting vegetation were suddenly whipped into a foaming maelstrom and we went away quietly, composing our retorts to the first fool back in England who said that those cricket tours must be glamorous affairs.

Glamour does not enter into it. The success or failure of a cricket tour stands or falls by the personal qualities of the men engaged in it. Cricketers have a phrase for it. A "good tourist" is a man who fits in, who wants to help, who doesn't raise hell if he is dropped, who doesn't sulk if he has to attend an official reception when he would prefer to go to the pictures, who will bowl flat out at the nets on the eve of a Test when he is not playing himself next day. A poor tourist is a moaner, a barrack-room lawyer, a clock-watcher who arrives at the nets on the minute and would not bowl a ball without a black look a moment after the appointed time.

A touring Test captain prays for a team of good tourists. He does not ask for obsequiousness, boot-licking or subservience. He appreciates that Test cricketers, like any other men at the top of their professions, are individualists with idiosyncrasies of their own. He accepts the fact that they are liable to show a little temperament if they are not included in a Test side when they feel that they ought to be. But, in the end, he is at the mercy of his men.

There are a number of ways in which cricket tours can be improved and the first is to continue the present trend of making them shorter. My first tour lasted thirty-two weeks, but that included three weeks on a boat. Now we always fly. I believe that the absolute now should be sixteen weeks and that twelve weeks would be better still. The reason is obvious. The majority of touring cricketers are married men and the strain imposed on a marriage by such abnormally long absences is immense. Some wives are self-sufficient and can accept it. Others find their lives virtually collapse when their husbands go away. I have heard it argued that since the wives knew what they were in for when they married a professional cricketer they have only themselves to blame. This is nonsense. In eight cases out of ten they are marrying a county cricketer who has not yet made the England team. He probably has no idea whether he will ever get that far or not, or whether, if he does, he will stay there. If he does become an established touring player then he faces a very real social problem because in a span of nine years he could expect to be absent from home for four of them. It imposes a real strain on the normal pattern of home life.

This unavoidably raises the problem of wives on tour. Should they be allowed to join their husbands or should they be banned? I am sure that it would be wrong to ban wives from tours altogether. But I am aware that as long as some wives travel and others do not this can create problems which are not necessarily in the best interests of team unity. On the other hand the cricket authorities could obviously never bring in a rule to stop them. The only proviso which is stipulated in the existing situation, and it must be right, too, is that wives are not present in the early weeks of a tour when a team is knitting together. But the real answer is in what I have already advocated: much shorter and more concentrated tours which might eliminate the problem altogether.

Another aspect of touring which requires reform is the system of "good conduct" bonus awards. On an Australian tour in the sixties, for example, players were paid £850 plus £150 bonuses for good conduct. Mostly the full £1,000 was automatically paid but there were still instances when, on the recommendation of the manager and the captain at the end of the tour, the whole or part of the bonus money was withheld. On one tour Freddie Trueman, Barry Knight and Ray Illingworth lost part of the bonuses. The question of who, and who did not, receive their full pay naturally became a subject of acute interest to journalists and although MCC never publish the decisions the information soon becomes public knowledge. The subsequent bad publicity which cricket receives more than outweighs any small merit the bonus system may have, and it is most unfair on the captain and manager.

More recently an additional incentive payment scheme was introduced which for the first time rewarded long-established players with slightly higher salaries than newcomers. An extra £25 was paid for every previous overseas tour a player had undertaken. A cricketer on his ninth trip, therefore, would receive £225 more than a player on his first. In view of the low scales of payment all round this was perfectly reasonable though, personally, I would prefer to see incentives from which all the players of both Test teams would benefit. It would seem realistic to reward them on a percentage of tour profits basis, thereby encouraging the brand of attractive cricket which is going to pull more spectators into the grounds.

Unlike England's World Cup footballers, incidentally, her cricketers have never quite got off the ground with commercial schemes to bring in money "on the side". This largely depends on the outlook of the captain and manager. On Hutton's 1954–55 tour, for example, we did quite an amount of team advertising which brought in a total of around £3,000. This provided money for drinks at our Saturday evening gatherings, allowed us to repay a great deal of hospitality with a large party at the end of the tour and still receive something like £150 a man. But there are great dangers in conflicting priorities when such schemes are launched. Peter May, as captain, kept them in perspective and although Ted Dexter later spent a good deal of his time on the telephone exercising his commercial ingenuity on behalf of his team, our new approach did not bring the team much goodwill.

Inevitably the throwing together of sixteen or seventeen individual personalities to live and work with one another for almost half a year, often under conditions of quite severe strain, can lead to other problems. For economic reasons only the manager, captain and perhaps two or three senior players have single rooms. The rest double up. In some cases this could do much to cement team spirit, in others it simply would not work. Tom Graveney, for example, was a man who liked to lead a most orderly and pre-determined life. He was always up at seven a.m. sharp for breakfast. Freddie Trueman, whose sleeping hours were geared to surfacing at nine forty-five and then shuddering at the mere mention of eggs and bacon, would not have made the ideal room-mate. A manager has to make time for details such as this.

One factor that all the players have to accept is that from the moment they leave England until the moment they return they are living a fish-bowl existence. Every move they make, on the field and off it, is watched by the now large contingent of pressmen who travel with the team. Usually cricketers and correspondents travel by the same planes, stay in the same hotels and attend the same parties. Down the years the English cricket authorities have done nothing to discourage this very close contact and I think that is probably wise. If they tried to seal off the team as a separate travelling unit it would only cause unnecessary antagonism and turn the journalists into detectives. As it is they do not need to snoop. They know our temperaments, our weaknesses, our characters. They know all the gossip and if there is an internal row blowing up within the party they will probably know it before some of the players. In the past this has led to a few trivial incidents being blown up into spurious dramas which would have been laughable but for the personal embarrassment they caused. But in recent years there has been a marked decline in dirty-laundry journalism. Correspondents now tend to write fewer personal stories about players and, on balance, I would rather have them living in our laps and using their own judgment about the mass of inside information which is freely available to them.

I have attempted, in this chapter, to give the reader an insight into the life of the touring cricketer. It would not be complete without a reference to the worst day for every player on every expedition: Christmas Day. I have spent nine of them abroad and I have always been glad when the next cricket day dawns. There are a host of invitations to spend the day with local families but, like most cricketers, I am sensitive about breaking into someone else's family Christmas. Over the years an established formula has emerged to combat the homesickness and misery of those twenty-four hours. Mid-morning the English journalists throw a champagne party. This is followed by a communal lunch at which everyone gambles in a sweepstake to be settled on a golf course immediately afterwards. Good golfers and golfers who could not tell a putter from a brassie then move off to play or hack their way round eighteen holes. A combination of champagne, brandy, turkey and a very hot sun are not the ingredients for championship golf but it proves an effective diversionary exercise.

# 18

The sixties in English cricket was a decade of unrelieved turbulence. Controversial figures came and went. There were increasingly bitter exchanges over throwing and the place of the coloured man in sport. But the centre of the turmoil was the England Test captaincy. One man was caught in the crossfire of the ceaseless arguments and I was that man. It was not a gratifying or amusing experience.

There would be no point in my denying that I had always expected to captain England in succession to Peter May. I was in no way after May's job because my respect for him as a cricketer and captain was total, and my loyalty to him absolute. But when he decided to stand down I saw myself as his natural successor. Although I was quite well aware that I had fallen foul of Walter Robins in West Indies I was not to know, of course, that he would later be appointed chairman of the England selectors.

I was also unaware of another factor. Despite my closeness to Peter May, despite knowing the disillusion and illness he had suffered, I never really knew whether or not he wanted to take over the reins again when he had recovered full fitness. Ironically, I did not know that until a late summer's day in 1970, when we lunched together at the Great Eastern Hotel on Liverpool Street Station. We had not met for some time and there was a great deal to talk about. Kent had just won the County Championship and I was just off to Australia, this time under Illingworth. "You know," said May, "I was very lucky. Everything came to me very early. I played in seven winning Surrey sides. I got into the England side quickly and became captain quickly. I played in an England side that won the Ashes in Australia and captained an England side that won the Ashes in England. I captained England in Australia, South Africa and West Indies. My only disappointment was that I didn't get my hundred hundreds. But apart from that I had done practically everything there was to do by 1960. I really didn't have any ambition to come back at all, you know."

Had we had that conversation in 1960 instead of 1970, and had cricket's administrators known what was in May's mind at the time, the pattern of things might have been different over the next ten years. Instead Peter May's shadow still loomed over the game in 1960 when we returned from West Indies to take on the South Africans in England. May was still ill, recuperating from a second operation. He played in none of the Tests and did not make a single appearance for Surrey. Yet he was only thirty years of age. Everyone assumed that in his own good time he would be back. That, at least, was the assumption of the selectors when they picked me, Test by separate Test, to lead against South Africa. And that was the situation as I saw it when, match by match, I accepted. I was caretaker captain in my mind and everyone else's.

If I could now have that period of my life over again I would do almost everything quite differently. I would have asserted myself without inhibitions. But at the time the consciousness that I was looking after the team for a friend in hospital was always with me. I do not offer that as an excuse for what turned out to be a dull and disappointing series. We won it so easily that it was an anti-climax and, in the absence of cut-and-thrust conflict, the critics turned their attention to wondering why Cowdrey wasn't insisting on faster runs or demanding more swashbuckling performances.

They were not slow to pounce on any incident and their biggest hue-and-cry came during the third Test at Trent Bridge when Jackie McGlew, the South African captain, was run out during the second innings. No one ever questioned the fact that McGlew, the non-striker, was still two yards out of his ground when Brian Statham threw down the stumps ahead of him with a direct hit. The storm was caused by the fact that another fielder, Alan Moss, had collided with McGlew and baulked him during the scamper.

*Wisden* records what happened next in these words: "Cowdrey and the other England players near the wicket promptly appealed and Elliott, the square-leg umpire, signalled out. Elliott's decision was correct because Moss had not deliberately baulked McGlew. McGlew never hesitates when given out, but as he hastened towards the pavilion the crowd voiced their disapproval of the circumstances of his dismissal."

The crowd were not the only ones to voice their disapproval. The press gave me hell. They were vehement that I should have brought him back and seemed unaware that that was precisely what I had tried to do. I went to the umpires and said, "Can I bring him back?" Their reply was, "No, you can't. There has been an appeal and he has been given out." My intentions, therefore, were demolished by the strict enforcement of the Laws of Cricket. What I should have done, as experience has now taught me, was to have withdrawn the appeal.

By the fifth Test Walter Robins was leading the criticism at the way England batted in the first innings. We struggled badly on a grassy wicket, were put out for 155 and then saw South Africa make 419 on a pitch which, by then, was playing perfectly. Although we had already won the series convincingly I still had the weekend to contemplate the possibility of a last-Test defeat at the hands of a South African team which was not really very good. As it happened I played my best innings of the summer on the Monday. I scored 155 in a record opening stand of 290 with Pullar and thrashed the ball all round the Oval. Most big innings have some motivating force and in my case it began and ended with Robins' criticism.

Although I was happy to finish that season on a successful personal note I had few pleasant memories of my first full series as captain. By the spring of 1961 Peter May was in the nets, preparing to come back into the game, and I was both relieved and content that he should resume control. Assuming that this would automatically be so I turned my attention away from England and concentrated on the rebuilding of a Kent team which had been struggling in the lower reaches of the County Championship. This so absorbed my time that, apart from anticipating that I would hardly be dropped from the England side as a specialist batsman, I gave no thought at all to the Test series that lay ahead against Richie Benaud's Australians.

My domestic world of Kent cricket was abruptly shattered, however, by a phone call to my home from Gubby Allen on a Saturday evening late in May. Allen at this time was still the selectors' chairman and was due to preside the following day over the meeting to choose England's team for the first Test in Birmingham. He asked me to drive up to his flat in Queen's Gate early the next day and join him for breakfast. I explained that I was due to play in a benefit match at Folkestone and therefore would not have much time to spare. But he said, "We shall probably need you for most of the morning." I understood why when I reached his home the following morning. "The situation," said Allen, "is that I am not sure that Peter is going to captain next week. He may do ..."

I would have been fairly stupid not to realise that I was now involved in a dilemma. Clearly Allen and May had been discussing the captaincy situation. May had already made some big scores that summer and had batted well against the Australians for Surrey at the Oval. But the shattering fact remained that in a few days' time I could now well be leading England into an Ashes series against an Australian team whose bowlers I barely knew from Adam.

And that was how it was to be. Peter May arrived an hour later and announced: "I have given this some thought and I would honestly like to be left out of this series for the moment." The other selectors, who apparently had no suspicion that this could happen, looked stunned.

These were the circumstances under which I was invited to captain England against Australia for the first time. It was not an auspicious start, nor was it an auspicious first Test. Nothing went particularly well for me as captain; on looking back I feel that I was not prepared. In the end the match was drawn, but only by courtesy of a magnificent 180 by Dexter in the second innings, a foretaste of the sort of batsmanship he was going to bring to the Test match scene in the next two or three years.

To illustrate how vital it is to have analysed opposition attacks and tactics before a game I might point to the evidence of what happened in the Australians' next match but one. They came from Birmingham, via Leicester, to Canterbury and there escaped by only seven runs from being the first Australian side since 1899 to lose to Kent. The match was encouraging for me personally, with a score of 149 in the first innings and 121 in the second. Sadly it was only a preface to the unhappiest day in my cricketing life.

By the time we returned to Allen's flat to pick the second Test team it was clear to me what was happening. Behind the scenes pressures were being applied to May to take over the captaincy again.

Perhaps because of his recent breakdown, possibly because of the way his authority had been challenged during the tour to West Indies, May was resisting. This time he said: "If the selectors want me back then I would rather go into the match just as a player, not as captain." So again I led the team, now in the unusual circumstances of having Peter May under me.

Looking back, this was the Test in which I should have clinched the captaincy for years to come. My loyalty to May was still as strong as ever it was. And although, as I have said, I did not fully understand how ready he was to abdicate for good, had the Lord's Test taken a different pattern I think I might have begun a long reign of leadership and so avoided the many rumpuses and embarrassments of the next few years.

It did not work out that way. I won the toss, England batted and Alan Davidson bowled superbly to get us out for 206. Despite this we got back into the match well. When Australia batted they were at one point 6 for two, at another 194 for six and at yet another 238 for eight. From that point Trueman and Statham barely got another ball past the bat. Those last two wickets added another 102 runs. We did not suffer any bad luck. They batted well. We simply could not get them out. In these circumstances the captain takes the blame.

The one consolation as we went back to Lord's on the Saturday was that Australia's tail-enders had proved how perfectly the wicket was now playing. This was confirmed when we started our second innings some while before lunch. We needed 400 and the scene, the setting and the conditions were perfect. We had not lost a wicket at lunch and as we started batting again afterwards Lord's was a picture that any cricket-lover would like to imprint on his brain for nostalgic reveries in his old age. The sun really did blaze down from a cloudless sky and that great and wonderful ground really was packed to its eaves.

It was the day on which I should have made a hundred. It was the day on which England should have got well on the road to 400 or more. Yet, on that perfect pitch, we collapsed quite inexplicably and were all out for 202. I was out playing the way I should have played: attacking. But instead of hitting the ball to the boundary I hit it in the air to cover and was caught for seven. For our whole performance there were no excuses and no explanations.

We lost the Lord's Test by five wickets and that Saturday was the blackest day of my life. Knowing now what was passing through Peter May's mind at the time I realise that he would not have accepted the England captaincy again, whatever the outcome of that match. And had I retained the captaincy then and fulfilled what I wanted to fulfil for English cricket in the subsequent few years, I suppose I could have retired from the game long before now and so missed a lot of fun.

Instead I was gently released from the captaincy. May took over for the third Test at Leeds. He did so with my blessing and full support. I was happy, in the short term, to be relieved of the pressure, though deep down I was too disappointed to discuss it even with my family.

At Leeds I batted very well for May and England and missed a first-innings century by only seven runs. England won the Test by eight wickets and so the series was squared. But that was not quite the end of the affair. Driving up to Manchester for the fourth Test I was feeling unwell. On the morning of the match I felt still worse and had a temperature of 101 when I went to see the doctor. May, who had more regard for my match temperament than my temperature, kept pressing me to play. The decision was left to me and I know I was right in dropping out of the side. The man who took my place was Brian Close. And it was Close, on the final day of that match, who became involved in quite a controversy when he was running down the pitch to hit Richie Benaud out of the ground.

The match was lost and Australia retained the Ashes. It was not for me to comment on Close's tactics. I had left Manchester on the second day and only watched it at home on television. But afterwards May seemed to think that those last-day misadventures justified his insistence that I should stay there and play unfit.

Apart from two hundreds against the Australians for Kent it had been a season I was pleased to have behind me. It had been a season that had promised so much and had left me flat and disappointed with myself.

# 19

During the American Presidential campaign of 1968 a young writer named Joe McGinnis infiltrated the Nixon party machine in the guise of a publicity adviser. He kept his eyes and ears open, his wits about him and his face miraculously straight. Six months later he emerged as the author of probably the most hilariously revealing best-seller ever written about the intrigues and shenanigans of big league politics. Had any English writer been able similarly to infiltrate the inner councils of cricket during the months of April to September 1962 he would have emerged with not one hilarious book but two. Hilarious, that is, to all but those few unfortunates caught up in the whirlpool. The first volume might have been called "The Making of an England Captain" and the second "The Making of an England Manager". At times they would have borne more relation to a comedy script than a credible documentation of the events.

The campaign for which the captain and manager were required was to Australia in the winter of 1962–63. The field was fairly open. Peter May had now left the playing fields for Lloyds. It was time for a rest and I dropped out of the tour to India and Pakistan the previous winter. Ted Dexter had taken the team and had his problems, but while Walter Robins was chief selector Dexter was bound to be a stronger contender than myself. Another candidate under scrutiny was Mike Smith, a fine batsman, but there seemed some doubt about his ability against really fast bowling.

It was at this point, on a biting spring day when there was no cricket to write about, that E. M. Wellings, the pungent cricket

Fiery Fred

Catching Fred Trueman's 300th Test
victim, Neil Hawke of Australia, at the
Oval in 1964

Cover driving Chappell at Adelaide, February 1966

Colin Milburn hooks McKenzie for four in the 200th match between England and Australia at Lords, June 1968

Pleading with rioting spectators at Kingston,
Jamaica in 1968, and supported by Gary Sobers
and the President of Jamaica Cricket Association.
But the game had to be halted.

Nevertheless we won the series, and the family was there to greet me at Heathrow on our return

This MCC team to West Indies and Guyana in 1968 was in fact the only team I ever captained abroad: (Back row) J. Jennings (physiotherapist), A. Knott, I. J. Jones, P. I. Pocock, D. J. Brown, J. A. Snow, B. L. D'Oliveira, C. Milburn, R. N. S. Hobbs, L. E. G. Ames (Manager)    (Front row) G. Boycott, K. Higgs, T. W. Graveney, M. C. Cowdrey (Capt.), F. J. Titmus, K. F. Barrington, J. M. Parks, J. H. Edrich

Three Test selectors: Alec Bedser, Walter Robins and Doug Insole

With former MCC President Gubby Allen and recently retired MCC Secretary Billy Griffith

Contenders for the England
captaincy, Close and myself open
the England innings against
Pakistan at the Oval, 1967

Fielding practice at Edgbaston on
the day Ray Illingworth was
chosen to lead MCC to Australia
in 1970

The 100th run of my 100th 100 at Maidstone v. Surrey, 1973

A dream come true: walking in with Asif Iqbal after that innings

A word of congratulation from
Alec Douglas Home at a lunch
given at Lords to celebrate my
100th 100

In front of the stand named in
honour, Frank Woolley with
Ames and myself, the three Ke
cricketers to score 100 100s.

correspondent of the London *Evening News*, threw an entirely new name into the arena. Had he recommended George Brown for Prince of Wales it would hardly have caused more astonishment. The name he suggested was the Reverend David Sheppard, a man who had played his last Test for England five years previously and who had now retired from cricket to work at the Mayflower Centre in the East End of London. Wellings, however, was adamant in his argument that Sheppard was precisely the type of leader urgently needed to restore vitality to England's international team. It was good journalism and, frankly, should have been seen for what it was.

One reader, however, was deeply impressed by Wellings's suggestion: the Test selectors' chairman, Walter Robins. So impressed that he reached for the telephone and rang through to the Mayflower Centre to talk to Sheppard. He wanted to find out if there was any possible chance of Sheppard taking a sabbatical year from his new work so that he could play a certain amount of first-class cricket in the English summer with a view to leading England in Australia the following winter.

Sheppard was out. So Robins left a message with his secretary. It simply read: "Mr. Robins rang. Would you please ring him back."

By one of those coincidences so familiar to devotees of the "Carry On" films, David had a parishioner whose name was also Robins. This second Mr. Robins had recently had a problem which had consumed a great deal of Sheppard's time and, anxious that he should spend no more at the expense of his other parishioners, Sheppard pushed the message into his pending file to await further developments.

The developments came three days later when Sheppard was out and about on his parish calls and, by chance, ran into the second Mr. Robins. To his bewilderment Mr. Robins greeted him cordially and passed on without so much as a flickering glance of reproach. A little later they passed in the same street again and Sheppard, anxious now to know what the phone message had been all about, stopped him and apologised for the delay in contacting him. "I've been rather busy," he said, "but I gather you wanted a chat." Mr. Robins's face remained a complete blank.

Sheppard might have forgotten the incident altogether had the phone message not still been in his file when he returned to his desk. Robins? Robins? The only other Robins he knew was Walter Robins, the cricket selector. So at last he made the phone call that was to hit front and back page headlines in England and Australia for months to come.

Walter Robins, never a man to take kindly to being ignored for three days, was prepared to be cool at first. But by the time the mix-up had been explained his remarkable powers of persuasion had been fully restored. Sheppard, who had had no thoughts of a sabbatical when he picked the phone up, was now planning to take a year off and come back to cricket by the time he put it down.

Walter Robins was a methodical man and the suggestion was that Sheppard should play a stipulated number of games for Sussex and the situation would then be reviewed. And so, on Wednesday, June 20th, 1962, David Sheppard walked out to bat in The Parks at Oxford, watched not by the customary three or four reporters who might have covered a match like that but a press, television and radio corps of the size normally assembled only to witness England battle against Australia. Sheppard, who had not played for England for five years or for Sussex for two, scored 108 in the first innings and 55 in the second. It was a sensational come-back and the press entourage followed him avidly, recording his every run, his every thought and the occasional dropped catch. Inevitably, however, runs were not so easy to come by against the county sides as they had been against Oxford University, and by the end of the game against Surrey at the Oval in mid-July Sheppard was prepared to call off the experiment. He scored four and twenty-four opening the Sussex innings in that match and when it was over he went to see Walter Robins and Gubby Allen. "It was an intriguing idea but I haven't done as well as I'd hoped," he told them. "It has not been easy coming back after so long a lay-off. My batting hasn't been quite what I expected and I found the fielding rather difficult. Perhaps we'd better forget the whole thing."

Robins persuaded him to keep on persevering. Sheppard had at least one more match to play, for he was already committed to appearing at Lord's the following week in the Gents' team against the Players.

Unaware of Sheppard's own misgivings the press now assembled at Lord's in force, less to report the game than to witness what had now become a straight fight between Sheppard and Dexter for the leadership in Australia. The official decision was shortly to be announced and this was to be the climax of a remarkable story.

Indeed the climax was to be more remarkable than any of them knew. Sheppard scored 112 in the Gents' first innings and though it was a long and laborious piece of batting it persuaded the journalists, almost to a man, that it was this quality of determination which would finally swing the captaincy Sheppard's way. But that was not all. From the windows of the press restaurant, six flights of stairs above the ground, a number of senior correspondents spotted Walter Robins walking round to the pavilion. Anxious to get the tip-off that would confirm that Sheppard was the man, they attracted Robins's attention and engaged in a number of long-range signals.

Robins grinned and mischievously gave them the thumbs up. And so they stampeded back to their typewriters, confident now as they composed their stories for the following morning's papers. Next day almost all the headlines proclaimed "Sheppard for Captain" in huge type and beneath them came many a story extolling the percipience of the England selectors, the dashing imagination of the whole experiment, the courage displayed throughout by the Reverend David Sheppard.

Later that day a layman by the name of Ted Dexter was appointed to captain England in Australia.

At the very moment that the official announcement of Dexter's appointment was being made to a stunned press-box, David Sheppard was back at the Lord's wicket batting really well in the Gents' second innings. He made only 34 but the style of his strokes suggested a man with a huge weight off his mind and he might well have thought that his hundred had clinched the captaincy. The decision had been taken as David began his second innings and because he remained at the wicket until the end he was one of the last people to know of the appointment.

Now he was faced with the prospect of going to Australia with no responsibilities other than those of an opening batsman. Could he justify asking for six months' leave of absence from his work in the East End of London? What now? would be the public reaction to a parson throwing in the towel as soon as he had been passed over for the big job. He was trapped by the publicity and he could not withdraw for fear of being misunderstood.

And so it was under Ted Dexter, with myself as vice-captain and Alec Bedser as Assistant Manager that David, now Bishop of

Liverpool, sailed to Australia in the good ship *Canberra* in October 1962.

On the same ship, as manager of that MCC expedition, was the sixteenth Duke of Norfolk, Earl Marshal of England, President of Sussex and a former President of MCC. To say that his appointment was a surprise is an understatement. In fact, the appointments were related, for it was only after the selectors had decided that Dexter, not Sheppard, should captain the side that they faced the problem of who should go as tour manager. It is essential for the well-being of any cricket expedition that there is an easy, compatible relationship between captain and manager. Here was a problem. Dexter has always been a strong individualist with a life-style all of his own. Then, more than now, he was unpredictable and not the easiest of men to manage. "There's no doubt that Dexter can handle a bat," said one of the selectors, "but who's going to handle Dexter?"

By yet another of those remarkable film coincidences the Duke of Norfolk, who had arrived to attend a meeting at Lord's, happened to be present when the selectors were mulling this over. He knew Dexter well and swiftly sprang to his defence. "I don't know what you're concerned about," he said. "I've had no difficulty with him in Sussex. I find him a straightforward chap and I enjoy his company very much."

"That's all very well, sir," said one of the selectors, "but *you're* not going to Australia as manager, are you?"

"Well," replied the Duke, with a twinkle, "I haven't been asked, have I?"

At that moment in English cricket history nothing was further from the Duke of Norfolk's mind. But his casual remark caused what lady novelists call a pregnant pause. Not a word was said but a swift exchange of furtive glances between the selectors confirmed that the same thought had occurred to each. Shortly afterwards, when the Duke rose to leave, Walter Robins followed him to the door. Outside he asked the Duke: "Look, sir, about not being asked to manage in Australia. Were you joking?"

"I suppose I was," said the Duke. "It's never crossed my mind. But now that you've decided that Dexter is the man to captain England and if you think that I might be the man to handle him, you must let me know."

The outcome, of course, was that the Duke of Norfolk's appointment as manager was announced to an astonished press shortly afterwards. He came and enjoyed it and, naturally, was a great success.

On reflection, it really was remarkable that the Duke should have loved cricket enough to be prepared to leave home for such a long stretch. It was a handsome gesture, too, to Ted Dexter whom the Duke admired tremendously. We were not to realise until much later that there was just one extra obstacle to his journey which had to be overcome. He had to be home at the New Year and it was arranged that Billy Griffith, then Secretary of MCC, should be released from Lord's for a few weeks to tide over this period. It was unfortunate that just at the time when he was due to come home we had a disappointing spell of cricket. The knives were out and the Australian press did not veil their contempt at his leaving the ship at such a time. The implied criticism was that he had slipped home for some unscheduled leave with his family at Arundel.

The fact was that the Duke of Norfolk returned to England to oversee a rehearsal of Sir Winston Churchill's funeral procession. This took place once every three months in the hours of the early morning when London streets were empty. That this was in December 1962 and Churchill died in 1965 only emphasises the immense preparation that lay behind all the Duke's masterpieces of British ceremony and pageantry. Indeed, the river section of the Churchill funeral had been the Duke's own idea and apparently Churchill himself had been delighted with it. We were to hear later that Sir Winston's failing health was something of a constant worry to the Duke in far away Australia.

All this, of course, was as unknown to the English players as it was to the Australian press. There was certainly no resentment among the players who hardly envied the Duke his two arduous flights from one end of the earth to the other. Anyone who has endured this twice in a fortnight will know that it is far from being a picnic. The fatigue, plus the early morning rehearsals in temperatures 90 degrees lower than those to which he had become acclimatised in Australia, certainly did little for the Duke's health. When he re-joined us in Adelaide he was a tired man, suffering from ear and nose trouble and afflicted once more by his constant enemy, insomnia. I felt very sorry for him at the time and sorrier still later when I realised how deeply he had been cut by the press criticism—and he had to be silent under it.

I admired the Duke of Norfolk most of all for the way he always sought to play second string to the captain, yet was willing to take any of the load off the captain's shoulders whenever it would help. Throughout the tour it was Ted Dexter who occupied the centre of the stage, supremely confident in every situation. Dexter, as a batsman, played magnificently and enlivened a generally dull Test series with some spectacular innings.

Both tours to Australia in the 1960s followed curiously identical patterns. In each, England went one up in the series only for Australia to win the very next game. In each the final outcome was a one-one draw with three Tests producing no result. In each the final Test was drawn before small crowds and we were conscious that the public was losing interest. In each Australia retained the Ashes by virtue of having held them in the first place. This dreary pattern was disappointing and we came home each time with a slight feeling of anti-climax.

I do not subscribe to the radical school which feels that the fight for the "Ashes" spoils the matches. The very term has an intrinsic value through its link with the great traditions of the past. But I would like to see England and Australia come to an agreement that, in future, the Ashes are not "retained" by the winning side. In other words that each series begins with a clean slate and that if a series is drawn then the Ashes become a prize shared.

# 20

The 1960s, when viewed in retrospect by future cricket historians, will doubtless be neatly classified as the Decade of the West Indies. There is something to be said to support such a claim, sweeping though it is. The team that Frank Worrell built and Gary Sobers inherited, comprised as it was of much electrifying individual talent and immense collective appeal, caught the imagination of a world-wide audience at the very moment when the game was going through one of its more somnolent periods. Suddenly, on a chilly December morning in 1960, news came through to Britain from Brisbane that Australia and West Indies had tied their first Test match. It was followed, almost daily, by accounts of epic innings and vibrant cricket, of a crowd of 90,800 watching a single day's play, of a civic farewell in Melbourne in which hundreds of thousands of Australians lined the streets to wave goodbye to a West Indies team standing like royalty in open cars. Yet here was the team that we had beaten on their home soil. There had been only one significant change: captain and vice-captain had swopped places. Gerry Alexander continued as a very effective wicket-keeper-batsman, and vice-captain Frank Worrell became the first coloured man to captain the West Indies. He was a great player in his own right and a man of great dignity and personal charm. The 1960s, therefore, began in style.

I well remember the warmth of England's greeting to Frank Worrell's West Indians in the spring of 1963 and, indeed, the apprehension of England's selectors approaching the first Test match at Manchester which West Indies won by ten wickets with more than a day to spare. It was a simple story: Ted Dexter lost the toss and first use of a wicket which, in the end, took a lot of spin. West Indies had Lance Gibbs to exploit it and our fate was written on the walls of Old Trafford long before the weekend.

That initial Test is only memorable to me now because in the first innings I was bowled round my legs by a fast bowler. I know full well the reaction it created in some quarters at the time. "Cowdrey losing his nerve, eh? He dodged it, looked thoroughly scared." This was not quite the case. I have already explained at some length how I had developed a method of coping with the speed of the West Indian new ball bowlers in the Caribbean. I tried to stand as still as possible at the crease on a guard of middle-and-off, move down into the line of the ball and either hit it or let it hit me. For some reason I convinced myself that the same tactics would work in England. This was the first occasion on which I had faced real speed since the Tests in the West Indies, but I was extremely confident of my method. So I took my middle-and-off guard, which had served me well in the West Indies, but which of course I now took in England, in the normal course of things. When Wes Hall let one fly down the leg-side, as I thought, I reacted just as I had successfully reacted to identical deliveries from him countless times in West Indies. I swayed out of its line, deliberately leaving it alone. Unfortunately I had misjudged the bounce. This was Manchester, not Kingston, Jamaica, and the ball did not bounce so high. Instead of rearing well clear of the stumps as it would have done in the Caribbean it only rose sufficiently to clip down the very top of my leg-stump, sending it cartwheeling. It was a long walk back to the pavilion. To go into *Wisden* as b. Hall 4 is embarrassing enough. To be reported in every newspaper the following day as being bowled by Hall behind your legs is harrowing. After applying penetrating logic to considerable experience I had succeeded in making two and two add up to five.

The next Test match, which was one of the truly great cricket encounters of all time, was also my last of the series, for in another confrontation with Wesley Hall my arm was broken.

I shall return to that match in a moment but first it is essential that certain aspects of that game, that series and, indeed, two complete tours to England in 1963 and 1966 by West Indies are drawn into perspective. All was not quite what it appeared to be from the pavilion, and the reason was the presence of a very fast West Indian

136

bowler named Charles Christopher Griffith. He is now, I am happy to say, and has been for some time, a very successful coach in Barbados. But to pretend that he did not exist, or that West Indies cricket administrators were not concerned about his inclusion in their touring teams, would be akin to writing a definitive account of the Protectorate without any reference to Cromwell.

The truth about Griffith was that he could bowl with a perfect action. On the occasions when he strove for extra pace, his action altered perceptibly and he could produce a most brutal, lethal delivery, fast yorkers or short-pitched bouncers. It raised the whole question of what is a throw. One thing is certain, that a cricket ball thrown, not bowled at above a certain velocity is quite capable of killing a batsman, and I do not think it is too melodramatic to suggest that it was more by good luck than any responsible judgment that there was no fatal injury during the 1960s. In fact, India's Contractor was very badly hurt in Barbados.

It is not easy to convince people who have not played cricket at a reasonably high level of the very real danger. But basically the difference between facing the legal delivery and the throw is this: against the legitimate fast bowler the batsman plays the line of the arm. In other words, as he sees the bowler's arm coming to the vertical he can anticipate the direction of the ball and begin to position himself for either an attacking or a defensive shot as soon as the ball is released. With the bent arm and snapping action, the batsman has trouble picking up the ball. He does not see the ball leave the hand and is therefore groping. The direction and trajectory of the delivery are unpredictable and therefore the batsman is faced with the difficult problem of trying to play the ball off the pitch. In a sentence, the legal delivery comes out of an arc whereas the throw comes out of a muzzle.

There are other, less emotional reasons why it is imperative that throwing is eliminated from the game. From the bowler's point of view, there is the ethical reason that the thrower is a fraud because he can achieve by a spurious knack the same results that men like Ray Lindwall, Alec Bedser and Wesley Hall have taken years of hard, dedicated work to attain. If throwers were allowed to proliferate, the long-term effect on the game of cricket would be disastrous: in a few years genuine bowlers would cease to exist.

It is a pity that this subject did not receive a greater public airing early in 1963, for it would have brought into the open a situation which, within the game, festered into an extremely unpleasant atmosphere. The reason was, I suppose, that in the opening Test of that series in Manchester, Charlie Griffith never really let himself go. On the other hand there was sufficient evidence to the experienced eye that there were going to be problems. In the Manchester Test, Lance Gibbs took the brunt of the bowling and there was not much pressure on the fast bowlers.

The next Test, at Lord's, was notable for a stirringly close finish and earlier in the match one of the greatest innings ever seen on that ground. No one who saw Dexter's 70 off 74 balls in the first innings will forget it. Hall and Griffith were warmed up and in full flow. They were after him. Many men would have ducked the confrontation. But this was the situation for Ted Dexter. He took Griffith on contemptuously. Not only did his innings reflect completely his volatile nature and almost arrogant confidence, it also thrust England right back into the game. It is not my intention here to recall its thrusts and parries, hour by hour, since anyone wishing to re-live those agonies of suspense can read Alan Ross's excellent book on the subject. Even so, there are emotions which only a contestant can feel and for me in that match there were many.

The first came on the Saturday when I had to take over the captaincy of England in the field. Dexter had been injured during his superb innings the previous day and now, with the game delicately poised, I had the responsibility of making sure he had not played in vain. There is always a unique tension before play starts on a Test match Saturday at Lord's, with thousands bustling behind the pavilion, huge and strangely hushed crowds around the nets, the ground itself packed as you go through the Long Room doors and begin to come down the steps. I have played before crowds three times as huge in Melbourne but nowhere on earth do my stomach muscles tighten up a full hour before play begins as they do in this special place. That morning, for the first time in seven years, Lord's had to turn crowds away. The gates were closed ten minutes before the start. When I led the team into the field twenty-five minutes before lunch, with England only four runs behind on first innings, I felt no different from the way I felt that first Test Saturday at Lord's, many years earlier. But now, with Dexter lying on the treatment table, there was a new responsibility.

For a long while we held complete control. West Indies lost two wickets at 15, their third at 64, their fourth at 84 and their fifth at 104. No captain could have asked more but few would have enjoyed what came next. Frank Worrell came in to do little more than hold the fort for Basil Butcher who was blazing away at the other end. Thrilling though Butcher's innings must have appeared from the boundary there seemed no possibility, in the middle, that he could keep taking such massive risks and get away with it. But he did. We could not separate them and at the close of the day Butcher was 129 not out and Worrell 33 not out. It was a disappointing finish to a magnificent day's cricket.

In the end England were set to make 234 to win. Rain had intervened to make it a contest against the clock as well as West Indies, but for me the innings remains memorable because it was as tough as anything enacted in professional sport since the days when both boxers had their noses broken for half-a-crown. The light had diminished to a heavy grey gloom and Hall and Griffith were at their most hostile and hard to pick up. I had made 19 when Hall switched round to bowl from the pavilion end where, in those days, there was no sight screen. He let loose two very nasty ones and then, by chance, pitched one only just short of a length. It reared straight up and would have struck me under the chin at full speed had I not flung up my left arm in an instinctive parry. The ball therefore struck a rigid arm, and snapped the ulna bone just above the wrist. I left the field knowing that for me the 1963 cricket season was over. I did not dream that I would have to appear again on the ground before that remarkable day was done.

It would not have been necessary but for an astonishing display of courage throughout the afternoon by Brian Close. Like Dexter in the first innings, Close in the second batted on a flood-tide of adrenalin. He charged the fast bowlers to such an extent that twice Hall actually pulled up before releasing the ball as he saw that Close had already advanced three yards down the wicket to meet him. There were many intelligent cricketers in the pavilion who believed that Close had gone berserk. I was not among them for I recognised in his tactics something far more than bravado. He was using logic that had been the art many years before of Frank Woolley: making room for his shot by taking a pace down the pitch as soon as the arm came over. Admittedly, this exposed all three stumps to the bowler but, assuming the ball was going to be well pitched up and straight, Woolley would then move into position and hit straight through the line of the middle stump. If the ball came where he had anticipated, it was invariably a magnificent shot. He would not be bowled because he was hitting straight. If the ball was wide or short he left it alone, again safe in the knowledge that he could not be bowled. The only real danger was in getting a nick to the wicket-keeper.

This was Close's reasoning so what, to many, looked like a maniacal innings of blind courage was, in truth, a carefully pre-meditated assault. It was an unforgettable spectacle, for several times, facing Hall, he was stranded down the pitch ducking and weaving like a desperate boxer. Many times he was inevitably struck and when he was finally out, for 70, and stripped off in the dressing room his torso looked like a relief map of the Atlas Mountains. There were black, blue and purple bruises from his neck down to his waist and in one or two places you could actually see where the stitching of the ball had left its impression on his skin. It had been, surely, Close's finest hour.

Close's innings had so thrust England back into the game that a tight finish was now inevitable. It was clearly going to be all hands to the wheel, perhaps even mine, broken though it was. Dexter was insistent that I should not return to the wicket unless it was absolutely imperative but even so, with exactly an hour to go, I was fumbling back into my cricket gear with a left arm now in plaster from just below the bicep to just above the top knuckles. I was also trying to work out how I should bat because the doctors had made it clear what could happen if I further injured that bone even by jarring it while making contact with the ball. One doctor went so far as to suggest that the left arm should be bound behind my back with adhesive tape, to stop me grabbing the bat handle with it in some involuntary movement. I avoided this by promising to tuck the fingers of my injured hand into my pocket. I was not going to be able to bat from a right-handed stance, so what I decided to do was to face up like a left-hander—in other words to play back-hand with the right hand. This I practised in the dressing room, knowing almost exactly the tactics which would be employed against me if I were required to return to the wicket. They would crowd me with close fielders and work for a prodded catch off the bat or glove.

Outside, meanwhile, it was becoming more and more likely that

I would have to go out again as the match moved to its tumultuous climax. With twenty minutes to go England needed fifteen to win. West Indies needed two wickets to win. At the start of the final over, from Hall, West Indies still needed the two wickets but England's target was down to eight runs for victory. Derek Shackleton was the facing batsman with David Allen at the other end. Shackleton took a single off the second ball and Allen a single off the third. But off the fourth, to a mighty roar from the crowd, Shackleton was run out sprinting vainly for the pavilion end.

So with six runs needed and two balls to go I walked out to the wicket. Although I later saw photographs of myself looking very grave I felt confident that even if I had to face a couple of overs I could keep the ball out of my wicket one-handed. As it transpired, since I went to the non-striker's end, the most I would have had to face was a single, final delivery from Hall.

The scene when I arrived out in the middle was incredible. David Allen was the calmest man in St. John's Wood. In contrast Wesley Hall, now required to win a Test match in two balls at the end of a long day's bowling, was so excited and tense that his eyeballs were staring out of his head. But he walked round in small circles, apparently seeing nothing. It was at this point that Frank Worrell, already taking up his position at short-leg, had a sudden astute thought. His head flashed round and he called to Hall: "Make sure you don't bowl a no-ball." What followed was pure farce. The crowd was so colossal that Hall had not heard what Worrell had said. He stopped in his tracks, inclined his head and cupped his hand to an ear straining to hear his captain's instructions. So Worrell repeated them, screaming at the top of his voice one of the most colourful orders that can ever have been bellowed down the length of the Lord's pitch: "What I said was for God's sake don't bowl a b..... no-ball." Hall got the message. He went back to his distant mark, pounding the ball from one palm to the other. Then he turned and hurtled in. Allen met him with an unwavering bat face. Hall turned and flung thirty hours of frustration into his final delivery. Again Allen played an imperturbable defensive shot. The Test match was over, drawn, and my one-handed batting technique had not been put to the test.

There was a good deal of subsequent debate about why England had so concentrated on saving that match in the closing minutes when, with a little more enterprise, we might have won it. But for my injury we must have won it. Frankly, they had not earned victory. From the moment Brian Close settled into his innings, West Indies had really only kept us at bay by reducing their over rate dramatically. From a grim thirteen overs per hour they dropped even further at one stage to only slightly above eleven. I appreciated Worrell's difficulties, but this had been a mistake, and I know that he looked back on it all with some regret. In the heat of the moment these things happen. Nevertheless it had been a wonderful Test match. My injury apart, it was perhaps the best cricket match I have played in for tension and excitement, and constant changes of fortune.

# 21

The most controversial features of the game in my time have been the sudden appearance of throwing, the gradual increase in the number of bouncers bowled, the new pressures upon umpires and the emergence of the fully professional game. Whilst I was never bowled a bouncer as a schoolboy this was one of the extras, not an optional one either, which went with batting in first-class cricket. In my early years there were only a handful of bowlers who could bowl a good bouncer. They used it occasionally, very much as an element of surprise. Seen in this light it was a legitimate part of the bowler's armoury. It was of particular value to him when he found a long-legged batsman thrusting his front foot out obstinately, even before the ball had left his hand. I have a very clear recollection of Easton McMorris, playing for Jamaica, keeping Brian Statham at bay effectively by thrusting out his front foot down the line. Brian Statham, a magnificent competitor yet the fairest sportsman in all the world, warned him quietly and courteously that if he continued in this vein he would be given one or two nasty bouncers. I have never known a warning being given like that before or since; I cannot envisage it happening in today's game. Unhappily, McMorris did not heed the warning and two overs later walked straight into a short-pitched delivery which hit him a severe blow under the heart. He was seriously hurt and had to be taken to hospital. No one was more upset about it than Brian Statham, but McMorris was taking advantage of his good nature and at the end of the match, when he had fully recovered, he was big enough to admit that no blame could be laid at Brian Statham's door.

Most fast bowlers have had spells of over-doing the quick stuff but the great fast bowlers at their best have been most dangerous pitching the ball up. I think of Ray Lindwall in 1948, swinging the ball away late to the slips, the batsmen playing hurried strokes and being caught in the slips. Every now and again he would produce the most lethal yorker to remove the leg-stump. But the knowledge that he could produce a really nasty, skidding bouncer was always in the batsman's mind, and made him just that bit more apprehensive.

Frankly, I have been disturbed at the number of bouncers bowled at Test level these last few years. On my first tour of Australia with Tyson and Statham on one side and Lindwall and Miller on the other, it was never over-done. Today, if there is any semblance of pace in the wicket one comes to expect a bouncer three or four balls an over—even more at times. This then becomes intimidatory bowling, contravening the law, and it has been terribly difficult for the umpire to intervene and adjudicate fairly. When there are too many bouncers bowled tempers fray and bad blood is spilt. The difficulty for the umpire, of course, is "What really is a bouncer?" This question was constantly asked in Australia last winter when Lillee and Thomson had us over the guns day after day. One batsman will tuck a short-pitched delivery away quite neatly and yet that same delivery will have another batsman in a tangle, perhaps hit him. I am all for the occasional bouncer inviting a challenging riposte from the great player who can hook, but I look forward to the time when a fair balance is restored.

Ever since bowling changed from under-arm to over-arm there have always been occasional cases of bowlers with unusual actions suspected of throwing. I am mindful of the controversy over Mold of Lancashire which so upset Lord Harris that he turned Lancashire off the Kent fixture list for a few years. I think, too, of Gilbert, the aboriginal pace man from Queensland who, I understand, was too unusual to be allowed to continue once he had started taking wickets. As I look back I simply do not remember the subject being discussed in my early years with Kent. The first thing I remember is the dressing room underworld starting to mutter about Surrey's Tony Lock, noted for classical action when he was using the air but distinctly suspect when he quickened up. Douglas Wright of Kent used to mix in a faster ball occasionally but there was no hint of a throw about it; yet when Tony Lock produced a quicker ball he looked almost as if he was running someone out from cover point.

There was a celebrated occasion in West Indies in 1953 when some money was collected to bring George Headley from England to play in the Jamaica Test match. It was a moving moment when he walked to the wicket to a wonderful reception. Len Hutton responded by putting the field back so that Tony Lock could give him one run. A charming gesture this which is probably unprecedented in Test cricket. George Headley moved into double figures and was just beginning to settle in, it seemed, when Tony Lock sent his leg-stump cartwheeling before he had time to get his bat down. I heard it said that it was probably the quickest ball bowled in the match. With Tony Lock it was not only this faster ball that was under fire. While Stuart Surridge used to let Jim Laker have his head and refrain from too much interference, he would be inclined to chide and chase Tony Lock, exhorting him to more explosive effort. In the delivery stride he would be seen to drag the back foot, giving the arm time to slow down, curl and bend before banging the ball into the wicket. This had the effect of making it cut and leap off certain types of wicket in the most alarming fashion. No other bowler achieved anything like the same result and one became suspicious of his action.

One of my proudest memories is to have played in Jim Laker's match, the Test match at Old Trafford against Australia when Laker took 19 wickets. In fact, I caught the only victim to elude him, at slip off Tony Lock, early in the second innings. This match might have been remembered for an exhilarating opening partnership of 170 between Richardson and Cowdrey, and later for a fine come-back hundred from the Reverend David Sheppard, hot-foot from the parish of Islington. However, the rains came and the pitch was transformed, but not before Laker had taken quite a few wickets on a dry, slow-turning wicket.

His consistent, nagging accuracy, making them play at every ball, was a masterpiece. He was fortunate to have such conditions in his favour, but he must take the credit for as superb a piece of attacking bowling as there has ever been.

Tony Lock beat the bat time and time again, and I shall never know why he did not enjoy a harvest of wickets as well. No one felt more humiliated than he did.

I do not recall anything unusual about his action in this match but as he did push the ball through faster in order to extract something out of the wicket, it was probably suspect. Here, at least, was one instance where the bowler with the genuine action, Jim Laker, could boast the greater success. More often than not the reverse is the case. In fact, the most telling argument in favour of being tough on bowlers with a suspect action is that so often the legitimate bowler, who has spent years perfecting his art, is at a disadvantage. I know that Ray Lindwall felt very strongly about this as he watched Meckiff and Rorke competing alongside him.

The real difficulties in detecting a thrower arose with a bowler who could bowl perfectly fairly, but who could produce by way of variation a faster ball with a suspect action. In Peter Loader's case there were two deliveries which caused people to pause and wonder. As well as the faster ball he had a well-concealed slow off-spinner and both were suspect. Yet, he was a magnificent match-winning bowler, a model for any youngster, with the away-swinger his basic stock-in-trade.

One of the cricketers for whom I felt the most sympathy was Harold Rhodes of Derbyshire. It was only when he won his England cap and was enjoying success at the top that his action started to be questioned. He was tall and lithe, with long arms and a whippy action, and he had the ability to produce the much faster ball which would take the very best players by surprise. With the help of the slow-motion film camera it appeared that he was double-jointed at the elbow. The arm looked bent at times, yet this was a natural phenomenon peculiar to him. Does this really constitute a throw? The debate went on and on and was never happily resolved. Unfortunately, his career was seriously affected by the controversy.

Roy Gilchrist of the West Indies was another who could bowl fairly and bowl quick too, but could produce a lethal thunderbolt when he was roused. Although a number of umpires studied this with great care, his arm never appeared to bend, and it remained something of a mystery. There will be many like him, I fear. Most of the time their action is perfectly fair. The occasional really fast ball breaks the law. How can any umpire be expected to cope with this?

There are clear give-away symptoms of the ball that is blatantly thrown, the open chest, the front foot splayed out in the delivery stride and the falling away from the wicket after delivery. It was fascinating to compare Wesley Hall bowling one end and Charlie

Griffith at the other on those days when Charlie Griffith was really letting it go. Charlie Griffith was one of those who could bowl quite genuinely and accurately at a brisk medium pace, but when he was at full throttle he would open up, and pound the wicket with enormous power.

I honestly believe that none of them had any intention of contravening the law. I believe that in each case the knack had been developed early in their cricket-playing days and should have been checked before the habit was formed. By the time they had enjoyed sufficient measure of success to win a Test place this faster ball had become a very important variation in their armoury.

In the case of Ian Meckiff, and Geoff Griffin of South Africa too, the arm appeared to bend at some point, and so the problem was fairly straightforward. It took a long time to resolve because it was all such a new and unknown phenomenon and understandably umpires went to great lengths to be as fair as possible to the players concerned. In consequence, their agony was rather long-drawn-out. I am confident that the blatant thrower will never get as far as first-class cricket again—we know so much more about the malaise now. But I believe there will always be a number who are clearly legitimate bowlers but attract our attention with an unusual delivery every so often. We may get more of these than we would like and the umpires will be set an unenviable conundrum.

While on the subject of umpires, they really do have a task and a half in the modern game. It is a fact of life, I suppose, that the more skilled we become in any walk of life, the rougher the road seems to appear. It is certainly so at cricket.

The standard of English umpiring is higher every year. Our Test match umpires today come under severer pressure and criticism than ever before. Yet, to my mind, their ability to handle tense matches is near faultless. Of course, they make mistakes, but the art of umpiring lies much more in the astuteness with which they handle the game without interrupting its flow unnecessarily.

When I started, the umpires were like protected birds, jealously guarded by strong and independent captains. Their role was just as important but there was a more natural allegiance and deference accorded them. Today, the umpire has to be a strong, resilient character and his lot can be as lonely as a lighthouse. The participants

147

are playing for high stakes and the captain is much more at one with his men on points of principle. The winning counts so desperately. Less and less can an umpire look to the good nature of the players in the tight decision. More and more he has to walk a tightrope, striking a balance between the aloofness of decision on the one hand and the warmth of consideration on the other.

Happily, all our top-class umpires have been good players themselves. They cannot easily be hoodwinked over small things. This cuts out a lot of pettiness. I am optimistic enough to think that the players are learning to live with the pressures of playing for big money prizes. Each year they will be making room for more expression of old-fashioned courtesies and with them will come the responsible contribution which enriches our game. No one enjoys seeing the umpire's decision being questioned, to the accompaniment of an unpleasant display of temperament. The cricket field is no place for ill-manners.

I want to turn to the subject of "professionalism" before I close this chapter because it has such a bearing on cricket's future. Every professional cricketer should examine himself and consider what contribution he is making to the game. His philosophy and attitude determine so much of the development of the game in the years ahead. The good professional seeks to make the best use of his talent and plays flat out to win. Yet there is more to it than this. Personally I see nothing professional about a contemptuous indifference to crowds, a calculated disregard for the game's public and patrons, a lack of social responsibility outside the boundary ropes, an attitude of envy towards those other sports whose players make more money, an attitude of "we" and "they"—"we" representing the democracy of the dressing room, "they" the autocracy of the administration and committee room. This is not "professionalism" but a sickness of some paid sportsmen. It reflects an attitude that has spread through many other walks of life in Britain and it is based on the quite groundless belief that the world owes us a living. I have seen this so-called "professionalism" come into football and this last year or two creep into our game of cricket. Those of us who care for the game and those who will play it in the years ahead must stand firm to uphold standards—true professional standards.

One evening, during the Melbourne Test match, two English

batsmen were playing out the day, clearly intent on preserving their wickets till the morrow. The crowd replied with the new Australian custom of banging empty beer cans on the concrete terracing. It was not a pretty sound but it raised a chorus of caustic criticism and bitter condemnation in the English dressing room. Sitting silently beside me in the dressing room was the Australian golfer, Peter Thomson. He had listened to our team's reaction with interest and later he spoke about the new relationship between crowds and professional entertainers, the theatre and sport.

"I believe that your players should be clear-minded about it," he said, "because although the crowd's demonstration was ill-mannered this kind of alien reaction is something that we, as performers, must now accept." He then quoted an instance of how his own nerve had been similarly tested in an important play-off in an American golf tournament. So intense was the interest in the game that as he and his American opponent came all-square to the seventeenth tee, the entire fairway and green were locked in by a huge gallery of spectators. Both men hit their drives into the centre of the fairway and were left with seven-iron shots to the green. Thomson played first, struck a fine shot only to see it catch the wind, veer fractionally off-course, hit the top of a bunker and then slowly roll back into the sand.

"What hurt," said Thomson, "was a sound I had never heard before on a golf course. A huge roar of delight went up as my ball went down into the sand. Hundreds actually stood there clapping. Then, when my opponent hit a fine shot right into the heart of the green there was a great cheer of relief. It was a big test for me. The next three or four minutes were very difficult to live through.

"What I had to realise was that crowd values have changed. They are not always going to lean over backwards to show generosity to the visitor. We've got to learn to live with it. I had to take a grip on myself and realise that we *want* those huge crowds lining the fairway, we *want* that kind of enthusiasm, we even *want* that kind of enormous spectator participation. The crowds pay their money and they are now demanding their pound of flesh. It is something that cricketers, like golfers, will have to learn to live with."

It is not the first time in this book that I have alluded to golf and golfers as examples of how we in cricket should be approaching our affairs. The reason, perhaps, is that while cricketers for many years were able to take a certain popularity for granted, professional golfers have had to pull themselves up by their shoelaces to establish their present status in sport. Not so many years ago they were only accepted in members' club houses by invitation. Today their status is unchallenged and, for the successful ones, the financial rewards are staggering.

What professional cricketers must remember is that this transformation did not just happen. The golfers worked at it, building up their prestige in a conscious campaign of self-discipline. They took great care with their dress, with their manners and their bearing, on and off the course. Before demanding more money they created a demand for more professional golf. What the world saw, it liked: men who were courteous, men who would put themselves out not only to become masters of their game but to speak well in public, to spare time for the customer with a smile here and an autograph there. They were conscious all the time that *they were* professional golf. No man living has been more conscious of the new dignity of his game than Arnold Palmer. No man could conceivably be more polite than Gary Player who does not call people "Sir" for obsequious reasons but because he believes that his game thrives on its reputation for politeness and consideration.

The result is that golf has attracted sponsorship and highly lucrative television coverage, which in turn attracts more sponsorship. It is a thriving, ever-growing concern and it has become so because it was the players themselves who cared.

The lesson for cricket is obvious. Its players, too, must care more and take on a more collective responsibility. Our fate could well hinge on whether the sponsors continue to find us attractive enough to support. Attractiveness does not begin and end with strokes at the wicket. It matters that we seek the best, avoiding pettiness, cut out bad language, control temperaments, spare time for members and be part of the club's social functions. We can learn something from the kind of impression that professional golfers, these past ten years, have left throughout the world.

There can be no alternative. If "we" and "they" remain burned in men's souls then cricket, as we have known and loved it, is dead.

# 22

It was only because of a casual telephone call to my home that I was not out of cricket for almost an entire year after breaking my arm in the Lord's Test of 1963. I played no more that season, and although I was invited to captain the England team the following winter, I was still not fit when the side left at the end of December. Mike Smith led them instead. My problems, however, were minimal compared with the holocaust of injuries and illnesses suffered by that team as soon as they got to the front. Instead of sending home cricket reports the correspondents were cabling casualty lists. As I have already mentioned in an earlier chapter, they were at one point down to four fully fit men out of a party of sixteen, and were actually alerting English journalists to stand by to field in a Test match if the situation got worse.

I had just finished reading about it in a newspaper at home one morning when the telephone rang. It was the MCC secretary, Billy Griffith, calling on a matter entirely unconnected with the Indian tour. Quite by chance he mentioned he had just received a letter from David Clark, the tour manager in India, explaining what an appalling jam they were in. He asked me if I could recall which players had been nominated as batting replacements should an additional player have to be flown out in an emergency. By the time we had found out who they were we had also discovered that both were at that moment coaching in South Africa. At that time of year there was liable to be some difficulty in getting them released from their contracts so, in a moment of rash loyalty, I volunteered to go. Less than twenty-four hours later, with my now healed arm punctured by injections against everything from yellow fever to fowl pest, I was in a jet which was making light work of the old tea-clipper route.

It was a desperate scene which met me on arrival. There were only five fit players. There was no plan for a team-selection meeting. The rule of this hard field was that if you could get on to the field you played.

I had not touched a bat for seven months but thanks to the enthusiasm of a long queue of Indian bowlers in Calcutta there was time for two long nets before the third Test began. I scored 107 in that Test and 151 in the next at New Delhi but both pitches were easy-paced and neither innings would be rated as a work of art. They served their purpose. England did not lose a Test and at the end of rather a stalemate series the score was India nil, England nil with five Tests drawn.

The tour was largely kept alive by moments of off-beat humour; during the Delhi Test, for example, the crowd began pelting us with stones, for no apparent reason, just before the lunch interval. There was, of course, a perfectly logical explanation and we were fools not to think of it. All the reserved seats had been sold twice over. Consequently every second spectator, having paid good money for a chair which was already occupied, was understandably prepared to stop the match until the chaos had been sorted out. Actually, they were fortunate to be seeing a Test match at all. There was a moment on the opening morning when, with tongue in cheek, we threatened strike action. For the third day running there was no water in the dressing rooms. We had discovered this after our first net practice and our manager, David Clark, had made several pleas for it to be put right before the match began. When we turned the taps on in vain the following morning David, with a twinkle, set off to issue the simple ultimatum: "No water, no Test." He took one look at the size of the crowd and realised that he had to modify his terms if we were to get back to the hotel alive!

As usual in India there was a simple explanation. At Test match time the local water board authorities had been in the habit of receiving an allocation of free tickets for the game. This time the cricket authorities had overlooked this little perk. The water board's reaction had been as uncompromising as Clark's. "No tickets, no water."

As soon as David discovered the reason he unearthed the number of tickets required and drove round to see the water wallahs. By the time he returned to the dressing room every tap and shower was already running full-bore.

In spite of the sickness which had ravaged the team early on the tour, I know that all the players enjoyed this tour as much as any before. India is a fascinating country, to say the least. The people are as fanatically keen about cricket as the West Indians but they do not bubble with quite the same fervour. Moreover, they are courteous, painstaking hosts and one cannot help being moved by the knowledge of giving pleasure every time one walks on to a cricket field. Because there are less sophisticated outlets for entertainment off the field a touring team blends more closely together. A good captain and manager relationship is vital to success. Mike Smith and David Clark were an excellent combination, and David Clark probably worked as hard as any manager on the tours where I have travelled.

David was in the Rugby Eleven just before the war and would have made his mark for Kent, I am quite sure. He was one of the many whose career was snuffed out by seven years of war and to him fell the misfortune of being captured at Arnhem. Our paths have crossed since his interest in me as a schoolboy, his selecting me to play for his Kent side and giving me my cap. In all the years I was captain of Kent he was at my right hand as chairman of the County Cricket Committee. For most of these years he was giving a tremendous amount of time to MCC affairs and the administration of county cricket. He headed the Clark Report on County Cricket in 1970. Knowing him as well as I did, it was no surprise to me that he was such a splendidly adaptable manager, widely respected wherever we went and much liked by his own players. A tour of India can test one's sense of humour but David Clark has patience and humour in abundance. Cricket owes a huge debt to men like him who, absorbed and committed as they are in their own business affairs, love the game so much that they are always ready to give freely.

Every city and street on that tour held a special interest for me. More, perhaps, for me than for other members of the team for, apart from re-fuelling stops en route to and from Australia, this was my first return to India since my upbringing there as a child. In those early years, though, I had never seen the big Indian cities. Bombay and Calcutta, with their teeming humanity and heart-rending poverty, came as a stunning shock. They were not in the India I had known in the hills.

## 23

We returned from India to resume arms once more against Australia. It was an evenly fought series, best remembered now for rain and a Manchester Test match which broke every bowler's heart; in five days, 1,271 runs were piled up for the loss of only eighteen wickets. I had been injured so did not play in that game but returned for the final Test at the Oval to play one of my best innings against Australia, finishing with 93 not out at close of play on the fourth day, only to return on the fifth to watch the rain fall steadily all day. But this was the match when Freddie Trueman ran bow-legged through the gates of history to become the first bowler ever to take 300 wickets in Test cricket, and as such it was a match to remember. With his unfailing sense of timing he chose a full-house Saturday to achieve it; but though the newspapers, rightly, devoted pages of tribute to their tousled-haired hero the following day, not one printed the astonishing story of how Their Fred finally pulled it off.

Trueman, in that summer of 1964, was just beginning to run out of steam. He had been a world-class bowler for some twelve years. Now the old theatrical gestures were intact but some of the fire had gone. Indeed the only real luck he had was to be relieved from bowling on the Manchester wicket where fast-bowlers looked like galley slaves. Poor Fred Rumsey was given this task and was duly dropped for the final Test. Trueman, who had been experimenting with a shorter run for Yorkshire, was recalled to the England team. To say he was pleased was probably the understatement of the season for he had never been indifferent to records, and at that point in his career he had 297 Test wickets to his credit. He realised that he had not much longer to go and I think we all felt that this was to be his last appearance for England.

He had reason to be disappointed when England won the toss and batted, for the pitch on that opening morning was grassy and would certainly have given him real assistance. Instead it improved steadily during our innings and by the time Trueman came to bowl on it with trumpets blaring and great flourish, back now on his long "international" run, it was clear there would be no immediate sensations. By the Saturday morning he was understandably tense and visibly nervous. He could not find his rhythm. He knew that he was bowling badly. To add to his depression Australia were rapidly running out of batsmen to bowl at, but none of them had fallen victims to Trueman.

The more anxious he became the worse he got until, in the end, Ted Dexter had to take him off. The words must have sounded like a life-sentence to Trueman. His jaw sank down on his chest as he walked from short-leg at one end to short-leg at the other, cursing his luck and visibly ageing.

It was at this point that England got stuck. We had begun the morning well but in the half hour before lunch we were bogged down again and Dexter was beginning to look as desperate as Trueman. He came in from the covers at the end of an over, tossing the ball from hand to hand, and as we met in the middle of the pitch he simply said, "We must try something different, any ideas?" Whatever plans he had in his mind, only one thing was certain. None of them included bringing back Trueman.

For once, however, Dexter was over-ruled. Before I had time to answer his question a frantic voice just behind me said: "I'm going to bowl." It was Freddie Trueman about to prove that possession is ten-tenths of the law. For as Dexter said, "Wait a moment Freddie," Trueman snatched the ball from his captain's hand and began striding away towards the sight screen to begin his run. Short of actually starting a punch-up in the very centre of a Test pitch, Dexter was nonplussed. He chuckled away, walked out to cover point and accepted the situation for the next six balls. It may not have been orthodox captaincy but in this instance it proved to be wise. After all, if your leading bowler, a great one at that, wants to bowl, why stop him?

Trueman's first three deliveries could only be described as wildly inaccurate. But with the last two he saved himself. They were just enough on target to earn him another over, the last before lunch, without any real argument. And it was in that over that he knocked out Redpath's middle stump and then, with the very next ball, had McKenzie flashing a catch which I held at slip. So Trueman walked off to lunch not only just one Test wicket short of his 300 but also on a hat trick. The Oval was buzzing with excitement.

No luncheon interval can ever have been longer for us or Freddie, or shorter for the spectators. Trueman never left the dressing room. He ate and drank nothing, merely sat down, stood up, prowled around and then sat down before going through the whole meaningless routine again. He was rarely a man to show nerves but that day he could not conceal his agitation. He wanted that 300th wicket more than anything in the world. Equally, no spectator intended to miss that first ball. Waitresses rushed to and fro in the Oval dining rooms and cleared away cups of untouched coffee. There was no lingering over brandy or cigars as everyone jostled back to their seats while we filed down from the pavilion and into the field again. The tension was acute, not only for Trueman himself but for Neil Hawke, the new Australian batsman, and for the English fielders who must all, like me, have been fighting down the nightmare thought of how awful it would be at this moment to drop a catch.

At least there was to be no further delay. Trueman's over before lunch had not been completed so he had to bowl immediately. He ran up to the wicket in total silence, bowled—and Hawke gently pressed forward and kept the ball out of his stumps. There was to be no hat trick and Hawke, with a tone of genuine sympathy called down the wicket: "Bad luck, Fred. Well bowled."

Yet happily the greater prize was eventually to come Trueman's way. For the next fifteen minutes or so he bowled with real inspiration. He was not perhaps quite so fast as he had been at the peak of his career, but all the skill and fire came flooding back and he was a wonderful sight to watch. It was as though he felt that this was his final act in Test cricket and he was determined to leave an indelible memory of his prowess. Ironically the wicket took some time in coming, but this time Trueman kept a firm control on his frustration and at last Hawke nicked a catch to me at slip. It was straightforward, but sharp, coming firmly at a good height just to my right, and I took it comfortably. But easy or not it was several minutes before my heart resumed its normal pace. It would have been on my conscience for the rest of my days had I dropped that catch on the day Fred Trueman hi-jacked the England bowling.

As it happened, of course, Trueman *was* chosen for the first two Test matches against New Zealand the following summer and, in the end, raised his haul of Test wickets to 307. But we were not to know that at the time. At the moment when he grabbed the ball from Dexter on that Saturday morning at the Oval he looked a spent force and I think it quite possible that, had he not overheard the captain's remark to me and reacted mutinously as he did, he might never have bowled in a Test match again. On such small turns of fate do great things happen.

Another astonishing cricket episode in this mid-sixties period occurred at Leeds the following summer when John Edrich scored 310 not out against New Zealand. I have never witnessed a more remarkable innings, nor have I seen one which so accurately reflected the character and temperament of the man playing it.

The point here was that England batted first on a pitch so grassy, so classically a seam bowler's paradise, that it would not have surprised me had both teams been shot out for little more than 200 in each of their first innings. Furthermore, New Zealand, though hardly one of the dynamic cricketing powers of the period, were on this occasion ideally equipped to exploit the conditions. They had Motz, Collinge, Taylor and Congdon too, who could all move the ball off the seam with the expertise of an experienced English medium-pacer. This they proceeded to do with the early encouragement of Bob Barber's wicket.

At this point Ken Barrington joined Edrich and took the England score from 13 to 382. All the while I was padded up and perched on the edge of my seat, for never an over went by when it did not seem probable rather than possible that a wicket was going to fall. Barrington, calling on all his experience in these conditions, batted extremely well. But it was Edrich's innings that was truly remarkable. He either played and missed completely or thrashed the ball through the covers, over extra-cover, wide of mid-wicket or over mid-on. It was one of those innings which continually keep bowlers' hopes alive, whatever punishment they are taking, for sheer logic tells them that it cannot last. But in Edrich's case it did last, from start of play on the opening day until long into the next.

Eventually I got to the wicket with him and had a closer look at what was going on. From that range it just did not seem to add up. The ball was still seaming around, leaving a damp lush green mark every time it pitched, and Edrich continued to play and miss once or twice an over. Yet between errors he still pasted the New Zealand bowlers all over the ground with apparent ease.

The contrast was still more extreme because I could not settle in at all. New Zealand's bowlers held few terrors for me since I had scored 85 against them in the first Test and 119 in the second. But in the third at Leeds, with the ball veering about unpredictably, I played quite skilfully but could not keep the momentum of runs going. Eventually, I was out for 13 and left, bemused by it all. By the time I had taken my pads off Edrich was pounding his way to his third century and, as it transpired, the New Zealanders never did get him out. He scored 310 not out in England's total of 546 for four declared and I am convinced I shall never see another innings like it. It revealed the temperament of a man capable of divorcing from his mind a wild passing shot played only seconds ago, and concentrating on the next ball as a completely new challenge. It is an ability which the really great champion golfers have. Herbert Sutcliffe had this, I am told. Certainly Bill Lawry. It is a quality no coach can instil but Edrich has it in greater measure than any other batsman of his era and it is something for which England, on many occasions, have had reason to be duly thankful.

Tragically it was less than three weeks later that Edrich suffered a set-back that seriously shook his confidence. By then the South Africans had arrived in England and in the second innings of their first Test at Lord's Edrich was struck on the head by a ball from Peter Pollock. He took no further part in that series and South Africa, an immensely improved and competitive side, won the short series by one win and two draws. I had not toured South Africa the previous winter but it was obvious they came to England thirsting for revenge. I, too, needed to make an impression at this somewhat critical stage in my career and did so with a century at Nottingham, and two good knocks of 58 and 78 not out at the Oval.

They had some fine cricketers in that team but my recollections single out one above all the others, because it must be rare in cricket history for any man to attract thousands of extra spectators by the brilliance of his fielding. Colin Bland, then an athletic figure who had spent countless hours hurling a ball at a single stump in Rhodesia, had that magnetic quality.

Since then two other spectacular fielders have emerged in Clive Lloyd, of West Indies and Lancashire, and Alan Ealham, of Kent. In some respects Lloyd is an even more volatile figure than Bland. If comparisons are made, I would judge Ealham and Bland the best fielders I have ever seen. Alan Ealham, short and stocky, and never seeking the limelight, has become the most feared fielder in English county cricket and a most exciting figure on Kent grounds. Bland's skill was illustrated to perfection in the Lord's Test that summer when he ran out both Jim Parks and Ken Barrington on the same afternoon. There must be many who never fully appreciated what happened in Parks' dismissal and I think it worth recording here. It began when Barrington, batting at the pavilion end, pushed a shot out into a huge gap towards mid-wicket and called for a single. Parks sprinted off only to be pulled up by a shout from Barrington who had suddenly taken fright at the sight of Bland eating up the ground in huge strides from mid-on. This left Parks with the task of turning and recovering his ground. As Bland picked up he found that Parks was in a direct line between him and the stumps at which he was aiming. This is when a batsman gets accidentally hit on purpose and, if his judgment is right, he will get away with nothing more than a bruise for his pains. Parks judged it perfectly but he still did not survive. It had all happened so fast that there was no fielder at Parks' end to gather the ball if Bland lobbed his return over the batsman's head. Instead Bland drew back his arm like an Olympic javelin thrower and hurled the ball under Parks' feet as he ran. Parks was still out of his ground when his middle stump went cartwheeling into the air. It was the most breathtaking piece of fielding I have ever seen.

By the time Bland had also run Barrington out with another raking throw, his impact on the Test series was such that all quick singles were banned, certainly in his area of the field. As soon as a shot was hit anywhere remotely in his direction the ground rang with two simultaneous shouts of "No" and the batsmen ventured not a yard out of their creases. Moreover, the crowd were beginning to let their eyes rest on the ranging figure of Bland, more concerned with what he was up to than the principal actors.

I was so intrigued by him that I asked Bland if he would consider putting on a short exhibition of fielding and throwing when the South Africans came to play Kent at Canterbury. Surprisingly, no one had ever made such a request before and he was rather embarrassed by it. But he agreed and when the day came it provided an unforgettable spectacle for some 2,000 privileged watchers. We set up three stumps in front of a net and after a few preliminary arm-looseners Bland got down to work. Someone took a box of six balls and rolled them out to him along the ground twenty-five yards distant, first ten yards to his right and then ten yards to his left about cover-point range. Bland never stopped moving. He swooped on them and in one flowing movement threw them on the run. With his first throw he knocked the stumps sideways, with the next two he missed, with his fourth he lifted two stumps out of the ground and with his fifth he laid the remaining one flat. The spontaneous ovation was well deserved and one of the warmest I have heard any cricketer receive at Canterbury. Tragic that it was not on video tape so that schoolboys could enjoy and study the film.

What I did not realise at the time was that the sun was fast setting on Anglo-South African cricket relations.

# 24

This book would be incomplete without a tribute to Sir Donald George Bradman, and the influence he had on my cricket and myself. One of the lesser known facts about Bradman is that soon after he retired from decimating bowling attacks all over the world he became severely stricken by the golf bug. One day, after a particularly bad round, he returned to his home on the outskirts of Adelaide, sat in a chair and quietly announced to his family that he was now going to became a scratch player. Lady Bradman, a delightful person with a rare understanding of the outrageous quirks of games players, immediately realised that this was going to mean another upheaval to her household. Working and meal-time routines would have to be radically rearranged and conversation would now be dominated by such earth-shattering themes as the overlapping grip and the dynamics of the downswing. Lady Bradman reckoned that it would take the little dynamo about two years and, as always, she was right. Sir Donald rose at five, worked feverishly on his papers, breakfasted absolutely on schedule, drove off to attend to the affairs of his companies with determination and then, at the appointed moment, headed for the golf course, there to slave for hour upon hour at his woods and irons. His handicap duly plunged to scratch and by the expiry of his self-imposed time-table Don Bradman was one of the finest amateur golfers in Australia. He had mastered one game; he did not enjoy being mastered by another. If only he had been fifteen years younger Gary Player and Peter Thomson would have felt the lash of his tail.

This quite ruthless ability to drive himself, to concentrate utterly, to exhaust any problem he regarded worthy of his attention, to waste no time on fools and frivolity, to live his life to meticulous schedules, made him the remarkable cricketer he was and the extraordinary man he is. If he begins to expound on rose-growing, Australian wine, building a swimming pool or the local rateable value it is worthwhile listening because he does not venture opinions unless he is master of the subject.

I have never quite lost the awe of him I acquired when my father hustled me on deck in the Mediterranean, on my way home to school from India, to see the ship in which Bradman was passing. But by the time I returned to Australia for my fourth tour, this time under the captaincy of Mike Smith in the winter of 1965–66, I had got to know him quite well. We exchanged Christmas cards and the occasional letter and, in Australia, I had visited his home fairly frequently. We also played golf together on his home course at Kooyonga, Adelaide, where he embarked on every round as though he were driving off for the World Match-Play Title.

In those friendly games he would be most helpful, advising which was the best line to take to the hole, where the hidden hazards were down the fairway, which were the difficult greens and why.

His brilliance at ball games made him a fine lawn tennis and squash player but I had the great pleasure, on that tour, of introducing him to a game he had never tried before—real tennis. He had seen the court at Lord's and was aware that there was another court in Melbourne where I played occasionally. I promised to take him for an introductory game when he arrived for the Test match and one Sunday morning he collected me at the Windsor Hotel, an alert little figure in grey flannels, white shirt and scarf. He was visibly excited.

Real tennis, with its origins back in the French monasteries of the fourteenth century and a bemusing vocabulary of its own, is a highly complex game. Directions like "laying a chase on the hazard side" are beyond most people's comprehension until they have been on a court for several long sessions but, during our knock-up, Bradman questioned everything and let nothing pass until he understood it fully. Several times he became quite impatient at my apparent inability to explain all the implications of a certain rule in a single sentence. In those moments he looked like a schoolboy who could not understand why bridge is not as simple as snap.

But so penetrating is his mind that by the time we began playing a game he understood every tactical situation perfectly. And that was not all. What staggered me was his fantastic speed about the court, racing from one corner to another to retrieve a ball which a man half his age would have ignored. Bradman at the time was fifty-seven and had already suffered one heart attack.

It was that morning, on that court at Melbourne, that I understood why Bradman was probably the greatest cricketer that ever lived. I was aware not of a man but a machine whirring at my elbow. He was conscious of no mortal thing outside those walls. His concentration and determination were absolute. Here was a man, at an age when most men would have been living out their past glories in a rocking chair, aggressively storming a new challenge. He was a power house.

In Australia they used to be proud of "our bridge, our harbour and our Bradman". He is universally respected but, among people who know him and millions in Australia who don't, his image is not one of a glamorous, popular idol. This may seem curious in a country where winning is in itself a philosophy. I think the explanation is that Bradman's insistence on getting to the heart of any problem as swiftly and directly as possible leaves little time for frills. It is not his way. He has no time to waste on what many would regard as the natural courtesies in argument. Whereas another man might preface his disagreement with "Well, perhaps one could take a slightly different view to that ..." Bradman would cut the preamble to "No, you are wrong because ..." He is entitled to be dogmatic because he does his homework, and is invariably well briefed.

He can only cram so many activities into his life by observing the strictest personal regimen. He rises at five a.m. and goes to bed at midnight. Every moment of those waking hours has to be used to a purpose. In earlier days he would guard his time and plan it as meticulously as a Prime Minister. When talking to him there is usually a theme for discussion, a point to pursue, a problem to solve. It is not difficult to see how, when he turned his attention to stockbroking, he was successful. Indeed, over dinner with the England team one night, Sir Robert Menzies said that in his view Bradman knew more about certain aspects of Australian finance than any other man in the country.

Inevitably he is at his most dazzling on the subject of cricket. He has the sharpest cricket mind of all the cricketers I have met. His knowledge is so extensive that I can quite understand the difficulties he occasionally faced in his capacity as chairman of the Australian Board of Control. There must have been other members who found it hard to keep up with him and, indeed, to tune in on his wave-length of thinking.

I regard it as a tragedy for cricket that in a game beset by problems so much of this brilliant talent has been so pathetically wasted. While the hub of everything revolves around Lord's, Bradman has been in the branch office in Adelaide. Of course, his influence has been considerable over the years. I cannot think there has been any major change without his view being sought. How much more could he have done for cricket had he been able to come to London each year. Every summer at Lord's there is an international conference at which Australia is represented. Only twice in twenty-five years has Sir Donald been present.

His method of dealing with the ugly throwing problem in Australia illustrated well the way in which his splendid brain and driving force could have been put to wider use. The irony here is that when he was concerned solely with selection of Australian teams he picked bowlers who later, it transpired, had suspect actions. That's how difficult the throwing problem was. But when he be-came chairman of the Australian Board we had all learnt a lot more about it and he sought to put things right. He accepted his responsi-bilities and recognised throwing as one of the main evils in the game. He decided that it should be eliminated as quickly as possible. His approach was the familiar one of giving it his undivided attention for some eighteen months. He collected reports on throwing, wrote reports on throwing, had films taken of every bowler in Australian State cricket, sent to England for films of many of the players in county cricket and in the end compiled so much information on the subject that he could give an excellent four-hour film lecture with his ancient hand-cranked projector. Armed with all the evidence, he assailed every administrator and umpire in Australian cricket with the new-found facts of his case and won the day. Throwing was banished from all levels of the Australian game in two or three years. It was a wonderful achievement.

It was fortunate that G. O. Allen was at the helm of English cricket over this period, guiding the decision making. They had been good friends over the years and in the days before the telex and easy telephone communication this rapport and alliance was important.

Gubby was one of Douglas Jardine's fast bowling battery in 1932–33, Larwood, Voce, Allen, Bowes and Tate, in the assault which came to be known as Body-line. But, as they drew up their plans, Gubby made it quite clear that whereas he would give the captain all he had, bowl as well and as fast as he knew how, with an occasional bouncer too, he was quite adamant that he would have no part in the new strategy devised in the main to snuff out Bradman's domination.

Gubby captained Middlesex, played for England against Australia in 1934 and led the MCC team to Australia in 1936–37, something of a making-good operation after the cracks Jardine had opened up four years earlier. By happy coincidence, Bradman was captain of Australia and largely responsible for turning a deficit of two into a three-two win to Australia. But it had been a successful tour in the widest sense, and Gubby, who had been the youngest man to sit on an MCC Committee was later chairman of Selectors, became President of MCC and for the last ten years has been Treasurer. His retirement this year is a severe blow and I doubt whether we can ever hope to find the same calibre of person to give as much time as he has done. Both "The Don" and Gubby Allen have really given the best part of their waking hours to the welfare and advancement of the game.

"The Don", it might be said, is an outstanding and unusual man. If he thinks something is worth doing he gives it all he has. I once wrote to him when we were setting up a trust fund for the dependants of a man very close to the English cricket scene who had died suddenly at an early age. I merely asked for a little advice about the possiblility of investing some of the trust in Australian shares. His reply was typical. Instead of a letter I received a priceless portfolio of investment information, meticulously detailed and immaculately presented. How could it have been otherwise?

To have met and come to know Don Bradman is one of the real privileges arising from my cricket travels to Australia. He came nearer to mastering the art of batsmanship than anyone. He had astonishing fleetness of foot, sharpness of eye and timing, but it was his mind that powered his success.

# 25

O ne of the best captains I have played with, and in striking contrast to "The Don", was Mike Smith, who has deservedly won a great reputation for impassive unflappability. This characteristic did not surprise me for I had known him longer than anyone else in the team. We had played in schools teams together at Lord's and at Oxford I had given him his Blue. Even then he was a quiet, pleasant, imperturbable man whose superb temperament was seen at its best in the Varsity matches when he became the only man to score three centuries: 201 not out in his first, 104 in his second and 117 in his third and last in 1956. These were outstanding performances in the context of his general batting ability at this period.

Ten years later this calmness had become a philosophy with him and what the Australians saw was a very different visiting English team which took its social responsibilities in more relaxed fashion, spent little effort on making any kind of impression, and tended to take time out when the last ball of the day had been bowled. The players predictably enjoyed this more relaxed policy, but it must have been puzzling to Australian administrators who had become used to visiting English captains involving themselves deeply with the wider aspect of an English tour. Many must have formed a mistaken opinion of Mike Smith, which was easy to do, but it did not appear to concern him in the least. Indeed an Australian said of him at the time that here was a man absolutely petrified of doing the right thing in case someone should interpret it as trying to court official approval.

His casualness extended to his dress and his attitude to people around him. His approach to a problem was to sit in a chair with the

*Daily Telegraph* crossword, doze off, wake up, finish the crossword and then fire some broadsides. It always reminded me of the photograph of Harold Macmillan, sitting in the corner of a first-class railway carriage, *en route* to the Yorkshire grouse moor, immersed in his favourite Greek Iambics, by his side the despatch box marked "Prime Minister", bulging with world-shattering problems. Sometimes his silences could last for hours on end but when he did eventually contribute to the discussion it was to reveal that all the while he had been searching his mind for an answer and, as often as not, found it. In fact he has an excellent, perceptive and analytical brain but also a disconcerting habit of giving the impression that he is a disinterested spectator. The greater the crisis the greater his ability to read Dante, and chortle away about trivialities.

In this 1965 tour England scored quickly, mainly due to some magnificent innings by Bob Barber, but like its predecessor this tour again saw us failing to make the best of ourselves and the series was drawn. When we returned to England to take on the West Indies Mike Smith survived only one Test. This, in my opinion, had nothing to do with his style of captaincy in Australia. The selectors were seriously concerned about him in the face of really fast bowling. Twice at Manchester, where we were heavily beaten in the opening Test, he had come perilously close to being hit and hurt very badly. With his glasses, it seemed, he did not pick the bouncer up as quickly as it required.

Whatever the explanation their decision was to have a huge effect on my life for now, five years after handing the England captaincy back to Peter May, I was asked to take it over again from Smith. I was uncomfortable about accepting it at the time because he had done well in Australia and had earned the respect of his players. I thought he was being harshly treated. Whatever defects might now be seen in his batting, he had batted well in Australia. Furthermore, he was losing the leadership after a defeat which had been determined more than anything else by losing the toss.

I accepted the invitation, knowing that the sympathy of the players would be lingering on with Smith. Looking back now it was a mistake to call on me. In those circumstances it would have been better for England had someone completely new taken over the position. It would certainly have saved me a great deal of personal pain.

My term of office this time was to last three Test matches. My first Test back as captain was at Lord's. Having established a first innings lead of 86 we then had West Indies buckling at 95 for five in their second—virtually 9 for five in the overall situation of the match. With plenty of time on our side and David Holford, playing in only his second Test, coming to the wicket to join his cousin, Gary Sobers, we needed just one break for victory. As everyone familiar with the saga of historic partnerships now knows, we simply could not part them. They stayed together for well over five hours until Sobers was able to declare just before lunch on the final day with his total 369 for five. Sobers was then 163 not out, Holford 105 not out. We needed an impossible 284 to win, and such was our demoralised state that, in the end, it was only a wonderful innings by Colin Milburn that saved us, and not West Indies, from defeat.

Upheavals like that traditionally demand a scapegoat and I had to be the victim. Quite rightly, as England captain, I had to accept the responsibility; but much of the scathing criticism of my tactics implied that I had not worked hard enough at finding the right tactics to break that partnership. The reason that I did not encircle Sobers with close fielders the moment he arrived at the wicket was that I knew him better than most of the critics who were simultaneously plotting his downfall from the safe side of the boundaries. I had seen him at close range in such situations before, and knew that far from stolidly digging in he was quite capable of accepting an irretrievable situation and playing accordingly. This reasoning was proved correct when he proceeded to play half a dozen strokes as though tomorrow did not exist. Had a ring of fielders surrounded him he could not conceivably have played like that and the last thing I wanted him to do was to steel himself into getting his head down.

Unfortunately, he did not mis-hit to provide the catch where I hoped, and, as soon as he saw Holford settle in to bat as though his life were at stake, his mood changed. As long as we could keep his concentration in check we had a real chance of getting him early. When he had settled in we had problems which we never solved.

From the disappointment of Lord's, we moved on to the distasteful disasters of Nottingham and Leeds. After Leeds we had lost the series and I was deposed as captain. Brian Close took over the reins for the final Test at the Oval and, as I looked at my own future in cricket,

I was certain that at least the captaincy chapter had closed. There was no overseas tour scheduled for the winter and the following summer's visitors to England were Pakistan and India. To me it was logical that the selectors should begin to re-shape their entire thinking for the future, a future in which a thirty-five-year-old Cowdrey who had not played particularly well that summer would have no part. When Close led England to a spectacular victory over West Indies in that Oval Test all these views were reinforced. In many ways it was a relief to me. I suddenly felt lonely but the emotion was tempered by the certainty that the pressures, sometimes rough and occasionally merciless, were about to be relaxed. As it happened all my thinking was wrong and the real pressures were only just starting.

But that was still some way ahead and it would be dishonest to suggest that I lived through the days immediately following my removal from the England captaincy with stoic indifference. Living with failure is the hardest lesson in top-class sport, nor does it come any easier the older one gets.

What helped a great deal at this time was the attitude of my own Kent players whom I had now rejoined on the County Championship circuit. They said nothing to me but I could detect sympathy in their sidelong glances and eagerness to contribute. I think they all played the harder because of what had occurred, and while that Oval Test match was in progress we won two excellent victories, first by an innings against Lancashire at Blackpool and then by nine wickets against Hampshire at Bournemouth. I scored 56 in the first match, 73 not out in the second and the therapy of a few runs and two victories worked. After that week I was determined to win my place back in the England team as a player, and hoped that the captaincy would never again be an issue. I enjoyed cricket too much, and I did not enjoy the in-fighting which the press liked to highlight. I became quite philosophical about it all. Today every move is investigated, every nuance of every situation picked up by the sharp antennae of Fleet Street and blown up out of all proportion. It can be quite unnerving if you happen to be the man in the middle but I consoled myself with the thought that it was not likely to happen to me again in my lifetime.

It was a good thing I had worked myself into this frame of mind because Kent's penultimate match that season was against Yorkshire at Harrogate, two weeks after Close's triumph at the Oval. York-shire had to beat us to win the Championship so packed crowds were guaranteed, not only to see the match but also to watch the sideshow of Messrs. Close and Cowdrey in man-to-man combat. Ironically all they saw for most of the first day was the rain falling steadily but this did not stop the photographers crowding round Close and me every time we walked out to inspect the wicket. They were clearly after a study of Close beaming, with me looking sour, but I managed to win that contest!

I must commend one of those press cameramen, however, for organising an exclusive picture which made me a hero all over Yorkshire by the following morning. There is on the Harrogate ground a Victorian mangle which is used to wring water out of the pitch-drying blankets. It was this photographer's idea to take a picture of me turning the handle as though anxious to get the pitch fit for play as soon as possible. When I agreed to do so the crowd erupted with applause at my "sporting gesture" and when the photo-graph appeared in a newspaper the following day it was accompanied by a large caption demanding "How's this for generosity from the Men of Kent?" It was a good question. I had not been rushing to get the game started at all.

The rain gave way to a magnificent cricket match. After a thrilling chase at the end we lost by 25 runs. So Yorkshire won the title, and as the players came off a huge crowd gathered in front of the pavilion to cheer their heroes—hopeful, too, that there might be some speeches. To my surprise John Nash, the Yorkshire secretary, asked me if I would speak first. I had not anticipated speaking at all, as I had imagined this was a family affair. In a few minutes, with nothing prepared, I was faced with the microphone in the tiny commentary box. I congratulated Yorkshire on their win, and I reminded them of Brian Close's great deeds in the Oval Test. It was not difficult to make them laugh and soon the cheers echoed and re-echoed out across the dales, champagne bottles kept appearing, and I was offered the freedom of Harrogate several times. I slipped away quietly before I was signed up to play for them. Close deserved his moment of triumph.

The following summer, the Tests against Pakistan and India saw Brian Close firmly entrenched as England captain. I threw myself more wholeheartedly into the leadership of Kent. We were now beginning to look a side. We had so many young players maturing that at last we stood a good chance of winning either the Championship or the Gillette Cup. It was a lean season for me until July and then the runs came. My form came just when I was almost despairing that I would ever bat well again. It was in a Gillette Cup game at Canterbury and I have rarely batted better in my life. There was a large contingent of critics present and most of them wrote articles the following day suggesting that I ought to be back in the England team, particularly in view of the forthcoming tour of West Indies. It was emphasised that I could produce the attacking stroke play that would be needed. I continued to play at peak form. Having been absent for all three Tests against India and the first against Pakistan, I was duly recalled for the fifth Test of the summer at Nottingham. Coming into the Tests so late in the summer I found it hard to muster a normally compulsive interest in the series. At that time I was completely wrapped up in Kent's performances. Driving to Nottingham I twice found myself pulling in to wayside telephones to ring Mike Denness, who was captaining Kent in my absence, and check on the latest scores.

I did not have a distinguished Test, nor did anyone else. That match is now best remembered for the 100,000 gallons of water which the Nottingham City Fire Brigade were reputed to have pumped off the ground before play could be resumed. I opened the innings both times, scored 14 in the first, two not out in the second and was happy when England won by ten wickets after losing the best part of two days to bad weather. This was England's fifth victory in six Tests under Brian Close's captaincy, a record which appeared to make still more nonsense of the press gossip which was just beginning to rumble: "Now that Cowdrey is back he is more the man to lead the tour to West Indies in the coming winter." It was not what I wanted to read. The publicity of the previous summer had left its mark, and I could not bear a repeat.

Then it all happened. From the Nottingham Test I drove to Burton-on-Trent to help the Kent team to a fine win against Derbyshire, while Close went to Birmingham to take over the Yorkshire side against Warwickshire. When our match finished we took to our cars again for the long haul down to Gillingham, stopping on the motorway for a quick supper. As so often happens, it is a meeting place for cricketers and we ran into someone who had just come from the finish at Birmingham. He was in such a highly excitable state recounting the rumpus that had gone on there that I did not gather it was Brian Close who was in trouble. Only when I saw the newspapers the next morning did I realise Close had been accused of using delaying tactics in the final hour in an alleged attempt to stop Warwickshire winning. Moreover, he was alleged to have struck some member in the pavilion. If it was as serious as the press were giving it space, then this was a delicate situation. I had no comment to make about it at the time, nor have I now. But *Wisden* begins its account of that game by saying, "This was the match with tremendous repercussions". I would not disagree with that statement.

Suddenly my telephone was ringing ceaselessly as one journalist after another phoned to ask me if I would be prepared to captain England in the West Indies. It was only when the question was put to me as bluntly as that that the full impact of the situation hit me. Surely I wasn't going to become involved in all *that* again? I was practically incapable of reply and retreated further into my shell. If I was to become captain, what a way to win one of cricket's highest honours! Anyway, I was otherwise engaged for the time being. Kent were doing well; we were in the Final of the Gillette Cup and just could win the Championship.

When the team for the final Test against Pakistan at the Oval was announced Brian Close was again named as captain and I was retained in the side. But by then Close had been asked to appear before a disciplinary hearing of the MCC Committee at Lord's to give evidence about the events on that controversial evening at Birmingham. Although I was aware that the hearing at Lord's was to be on the morning of our eve-of-Test practice at the Oval, I knew little of what was involved and had deliberately shut my mind to the case. When I arrived for the practice, however, a selector promptly asked me to take charge of the nets. Close had not yet arrived. His day had begun badly when his car had broken down on the motorway from Yorkshire and he had to hitch a lift from a passing motorist. Eventually, Close arrived and the enquiry was held with Brian Sellars representing Yorkshire as an observer. Obviously, there could be no immediate decision, and later, with the match about to start under Close's leadership, the disciplinary committee had decided out of courtesy to Close to withhold their findings until after the match. When Close finally arrived at the Oval his team were already changing after nets. Someone called: "How was it at the Old Bailey?" Close was fairly voluble about who said what to whom, but I was determined not to become involved and went off to take a bath.

Close was still talking when I returned and the headlines next day were full of strong speculation. By chance Geoffrey Boycott went sick just before the match started and so we were thrown further together when Brian Close decided to open the England innings with me. Once again, judging by the number of cameramen who waited at the pavilion gate as we entered the field together, it was clear that several sports editors had a pretty shrewd idea, knew more than I did in fact, about what was going on behind the scenes. I knew nothing, and still did not wish to get embroiled. The whole saga, on reflection, must have put Douglas Insole, the chairman and the selectors into an appallingly difficult situation. A decision had to be taken before the end of the Test match as the team had to be announced immediately afterwards.

There was no development until the Saturday of the Oval Test. That day I was among the last players to leave the dining room at the end of the luncheon interval and as I walked out Insole drew me aside.

"The Selection Committee will select the captain for West Indies on Monday morning," he said. "I want to know that you are definitely available for West Indies and that if the disciplinary committee at Lord's takes action against Close, that in spite of a very embarrassing set of circumstances, you would be a candidate to be considered for the captaincy. Time is our problem here, for we have undertaken to let the players know who the team will be after the Test match. I shall take it that you will say yes unless I hear by the start of play on Monday morning."

Nothing more was said but the press talked of little else, and by Sunday morning Close and I were top billing as rival contenders and they enjoyed fixing the odds 60–40 in my favour.

My immediate reaction was one of horror. I thought of Brian and his wife and how they must have felt. I could think of nothing at all that could happen outside my own family circle to cause me more personal anguish. I was right back in the nightmare of the previous summer when the whole question of the England captaincy had been transformed into a public debate.

On the Sunday I was so concerned about it all that I felt I must discuss it with Leslie Ames. What could Leslie say to me? He knew little about the details of the case. He understood my plight but could do little to console me. All he did say was: "You help no one by making yourself unavailable—that's the easy way out. If you are picked for West Indies, you must go. If you are invited as captain, again you must accept. You do not alter any decision that may be made over Brian Close by moving out of the picture."

These were all straightforward comments as I think back about it now, but at the time it was a relief to have an objective view, especially coming from such a good cricketer and fair-minded man.

On Monday the match came to a close soon after tea. Doug Insole informed me that I would be named as captain to the West Indies and that he would tell Brian Close before he left the Oval—an unenviable task for Insole, a blow to Close and, at the moment, a doubtful honour to me.

For all their fervid speculation the press were never certain who would get the job, but of one thing they were sure. If Close was appointed captain he would have to stay in London overnight to help select the team the following day. So they tailed him. They followed him to the Clarendon Court Hotel. He stayed the night. They waited for the next move. In the morning he left with his wife and luggage and headed for the motorway and Yorkshire. Only then could they be certain that he was no longer England captain.

Their vigil moved to Lord's to see who attended the selectors' meeting, but this was not the venue. Mercifully, I was spared comments and photographers.

The selectors were already seated when I entered. Whether they had been divided over Close I shall never know, but I could hardly hide my discomfort. After expressions of good wishes for a successful and happy trip, we sat down to select the party to tour West Indies.

Sadly, I was at a disadvantage. Instead of speaking from strength about the players I knew I wanted, I had not had time to do the necessary homework. To select a touring party of sixteen players should be the culmination of three months of ceaseless watching and planning. Nine of the party, perhaps, would pick themselves, but the balance of the fringe men was vitally important and would cause the difficulties. I longed for more time to think it out. I feared that we were rushing through decisions over which I had little or no control. This, after all, was now to be my side, and my contribution towards

174

the selection of it was not as thorough as I would have liked. But I had good judges around me who had done their homework (Insole, May, Bedser and Kenyon) and I need not have feared too much.

Any difficulties which I had at that meeting were as nothing compared with the storm which broke next day. The moment the words "Cowdrey, captain …" were announced at the press conference at Lord's the balloon went up again.

There was still one more sensation to come. Naturally I was not present at the Lord's conference but I know that Insole, as spokesman, was subjected to tremendous pressure on one point. Again and again he was asked: "Had there been no Edgbaston incident, which man would you yourselves have chosen as captain: Cowdrey or Close?" Eventually he answered "Close."

At the time the cricket world was astonished that Insole should have allowed himself this apparent indiscretion. After all, he did not have to give an answer to this question. By doing so he was conceding that MCC were having to go to West Indies under the leadership of their second choice. It was no help to the Cowdrey cause, it seemed.

Yet, in the event, it rallied people round me. The mists began to lift and by the time we left for West Indies I felt I had more support than I had ever had before as England captain.

I would like to pay special tribute to Insole for his devoted services to the game. I met him first as captain of Essex, got to know him a little at the Scarborough Festival and we became good friends on the MCC tour to South Africa under Peter May. He was an outstanding games player, of cricket and football, and one who loved every minute of practice as well as match play. He has a very quick mind and is an excellent chairman of cricket debate, whether handling the county captains, the first-class umpires or groundsmen. After a long spell as selector he became chairman of the most important committee in English cricket, the Cricket Committee. He would have made an excellent manager abroad, but he could not be away from his business for that length of time. Cricket and cricketers owe a great deal to Doug Insole who has given a lot of time in the interests of their well being.

# 26

When the air had cleared and the blood-letting had ceased there was only one way to approach my recall to the England captaincy. It was to put the whole unsavoury episode out of my mind and attack the job in hand. That job, for me, extended far beyond the immediate challenge of a Test series in West Indies. Whether or not I was to be in charge throughout, English cricket faced a period of furious activity which decided, by early in the 1970s, which was the most powerful cricket team in the world. After the West Indies tour England were due to meet Australia in England for the Ashes, which we had not won since 1956, and then go to South Africa, to face a team which had suddenly welded itself into a very formidable force. After that we planned to play South Africa in England and tour Australia in the winter of 1970–71. Five campaigns of the highest and most demanding order. I knew that, physically, there was no reason why I should not last that long and I now hoped I would be given charge of the England team throughout that period. I saw it not as a series of isolated challenges but as an era of cricket in itself.

Mercifully time, at last, was on my side. I had had no time at all to gather my thoughts on the evening the touring party was chosen for West Indies, but I now had almost four months to plan that campaign and scheme for the future before we left for Barbados on Boxing Day.

If we were to become a united team the most vital thing was to get the players together and clear the air of all the confusions of the recent months. The changes of captaincy over the last few years had also left their mark. So late in November, a month before we were due to leave, I called a two-day gathering of the routing players in London. Ostensibly it was for practice in the Crystal Palace indoor nets, though anyone with a grain of cricketing intelligence will know that batting indoors in England bears not the slightest resemblance to the conditions in West Indies. In this respect the get-together had little value. Yet for me it was of the utmost importance. I wanted to talk to my team and spent about a week carefully preparing what I was going to say. I spoke to them for almost an hour. I cannot now refer to any notes because I was so well rehearsed I did not need them. But from memory this would be a fair précis of my theme:

"The practice can come later. You're only here for a loosener and to be photographed to let the public know we haven't all died since the cricket season. I want to talk about English cricket at this point in time.

"Apart from one or two bolts from the blue our playing record in the past is not as good as it should have been. In this last year, there have been difficulties and embarrassments, much politics, too. I want you to know that I only accepted the captaincy again because of circumstances beyond the control of any of us here. I did so at the time only with very real anguish and not a few misgivings. But now that I *am* captain again I am delighted to be so, in the hope of filling a few vital needs."

I then outlined my Five-Tour-Plan and went on: "My idea for this period, ending with the tour to Australia in 1970–71, is to steal an idea from soccer and establish a basic squad of players, keep them and maintain faith in them. I cannot tell you whether I shall be the person in charge throughout. I may even be shipped back from West Indies before the last Test. But now that I am entrusted with this honour and responsibility, I am determined to be captain throughout these five series, not merely from any sense of personal ambition but to establish some real continuity in the game.

"You are obviously the nucleus of the best players in England, not merely for this immediate tour but for the next four years. One or two of you may fall by the wayside—your (and my) performances must inevitably decide that—but I hope we shall unite as one in this period to achieve solidity, both on and off the field. Apart from whether we win or lose in West Indies, cricket—English cricket —has so much to gain from a strength born of this approach."

I feel that was an important gathering. It helped to clear the air of the rancour and bewilderment of the past summer and it set us an objective.

We practised twice and the newsreel cameramen had their fill—vital publicity material sent on to the islands of the Caribbean as preliminary public relations to the tour.

That evening Edward Heath, then Leader of the Opposition, was good enough to entertain us as a team at the Junior Carlton Club—a very happy evening. We did not discuss cricket techniques or cricket tactics at all: "We shall take that up on our first afternoon in Barbados," I said. "For now I merely ask you to get plenty of exercise and keep fit."

We flew to Barbados to start our tour a month later and would have been hard pressed to make a less propitious start. We came close to being beaten by the island's Colts in our opening match, and although Boycott and I both scored centuries in the next game against the President's Eleven we took time to settle. We still could not make much impression once we had moved to Trinidad, the scene of the first Test match. Time was now running out. John Snow had suffered a nasty virus before Christmas and had taken a long time to throw off the effects. He seemed well enough in himself yet he could not muster enough energy to bowl long spells under a hot sun. Try as he did he looked innocuous in the early games and we could not risk him in the first Test match. This was a great blow for he featured very highly in my plan for the campaign ahead. Moreover, it only added to the general criticism of our team, now rated so poorly that the attendances were seriously affected. Fortunately, we were being under-sold.

Six days later the situation had switched dramatically. Far from struggling to survive we almost won on the final day. West Indies followed on behind our total of 568 and seemed certain to achieve a draw, when suddenly on the final afternoon Robin Hobbs had Kanhai caught by Tom Graveney at short extra cover. It triggered off a remarkable collapse in which David Brown came back for a short burst and took the wickets of Butcher, Murray and Griffith in a single over and then, with his last ball before tea, nipped the ball back between Wesley Hall's bat and pad only to miss the leg stump by a fraction. Had that ball struck we would have been away to a flying start with victory in the first Test. Instead Hall returned afterwards with Sobers and they held us at bay. At one point Hall offered a sharp chance to Geoff Boycott at short-leg. It would have been a difficult but straightforward chance to any specialist in that position but Boycott, who was only one of many fielders crowded round the bat, was not accustomed to fielding there. Neither batsman offered a further chance. Our real problem, though, was that Brown had exhausted himself with his earlier exertions. He had nothing left, Jeff Jones had bowled magnificently and was well nigh spent, and I had no John Snow to throw the ball to. The match was drawn and even the huge relief that we had at last come good on the tour did not compensate for our deep disappointment at having been so close to victory and not achieved it. Knowing what good batsmen they are on their own wickets, I wondered to myself whether we would find ourselves in such a favourable position again.

The difference that a fully fit John Snow might have made was immediately underlined when he started bowling in the next Test at Sabina Park, Kingston, Jamaica. In reply to England's first innings 376 West Indies could muster only 143 and Snow, with seven wickets for 49, was so devastating that their innings lasted a mere 48 overs. Unquestionably we were sailing home to victory when a bottle, swirling high up in the sunlight, not only changed the course of the match but transformed it into one of the most extraordinary Tests ever played. The following day newspapers around the world carried huge front-page pictures of helmeted riot police charging spectators and palls of tear gas drifting over the ground. No newspaper, however, has ever given a full account of that upheaval and its aftermath and I make no apology for devoting a little attention to it here.

I have heard a number of attempted explanations for the crowd's violent mood that day. One was that it was a local political demonstration, entirely unconnected with cricket, and another that it was a Communist-inspired plot. I cannot deny either. All I do know is that, coincidentally, the West Indies cricket team was falling apart at the seams when it happened. They were following on and had lost half their side for 204 in the second innings when Basil Butcher touched a leg-side catch to Jim Parks behind the stumps. As so often happens in these circumstances Butcher did not actually see the catch completed and, quite justifiably, paused to check whether he was out or not. His hesitation proved fatal. The crowd completely misinterpreted his action and exploded. They thought that there might have been some doubt over the decision and showed their teeth.

As Butcher turned and left for the pavilion the jeering from one section of the crowd turned into an angry, unbroken roar, and as we fielders gathered round the wicket the first bottle came over the fences and skidding across the ground. The players were physically safe provided we stayed in the centre of the pitch but when the storm showed no signs of abating I decided to walk across to the rioters and appeal to them to stop.

This was not an impulsive action. I had experienced a similar bottle-throwing demonstration in Trinidad on my previous tour to West Indies and I agreed with Peter May after that affair that had a cricketer walked across and appealed to the crowd he would probably have had a great deal more influence than the police. It was worth a try in Jamaica so I walked down to the boundary, an action which was neither as brave nor as foolhardy as it sounds. There was an eight-foot wire fence separating the spectators from the playing area which was difficult to scale and, although the bottles were still raining over they were easier to dodge than a slashed top-edge slip catch. When I got to within twenty yards or so of the wire I found the noise was so deafening that any reasonable exchange of words was impossible. I was astonished how angry they were. Whereas in Trinidad they had demonstrated because they were disappointed with the cricket and could be humoured back into reasonable behaviour, here they just stood and screamed. All I could do was to put up my hands and shout "No, no. Calm down. We must get on with the cricket." Some of the crowd clapped and laughed and shouted their thanks, furious with the demonstrators, but there were too many out of hand. From the expressions on their faces I realised I had little chance. Manager Leslie Ames had now come on to the field to make a decision and the Chief of Police came across to us and said: "There is a good deal more than cricket behind this. We will have to clear them. We are going to use tear gas. It isn't safe for you and your boys out here, so please take your players to the pavilion." Dejectedly, we trooped off, sad for Jamaican cricketers and disappointed, too, for ourselves when the game was so well poised for us.

I was stopped many times by other spectators who were desperately anxious to explain that the disturbance was in no way directed against the English team but was, instead, politically inspired. I believed them. Unfortunately, the effect on the course of that Test was to be considerable.

The tear gas attack was not a stroke of tactical genius since an afternoon breeze had sprung up. Instead of enveloping the rioters the thick white clouds blew down the ground and swirled into the pavilion to have the innocent, instead of the guilty, choking and gasping for breath. Several of the players were caught and the England dressing room was an unusual sight. Men stood with tears cascading down their cheeks or heads bound up in damp towels.

When the gas cleared we needed to decide quickly what should happen next. We had lost valuable time at an important juncture of the match. We had to decide what was best for cricket. From our point of view, we would have preferred to have called it off for the day.

This was in our minds when Leslie Ames, as manager, and myself, together with Arthur Gilligan, the visiting MCC President, went to discuss the situation with the Jamaica Cricket Association officials in their secretary's office. It was, by now, mid-afternoon on the fourth day of a five-day Test.

Our hosts were distraught, repeatedly apologising and expressing their shame at what had occurred. They saw our point of view completely and their chairman, Cecil Marley, said to them: "We have proved such poor hosts that it is hard for us to have any further say in the matter. If the England team insist on no further play today, we must agree to that." But he added: "As you see this will create immense difficulties. I fully understand your position and all I will say is that if you *could* start again today it would be enormously appreciated."

Their distress was moving in the extreme. Moreover, the police were most apprehensive about our safe passage back to our hotel if we decided not to continue. We had to play on. It was the right decision.

The Jamaican officials were relieved and one of them was swift to see that the time lost could only be a disadvantage to England. "This is a fine gesture on your part," he said, "and we must give something too. We have now lost one and a quarter hours' play because of this trouble. You are not going to need it to beat us, but just in case of interference by rain tomorrow I think we must be prepared to play an extra one and a quarter hours on the morning after the match is scheduled to finish. That is the least we can do." His colleagues immediately agreed.

This was highly irregular as the playing hours in first-class cricket are predetermined and cannot normally be altered. However the riot too, had been highly irregular so, despite the chaos that it could cause to our travel arrangements, I agreed. The umpires and Gary Sobers were duly informed that there would be seventy-five minutes available should it be necessary, and they would be played out on the sixth morning of the game. We were winning so easily that we would only need that extra time if rain intervened. They had followed-on 233 runs behind and had already lost half their side a second time for only 204 runs when the bottles started flying. Indeed when Sobers came to the wicket he said: "We've batted so badly here that we don't deserve to get out of this one." There was no doubt in his mind that the match was over.

But, as the records of that incredible Test match now show, that was not the case. By the time we filed back down the pavilion steps to resume play the ground had been completely cleared of bottles and debris, though not entirely of demonstrators. There were a few more sporadic outbursts of stone-throwing but though these were swiftly quelled by the police they had a further unsettling effect on the English players. It was fully twenty minutes before we could collect ourselves and by then the rhythm of our bowling and impetus of our attack had utterly disappeared. We had a further hour bowling at Sobers and the new batsman, Holford, and during that time we did not get a single ball past the bat. We never looked like getting another wicket.

Sobers, whom we had dropped when he had scored only seven, returned the following morning to play an astounding innings, without giving the semblance of a chance. As at Lord's, five years earlier, his mood had changed completely. Nothing got past him despite the fact that the huge cracks in the wicket were now making the ball shoot and fly unpredictably. He batted so well that he scored 113 not out and was eventually able to declare with the West Indies total at 391 for nine in their second innings.

The whole episode knocked the stuffing out of us. There was now no way we could win. We were left the unenviable task of playing out time in the final session of that fifth day. It happens so often in cricket that this is the ideal climate for disaster to strike and it certainly was this day. After exactly forty minutes' play we were 19 for four. Sobers, as effective with the new ball as he had been with the bat an hour or so earlier, bowled Boycott for a duck and then had me leg-before for a duck. Hall bowled Edrich for six and then Barrington was leg-before to Griffith for 13. The wicket had gone and in the frenzied atmosphere the pressure was on England, not West Indies. Eventually five-thirty came. It was then that Gary Sobers came to see me in the dressing room and said: "Well, we'll just have to claim that extra time, Colin." The day finished 30 for four and we spent an uneasy night wondering if our tail could hold out.

It was quite an ordeal for, with the West Indian crowd now roaring at every ball bowled, England lost a further four wickets in that time before we just escaped defeat with our score at 68 for eight.

At the airport a plane carrying a number of American tourists had already been held up for several hours to await the departing English Test team. They were furious at the delay and still more angry when there was a further hold-up so that I could give filmed interviews for both the BBC and ITN camera teams. The riot and its sequel had made big news in Britain and I was required to give the English point of view. Few cricket tours received such immense publicity after two drawn Tests, yet we were desperately disappointed not to have rammed home our advantage and won.

There was another sensation in store before the next ball could be bowled. From Jamaica we flew down to Barbados and it was there, during a day's relaxation on the idyllic Sandy Lane Beach, that we lost the services of our most experienced spin bowler, Freddie Titmus.

The accident happened just off-shore when several of us were clinging to the outside of a tiny motor boat of, as it happened, tragically unusual design. Instead of being in the usual position at the stern the propeller was set immediately under the centre of the hull, a fact certainly unknown to Titmus when he let his legs float up beneath the boat. In that instant the propeller severed four toes from his left foot.

His leg was a terrible sight as we hauled him out of the water and a moment later I was as close to personal panic as I have ever been in my life. For a while I was demanding that we should drive him into the big modern hospital in Bridgetown, the capital, but two coloured beach boys were equally insistent that he should be taken to Speightstown seven miles in the opposite direction. "It's much nearer. Much better road," they said. I did not doubt their knowledge of local geography but, having driven through Speightstown on a previous visit and formed the impression that it was little more than a rambling village, I was hardly confident that its facilities would include the kind of clinic and instant surgery that Titmus so urgently needed if his foot was to be saved. It was a bad moment. Every instinct told me that Bridgetown, despite the longer distance and the winding road that was always congested with tourist traffic, donkey carts and cyclists, was the place that we should be going. But the beach boys were so passionate in their argument that in the end they almost forced us to swing left instead of right. As Robin Hobbs and I lifted Titmus into the car they clambered in too, not only directing us but nursing Freddie's leg in the most moving way. We all had reason to be extremely grateful to them. Denis Compton, a member of the press party travelling with us and enjoying the day on the beach, had alerted the Speightstown hospital by telephone. The moment we arrived Freddie was wheeled straight into the operating theatre of one of the most modern clinics in the world. And through another door came a Canadian surgeon, still wearing the beach shorts in which he had been basking in the sun only a few minutes earlier. The beach boys had certainly come good. They had brought us to a man who had carried out dozens of operations on ice-hockey players who had had toes severed in sports accidents. From the time we carried Titmus out of the water to the time that the surgeon removed the towels from his leg to examine the damage no more than twenty minutes had elapsed.

I shall never forget the next few seconds. Freddie himself never looked at the awful sight of his poor foot as the towels were removed. Instead he looked at the surgeon's face, searching for some reaction, some sign, which would tell him whether he would ever play cricket again. But not a muscle moved in the surgeon's face. That total lack of expression gave Titmus great confidence as the surgeon said: "Right, we'd better get down to work." As Freddie went under the anaesthetic we returned to our car and drove back round the coast to our hotel to await the outcome. I, for one, feared that his cricket career was over.

At the hotel almost every journalist in the island had gathered to hear the surgeon's report when he telephoned me from the hospital.

It came after almost two hours. "He's a very lucky man," said the surgeon. "Had the propeller struck him even half an inch further back on the foot I would have had to amputate at the ankle." Instead he had been able to create a sort of flap with what remained of the four toes. I then asked him the dreaded question. "Play again? Why ever not?" he replied. "The ice-hockey boys are usually playing again in four or five weeks after something like this." Freddie Titmus's recovery, in fact, took a little longer than that but he resumed playing for Middlesex.

The Titmus accident, coming hard on the heels of the Jamaica affair, sent us into the third Test match in Barbados under something of a cloud. It had no great effect on the outcome since the wicket was so slow and dead that the result was certain to be a draw from the outset. But we played uninspired cricket. The game's only real highlights were an exhibition of stupendous hitting by Clive Lloyd in the West Indies second innings and the excellent bowling of Pat Pocock for England. Pocock had taken over from Titmus, who was waiting to be flown home to England, and he seized the chance well under dispiriting bowling conditions. I had the hope that we were seeing the emergence of one of the most promising off-spinners in the world. It is a major disappointment to me that he did not build on this promising start and become an established off-spinner in England. He has been a fine bowler for Surrey in spite of slow wickets at the Oval. He would have been a good overseas cricketer, too.

By now, despite a first Test we might have won, a second Test we should have won and a third Test that no one was ever going to win, the series seemed to be heading for stalemate as we returned to Port of Spain, Trinidad, for the fourth. It was important that our batsmen should be in the runs and be looking to score more quickly. We badly needed Colin Milburn in form.

One of the happiest memories of my captaincy was my link with Colin Milburn. Sadly, on his tour of West Indies he was unsuccessful with the bat, yet no one could have made more of a contribution off the field. Like Harry Secombe, he is a natural figure of fun. Everything seems to happen around him. He has a genuinely good voice, too, and it was a happy moment for the MCC touring party when he held the spotlight at midnight on New Year's Eve singing "The Green, Green Grass of Home" to a full house. The audience were ecstatic and the encores rang again and again. How they would have loved him to have done well with the bat, and this he would surely have done on later tours but for the tragedy of losing an eye in a car accident.

On that tour there were few matches before the first Test and unless you clicked early it could be difficult for a batsman. He was an instinctive stroke-maker, seeing the half-chance and going for it with wonderfully quick reaction for his size. If it was not to be his day he would look rustic and out of his depth. He kept getting out in the opening overs but he never became dispirited.

The following winter he was playing for Western Australia and this helped his cricket enormously. He had two very successful seasons in the Sheffield Shield and at the end of one of these we sent an emergency call to him for our final Test against Pakistan in Karachi. That he brought good cheer and lifted our spirits was inevitable, but he also obliged with a mature, fully Test-class hundred. Just when it seemed certain he would become established the blow fell. He has played again since and, encouraged by the example of the Nawab of Pataudi who also lost an eye and came back into Test cricket with some success, Colin Milburn has fought his way back with great courage. He is still playing but, alas, he has not been quite the same again. I can only say that he was a wonderful companion and colleague and I am lost in admiration for the way he has borne the disaster which brought his Test career to such an abrupt halt.

We played in Antigua before the third Test on a perfect wicket, and we badly wanted Colin to get some runs. I won the toss and he walked to the wicket with Geoff Boycott. Boycott went to the far end to take the first ball and the umpire at the other end, finding himself face to face with Colin, just could not contain his excitement. He almost embraced him, reminding him of how he had listened to his wonderful innings at Lord's on the radio and recounting one or two of his other triumphs.

The game at length got under way. Boycott took a single. Colin Milburn took guard from his new-won friend and could well have been justified in thinking he must be pretty safe from being given out. The first ball leapt off a length, hit him high on the leg and there was a vain appeal from gully. The umpire leapt in the air and gave him out—first ball for nought in Antigua, would you believe it, and the umpire highly honoured at participating in the great man's dismissal!

In the pavilion we were terribly disappointed for him. He walked in with disbelief written all over his face but within a few minutes he collapsed in a heap, laughing. I heard him tell the story time and time again, with no trace of malice, just plain, warm, lovable humour.

When West Indies batted first and declared at 526 for seven it seemed that the most England could hope for there, again, was a draw. This was not to be. It was a Test full of incident, although only two years later did I learn the truth about one extraordinary turn of events.

From the outset we were slightly fearful as a result of one team change the West Indians made. It was a clever move bringing in Willie Rodriguez, a leg-spin googly bowler who had caused havoc among us in the earlier match against Trinidad. Without looking a class bowler he had taken six for 51 against us, supporting a curious legend. The theory was bandied about that he was only really effective on one ground, the Queen's Park Oval, in the entire world and also that he could work his magic only from one end of that ground. It sounds so absurd that only a batsman who has faced him bowling from the pavilion end at Port of Spain knows what a problem it can be.

Port of Spain is one of the few grounds which do not have sight screens at both ends. They have not erected one at the pavilion end because it would block out too many seats in the pavilion. By chance Rodriguez's build and bowling action are such that when he bowls from that end, at the critical moment his hand is completely invisible against the grey background of a pavilion bar recess. He is tailor-made for the ground and it is difficult to read his action to distinguish the leg-break from the googly.

This was very disconcerting to us when we set out in pursuit of West Indies' mountainous total. The ball was beginning to spin and, with Rodriguez in their ranks, our opponents had every reason for thinking they had us in trouble. We lost early wickets, Rodriguez trapping Graveney and D'Oliveira. Happily for us, however, Alan Knott was dropped off Rodriguez very early in his innings at a crucial stage of the match. He stayed with me, making 69, while I got 148 and we avoided the follow-on.

By lunch time on the final day, this Test seemed destined to go the way of the rest. West Indies were not scoring as fast as they would have liked in their second innings. On the West Indian dressing room balcony we could already see several of the players changed out of their flannels and day shirts, convinced there was nothing left in the match. The whole atmosphere, as we returned to the field after lunch, was one of sleepy indifference. It did not seem then that West Indies were going to declare. The match was dead, we were weary and quite relieved to play the day through.

But after only two overs of the afternoon session I was surprised to see Robin Hobbs, our twelfth man, racing on to the field. No one, to my knowledge, had signalled for anything. Certainly I had not, but Hobbs came straight up to me in great excitement. "You'd better watch it, skipper," he said, "the moment you left the pavilion all the West Indians went in and changed into their flannels again. It looks as if they are going to declare." I cannot remember now what pretext Hobbs had for coming on to the field but I appreciated his initiative. There was not much that I, as fielding captain, could do about it, but it was valuable to be forewarned of these new West Indian tactics.

When the declaration came it challenged England to score 215 in 165 minutes to win. It has since been written that there was a dispute in the England dressing room about whether we accepted the challenge and went for those runs or not. There was none. Any caution I had was because I knew there was a tendency in these situations to get over-excited. I had seen them before: the quick burst of runs, the mounting excitement, the sudden loss of four wickets and then the desperate rearguard action to get out of trouble. I did not want to have to fight a rearguard action against Rodriguez when neither Tom Graveney, Basil D'Oliviera nor myself, all good players of the spinners, could guarantee to pick his googly from the pavilion end. My whole approach was to keep the temperature down and see how we went. Nevertheless, Tom Graveney and Ken Barrington were most reassuring. We had a very good chance of getting the runs if we got off to a good start.

We did. Rodriguez bowled Edrich for 29 but Boycott and I then batted confidently. We hit Rodriguez so hard that, in the end, we actually had him changed round from the pavilion to the top end where he did not take a wicket. In eighteen overs we made 100 runs between us, and although I was out for 71 the victory was on. Significantly Charlie Griffith, for so many years a thorn in English flesh, was not on the field. He had gone off injured and did not return. In this respect Sobers was distinctly unlucky, for without him West Indies was eventually doomed. We won the Test by seven wickets with three minutes to spare.

It was an exciting victory because the target was never easy. As the news spread through the Caribbean the sky fell in upon Sobers's head. For days afterwards his motives, his character, even his right to continue captaining West Indies were fiercely debated throughout the islands. They had lost and Sobers was held solely to blame. This was unfair because what no newspaper revealed at the time, nor any cricket history book since, was that that most controversial declaration of modern Test cricket had the blessing of Everton Weekes and, maybe, many of his senior players.

It appears that at lunch time on that final day there was a considerable discussion in the West Indies dressing room between Sobers and Everton Weekes, the former Test player who was their manager. Although they both felt the pitch would not take much spin they knew that the England players were weary with the heat after five days of the Test match, and were apprehensive of Rodriguez's leg-breaks. It was worth a chance. Moreover, he assumed that we would not go for the runs. If he had got an early wicket or two Rodriguez could have put us under great pressure. He is one of the few bowlers I have played against who really might bowl a Test batting line-up quickly. And when it came to trying to shut the game up Sobers missed Griffith. He accepted the criticism without once hinting that Everton Weekes had in any way been involved in the decision to declare. He is a big man, with a warm, generous approach to cricket and life.

Victory in Trinidad put us one-up in the series with one to play, and after four such eventful Tests we found in Guyana a wicket living up to its reputation, the most lifeless on the Caribbean circuit. The crowds turned out in their anxious thousands to will West Indies to the victory which would have squared the rubber, but though that game was of six days' duration, the first five passed with us reasonably on top.

Kanhai and Sobers, who did not share many big partnerships, brought a few grey hairs to my head as both of them scored 150 and

189

put on 250 together. John Snow bowled magnificently on a slow wicket and took ten wickets for 142 runs in the match, a rare feat in Georgetown. Boycott made a good hundred, I got 59 and 82 and Alan Knott was 73 not out at the end.

But I must pay tribute to Tony Lock, cricketer extraordinary. Confronted with the problem of replacing Freddie Titmus so late in the year, we needed experience and we needed match fitness. Tony Lock had just led Western Australia to victory in the Sheffield Shield, a huge triumph for him. But more than that, he had bowled magnificently throughout and was in the process of becoming the most successful slow left arm bowler in the history of Australian cricket. This, then, was the background to our thinking when we telephoned him in Perth to join us for the last two Test matches. He was as excited as a young schoolboy.

If there were no outstanding figures to boast, his contribution was tremendous: he was dynamic in the field and bowled his heart out for me. Yet his greatest performance, and something quite un-expected, came at Georgetown in the fifth Test when we were in trouble at 259 for eight, chasing the West Indies total of 414. He batted for two and a half hours and together with Pat Pocock put on 109. He finished up with 89, an innings made up of a mixture of cussed obstinacy and West Indian extravaganza. At the end of that day he was the happiest Englishman alive. He had deserved some-thing to crow about after the agonies of previous years.

He had come a long way since the tour of Australia in 1959, when he had seen his suspect action on film for the first time. We had been dining with Lord Cobham in New Zealand and our host was good enough to gather some films to show us after dinner. Tony Lock could not believe what he saw and left for his hotel a shattered man. It speaks volumes for him that on the next day he came to terms with himself and pledged that he would never resort to that action again.

Our next match was against Northern Districts in Hamilton. Tony had quite a long spell but now he was back to his early days at the Oval, floating the ball gently but very high in the breeze. He trapped two wickets, both caught at deep long-off. The clock had been put back thirty years to J. C. White and Colin Blythe. But to us it was unrecognisable as the Tony Lock we had come to know.

On return to England he had long discussions with the Surrey

Cricket Committee. He acknowledged that he had got to re-shape his action, that it would take him a long time and that he might never be a great bowler again. Quite voluntarily, he immersed himself in Second Eleven cricket for a year. Soon, as it was clear that there was good cricket left in him, he was cajoled into moving to Leicestershire. In seeking to establish his personality in the new surroundings he appeared to set out to be controversial and did some highly unorthodox things. But, at heart, he was a genuine cricket man and in partnership with Michael Turner, their devoted and hard-working secretary, he was responsible for the renaissance which Ray Illingworth has the privilege of seeing come to fruition.

After our experience together in West Indies, Tony Lock and I have a bond for life. I have spent many happy hours with his family in Perth, and when I was practising hard to get fit for the Test match in Perth in 1974, Tony Lock went out of his way to be my chief net bowler.

On the final day of the Guyana Test, with the pitch looking as perfect as it had on the first, we suddenly plunged towards disaster. Inexplicably, with the ball still spinning slowly, Edrich was out, then Graveney and Barrington for ducks, D'Oliveira for two and Boycott for thirty: in exactly 95 minutes we were knocked from 33 for nought to 41 for five with every prospect of relinquishing in minutes the prize we had toiled and sweated for months to win. By lunch time Alan Knott was with me at the wicket and the afternoon loomed ahead like an eternity.

It felt the longest day of my life with the pressure constantly increasing. We could not win, so runs were of little value. All that mattered was the minute-hand creeping round the clock. I recall Knott at one stage leaning back to cut a superb four off the very top of his off-stump. In a Gillette Cup match it would have brought the house down but in those circumstances I think I turned white. I went down the pitch to him and said: "Thank God there is still one batsman in the world who intends to hit every bowler out of sight." Knott grinned and acknowledged the point. It was the last risk he took. Later during a drinks interval, I roused the crowd to anger by laying my bat down in the crease and dashing for the dressing room. If they suspected I was wasting time they were wrong. Nervous tension of that intensity can play havoc with a man's inside. I ran both ways and they soon forgave me. But we were both batting well and when the hour-hand began to take over from the minute-hand, and we had put on 127 together, it looked once more as if we were going to escape. Then, with 70 minutes to go, I was out. I had made 82 but that was little consolation. The gate was open again and Sobers and Gibbs stormed through. Only Alan Knott clung on as I joined the other helpless batsmen. All we could do was to wait and hope.

The England dressing room was a strange picture. Three or four players were at the window, occasionally averting their heads as the ball was bowled. Basil D'Oliveira was lying on a bench with a towel stretched over his face. John Edrich was in one corner, behind the door. In another corner, staring sightlessly at the wall and praying fervently that he would not have to move from that position was Jeffrey Jones, a charming Welshman, an excellent opening bowler, but, more significantly at the moment, our last batsman.

His prayers were not answered. When Pat Pocock was caught, Jones was exposed to the final six balls of the day from Gibbs. On his survival, or otherwise, the entire rubber depended. It hardly seemed possible. He was not a batsman, it has to be admitted, but he would watch every ball like a hawk and put a straight bat in the way. I gave him no instructions. There were none to give him. Neither did Alan Knott, who came from the middle to meet him. It is true that they were seen in a confidential huddle for a few seconds but what they were doing, it later transpired, was singing the opening lines of "We'll Keep a Welcome in the Hillsides" to lighten the atmosphere in the torrent of noise!

And well they might: the situation was desperate. Jones was entirely hemmed in by West Indian fieldsmen crouching so close that Gibbs, the bowler, seemed to be propelling the ball from another planet. I cannot give an exact description of what happened since I saw the first part of the over from the dressing room and the last part through cracks in doors and windows, relying mainly on the noises. In the end it was a Welshman who won England the day. Jones survived, the match was saved and the series was ours. Part one of my Five-Tour-Plan had been achieved.

Kent, after winning the county championship in 1970

Toasted by the Prime Minister, Edward Heath, in the Oval dressing room after our victory: (left to right) David Clark, myself, Stuart Leary, Leslie Ames, the Prime Minister, Bob Woolmer

Kent celebrating their victory in the Benson and Hedges Cup Final at Lords, 1973

Introducing the Duchess of Kent, President of Yorkshire Cricket Club,
to Asif Iqbal; her husband, Patron of Kent Cricket Club, is meeting
our Yorkshire opponents

A new way of getting out: knocked unconscious and bowled by Andy Roberts at Basingstoke, 1974

Three uncomfortable moments in the second Test against Australia at Perth, 1974: ducking a ball from Lillee; in pain after being hit by a ball from Thompson; and finally out, bowled by Thompson

A warm gesture from Melbourne Cricket Club in 1975

Friends from many different fields
of interest:

Discussing golf tactics with my
neighbour, Ryder Cup golfer Brian
Huggett

On our way to inspect the wicket,
myself and opposing captain
Harry Secombe

After receiving the CBE at
Buckingham Palace in 1972, with
my wife Penny and sons
Christopher and Jeremy

Batting in Canterbury, Kent v.
Somerset, 1974

Shape of things to come under the new Discrimination Act: the England ladies putting me under pressure at Sittingbourne

My eldest son Christopher making his first run at Lords, for Young England Cricketers against Young West Indies Cricketers, 1974

# 27

The extraordinary thing about my relationship with Basil D'Oliveira was that he had been in Britain six years before we ever had a conversation. I had read about his arrival from South Africa to play league cricket in Lancashire, seen him play in a Cavaliers' match on television and felt pleased for him, in a detached sort of way, when he joined Worcestershire. But his impact on me had been no greater than that. He never really shone on the few subsequent occasions I saw him in county games and I formed the impression of an apparently personable chap whose back-lift was very restricted and who relied on strong forearms. I could not see him as an obvious Test batsman. I was surprised, therefore, when he was chosen for the England twelve for the first Test match against West Indies at Manchester in 1966.

We both arrived early for the net practice at Old Trafford on the eve of that game and found ourselves in the astonishing position of being fellow members of an England side and having to introduce ourselves. I said: "Hello, I'm Colin Cowdrey." He said: "I'm Basil D'Oliveira, I saw you play in a Test match once, in South Africa in 1956. I never thought I would one day play with you. Times have changed."

Had we pursued that line of conversation I would have been forced to admit, to my shame, that the word "apartheid" did not have a prominent place in my vocabulary before my one and only tour to South Africa in 1956. Indeed I did not know what it meant until the day we boarded a Union Castle liner at Southampton *en route* for Cape Town. Then a mysterious parcel was delivered to the ship containing a number of books and a message asking our manager Freddie Brown to give each player a copy. I took mine down to my cabin, glanced briefly through a few pages without registering what it was about, then put it aside. A few days later, just as mysteriously, our manager received a radio telegram from South Africa warning us that we would be in trouble at Cape Town if we tried to get our books through customs. This, obviously, was an instant challenge to go back to my cabin and read the book thoroughly. I did. As I turned the pages a whole new complexion on South Africa opened up. It was Father Trevor Huddlestone's *Naught for Your Comfort*.

On board ship a South African university professor approached Freddie Brown and offered to talk to the team one evening about the complexities of his country. We kept him going for two hours and he inspired me, at least, to keep an open mind until I had time to absorb. Too many rush to premature judgments. Some people adopt a harsh attitude without ever seeing the country at first hand. With priests I visited coloured townships outside both Johannesburg and Kimberley. It was in one of those compounds one Sunday evening that we ran into a group of young Africans playing cricket. I asked the priest I was with if I should go and join in their game for a while. He said: "They'd love it—but I think you'd better not." He was thinking, I knew, of the consequences for me if it was written about in the newspapers. That was in 1956. When I revisited Cape Town in 1972 I was given a warm welcome in the colour compound and the general atmosphere had moved on in an encouraging way.

For a young English cricketer, it was a wonderfully happy journey, full of fun, and a variety of interest. It was a highly competitive world of cricket where the sun always seemed to shine and there was a charming host always ready to entertain you in his house. When I was alone with time to think I was confused about apartheid; it worried me deeply that so many coloured folk should take such a close interest in the cricket, yet we could have no social contact with them. Moreover, they always cheered our side and took delight in our success. I was very sad that I was unable to return to South Africa with Mike Smith's team in the winter of 1964–65. By then I was equipped to learn a great deal more about a country in which sport tangled with politics, but the opportunity was lost. It was lost, again, of course, in the winter of 1968–69, but this time by the amazing chain of events which became known as the D'Oliveira Affair.

Few people were concerned about the political implications of D'Oliveira's selection for England in that summer of 1966. But by the time we returned home victorious from West Indies in the spring of 1968 it was a national issue. We were due to leave for South Africa within six months. Would D'Oliveira be chosen? If he were chosen, would he be acceptable to the South African Government? Would he recover his form after a largely indifferent tour of West Indies even to be in the running? The press were posing the question in public but so, in private, were MCC. In the January of that year they had written to the South African Government asking them for their views. By the first week in June, when we went into the first Test against Australia at Manchester, no reply had been received. The South African Government, it appeared, did not acknowledge hypothetical questions. At least, not in writing.

Australia won the match by 159 runs but on the final day D'Oliveira batted splendidly for 87 not out. It was a more significant effort than he ever knew at the time for among the spectators was Sir Alec Douglas-Home. He had been speaking the previous evening near by and called into Old Trafford to see the last two hours' play in the match. Sir Alec had just returned from a visit to South Africa and a meeting with Dr. Vorster. I asked him what he felt about D'Oliveira's inclusion in the England team throughout the summer in view of the impending visit to South Africa the following winter. I cannot quote his answer verbatim, but in view of the subsequent accusations of pressures and counter-pressures in the D'Oliveira Affair I think it is important to record the sense of his remarks, which I recall with complete clarity.

He told me that as captain and a selector my course of action was absolutely clear. I should not be misled by the press or swayed by public opinion. I must pick the strongest team, whether it included D'Oliveira or not. I must be absolutely honest and straightforward about it and not deviate. If D'Oliveira were picked to tour South Africa, Sir Alec could not say whether he would be accepted or not. He had spoken to Dr. Vorster about it but the South African Prime Minister wasn't in a position to say. Things are changing in South Africa all the time. No one in the world could say what the political climate would be in October.

For this reason he was totally opposed to MCC attempting to force the issue by insisting on a South African reply to their January letter. It would be simple to insist that if we hadn't heard by a certain date then we should call the tour off, but this was not a good idea. We wanted relationships kept as warm as possible in the current climate.

He added that he believed the moral issue was not Britain's to enter into. He was certain that to break off cricket relations with South Africa would have no effect on her attitude to apartheid, however long we refused to play against them.

I found Sir Alec's decisions very reassuring. I respected his wisdom and integrity and I left that Test match with my mind cleared about my role in the D'Oliveira issue. It was to remain solely a matter of picking the best team for the tour. His words sustained me greatly when, after choosing D'Oliveira in the twelve for the second Test at Lord's, we left him out of the team on the morning of the match. It was inevitable, I suppose, that a number of people leaped to the wrong conclusion. Many wrote me abusive letters, others wrote begging me to speak out about the political pressures that were being applied. There were none. It was purely a *cricket* decision—just as all the other decisions which kept D'Oliveira in and out of the headlines in the next few months were based on cricket thinking.

He was dropped from the side at Lord's, despite his excellent second-innings batting at Manchester, because of his bowling. At Manchester I had used him as first-change. He had bowled tidily but without the thrust to keep the pressure on at that point in the game. At Lord's we wanted more of a seam bowler than a swing bowler to follow up the initial assault of Snow and Brown. We brought in Colin Milburn as a batsman and Barry Knight as a seam bowler. After talking the matter over for some time on the eve of the game the selectors agreed that D'Oliveira was not a justifiable choice. Our thinking was right. Milburn scored 83 in England's only innings and Knight took three for 16 in Australia's first innings of 78 all out, their lowest score against England for thirty years. It was the 200th Test Match between the two countries and if rain had not flooded out fifteen of the scheduled thirty hours' playing time we would have beaten Australia out of sight.

The cynics refused to believe that D'Oliveira's exit was not some sort of a fascist plot and their letters rolled in. Unfortunately, it took two months to prove them wrong. Although he had been batting well early in the season he suddenly ran into a string of low scores.

He made only two and four against Kent at Worcester; then sixteen, nine and nought in his three innings immediately before the team for the third Test was chosen; then, just before the fourth Test, thirteen and four against Somerset and a duck against Leicestershire. Apart from one excellent innings against Yorkshire he had done nothing at all to attract the selectors' attention. But then, while England were engaged in the fourth Test at Leeds, D'Oliveira suddenly soared back into the news, not as a batsman but as a bowler. Three hundred miles south, in Portsmouth, he almost beat Hampshire single-handed with five for 39 off 26 overs in their first innings and six for 29 off nine overs in their second.

Two Sundays later the team for the final Test at the Oval was selected. We met at the RAC Club in Pall Mall against a background of speculation about D'Oliveira's inclusion. Most people, including Basil himself, I suspect, believed that this was the key to whether or not he would tour his native South Africa as an England player. When the names were announced shortly after lunch, D'Oliveira's was not among them. Those who suspected collusion were now convinced that the politicians had won.

They were wrong. One down in the series we had chosen the five best bowlers in England to win the match and Snow, Brown, Higgs, Illingworth and Underwood were nominated. Nine times out of ten I would have been quite happy with that principle but by coincidence—indeed the coincidence which in the end detonated the whole D'Oliveira Affair—I had played for Kent against Surrey at the Oval only the previous week. I had been out of action for a month with an injury but, on a pitch only eight yards away from the strip on which the final Test was to be played a few days later, I scored 109. The whole character of the wicket attracted my attention. The genuine fast bowlers could get nothing out of it. It was the medium-pacers, Stewart Storey for Surrey and Alan Dixon for Kent, who were beating the bat and causing problems. It struck me so forcibly that, with my mind on choosing the Test team, I talked about it to Mickey Stewart and John Edrich. They confirmed the wicket had been playing this way for several matches and that, with the weather hampering the groundsmen's work, it seemed the Test pitch was sure to play the same way. I was uneasy when we plumped for a predominantly fast bowling attack at our Sunday meeting but I accepted that it was probably sound. "If the conditions change to favour a medium-pacer before the match begins," I asked the selectors, "do I have your permission to approach another player?" Almost to appease me, I feel, they agreed. It was decided that should another type of bowler seem necessary I should first go for Tom Cartwright of Warwickshire, then Barry Knight of Leicestershire and since there seemed to be some doubt about the fitness of both of them, Basil D'Oliveira was the third name on the list.

This private arrangement was never revealed to the press which was why, the following Wednesday, they were stunned when D'Oliveira was suddenly drafted into the England team—and what few people know to this day, the quite astounding sequence of events which made it possible.

I had telephoned Birmingham from Canterbury immediately after the selection meeting to check on the fitness of Cartwright. Cartwright had bowled well in their Sunday match, I was told, but no decision could be made about his physical condition for a five-day Test until the following day. Next day I was called off the field at Canterbury to be told that he could not make it. Reaction had set in and he could not guarantee to stand up to the strain of a long match.

The next agreed name on my list was Knight. Leicestershire were playing Essex at Leyton, but I could not contact him on the telephone. It was a frustrating time with the line continually engaged and my presence required on the ground at Canterbury. Eventually, a most helpful telephone operator, who by chance was a cricket fan, took the task over. She got a message through to Barry Knight, asking him to ring me the following morning to report on his fitness. When Knight rang the following day he was disappointed to have to express doubts. He was only eighty per cent fit. "I'll play willingly," he said, "but I must say now I won't be able to give you everything."

There were forty-eight hours to the start of the Test. From my home I mulled over the problem for half an hour. Knight could not play in a five-day Test as an unfit all-rounder. I then telephoned Doug Insole, the selector's chairman, to tell him I was going for D'Oliveira. Insole was in a meeting and unavailable so I rang the Worcestershire ground myself and left a message asking D'Oliveira to report at the Oval the following morning—the pre-Test practice—instead of playing against Yorkshire at Worcester.

What must be emphasised at this point is that D'Oliveira was still not *in* the Test team. He was still only a stand-by and the chances were that he would not play. He was, however, on his way to the Oval, which proved just as well. At mid-day on the eve of the match Roger Prideaux, one of our opening batsmen, dropped out of the team through a virus infection. The solution was simple. Colin Milburn moved up to open the innings. And D'Oliveira came into the side, mainly as a batsman though his bowling could be useful.

The next two days brought one of the most significant innings in modern cricket. Although I won the toss and first use of a slow, brown wicket on a glorious morning, England were soon in trouble. Connolly, particularly, vindicated my Sunday reasoning by swinging the ball tremendously. Milburn was out for 8, Dexter for 21 and I was leg-before to Mallett for 16. An hour before the close D'Oliveira walked to the wicket: an utterly calm figure, betraying none of the huge tension there must have been within him. This, so far as he was concerned, was the innings which must decide whether he was to have the chance he had dreamed about for years — to return to South Africa as a free, equal member of an English Test team. It was a big load to carry.

He began slowly and rather tentatively. Quite often, with his short back-lift and staccato sytle, he can look like a novice in the early moments of an innings. But it is misleading. This day he was lucky to be dropped at 31, but thereafter he played a superb innings, full of attacking shots and commanding presence. The next day, batting now as if this was a mission utterly divorced from a Test match, he dominated the scene. The slow wicket suited him perfectly and he took his personal score to 158 before he was at last out. He returned to the pavilion to a standing, emotional ovation. Public opinion was convinced that the die was now cast. D'Oliveira, they maintained, was now a certainty for South Africa.

D'Oliveira himself merely sat very quietly in the dressing room. He is a remarkable man. The previous evening, half way through his innings, he had phoned his wife in Kidderminster. She was very nervous and excited. "Don't worry," he told her. "Don't bother to look at the television. I shall make a hundred all right. I've never played so well."

D'Oliveira himself, I feel sure, believed he had done enough to justify his selection for the tour. On purely cricketing grounds I was not so sure. Earlier that summer, by yet another curious chain of events, I had the honour of being invited to one of the Queen's informal lunch parties at Buckingham Palace. Unfortunately, I was playing at Leicester on the appointed day and could not go. In its place my wife and I received an invitation to attend a Palace cocktail party at which the Australian captain, Bill Lawry, was also to be present. I had a long conversation with him, mostly a lucid explanation on his part how cricket wickets had changed in South Africa. "It's a very different game there now," he said, "to the years when you played against Heine and Adcock. They've left a lot more grass on the pitches. It's not so much a fast bowler's tour. It's a seamers' paradise." In view of our coming winter tour there I was vitally interested. We continued the conversation over dinner and on the way home I came to the conclusion that if what Lawry had said was accurate, then both Cartwright and Knight might be more effective than the fast bowlers in those conditions, D'Oliveira too, but I saw D'Oliveira as a batsman who could bowl well. This, of course, had helped form my list of priorities when I pleaded for my extra bowler at the Oval. Now the same argument held good as we came to think about picking our side for South Africa.

The team was to be chosen on the final evening of the Oval Test and this, I knew, would be a major subject for debate. It would involve me as I had already been named captain.

First, however, I wanted to talk privately to D'Oliveira himself, to discover how he felt about the inevitable pressures to which he would be subjected if he were picked. The opportunity came after the third day's play at the Oval. I had been called away to take a telephone call as I came off the field and when I returned to the dressing room D'Oliveira was the only man there. I asked him, "Can we get away with it without getting too involved in politics?"

D'Oliveira was under no illusions at all about how the microscope would be on him every day, every hour, every moment. He had clearly thought it all out. "Everyone will be looking for the slightest flaw in my behaviour, both on the field and off it. There will be plenty of them just longing for me to get involved in an incident." He had worked it out, even down to the kind of social functions he would attend and those he would not. There were a hundred-and-one do's and don'ts to avoid deliberately provoking publicity. I was very impressed with his outlook, and equally appreciative when he said: "Look, I know I have put you all on the spot. I want to go, of course. But the whole situation is beyond me. I'm in the hands of people I trust and I will accept your judgment."

If this implies that, in the end, anything beyond cricket was involved in our debate over D'Oliveira, then I must firmly refute it. I left the Oval after a thrilling victory over Australia on the final evening, driving straight to Lord's where the other selectors were waiting for me. Doug Insole was in the chair. With him were Peter May, Don Kenyon and Alec Bedser. Gubby Allen was there as Treasurer of MCC, Arthur Gilligan as President and Leslie Ames as the already-appointed tour manager. Billy Griffith and Donald Carr were also in attendance. All selection meetings tend to go on, as one tends to get stuck on the last two or three places and the replacements in the event of injury. This one was no exception and ended at two o'clock the following morning, with the required sixteen names. Basil D'Oliveira was not among them.

The public announcement of the tour party was to be made the following day and we knew there would be an explosion from the press. We also knew quite well that few people would believe us that this was the selectors' best England team to win in South Africa.

I spent that night at the house of Brian Johnston, the BBC cricket correspondent who lived close by. I was playing at Lord's for Kent against Middlesex in only a few hours' time. The waiting was painful and the repercussions every bit as bad as we expected them to be. The heavy artillery was brought out at the Lord's press conference, the abusive letters began pouring in again, our great win at the Oval against Australia only a few days before was forgotten. People were now asking sarcastic questions like, "Let's see, how many did Dolly score for you in that match?" I expected it. I know how I would have been tempted to react. I was very sad for D'Oliveira. I did not phone him because I knew how the press could have misconstrued it. Instead my wife sent flowers to Mrs. D'Oliveira. Even this gesture made the front pages.

There was nothing to do but to wait for the furore to die down and then go to South Africa and win. There was, it was true, the small formality of checking the fitness of Tom Cartwright and Jeff Jones. Cartwright, the man who had taken D'Oliveira's place, was due to visit Bill Tucker, the surgeon, in London on the last Monday of the season and then meet us at Lord's at four o'clock that afternoon. As it happened, I had reason to know that his journey was hardly necessary. On the previous Saturday I captained an England eleven against Warwickshire, the Gillette Cup winners, at Birmingham. Cartwright was playing for Warwickshire and he bowled beautifully. He bowled me out with a perfect ball, went through his dozen overs without any sign of discomfort and then went to see his local specialist. To convince myself of his fitness for the tough tour ahead I went to see the specialist too. "He's absolutely fit," I was told.

On the following Monday I went to Lord's at the appointed hour of four to hear the fitness reports with my fellow selectors. It was going to be such a short, formal meeting that my wife was in the car outside, waiting to be driven home. By three minutes past four p.m. we were half way through our business. Jeffrey Jones was reported clear to tour. I then became involved in a conversation of remarkable cross-purpose.

Doug Insole, chairman: "Colin played at Birmingham on Saturday. Do you have anything to add about Cartwright?"

Cowdrey: "Yes, he was very good. There's not much more I can add."

Insole: "Amazing, isn't it? Anyway, bad luck."

Cowdrey, assuming Insole was referring to the excellent delivery with which Cartwright had bowled him at Birmingham: "Yes, it was pretty good. It pitched on middle and knocked the off-stump out. I want a few more of those in Cape Town."

Insole: "What are you talking about? Haven't you heard the news?"

Cowdrey: "What news?"

Insole: "That Cartwright is out of the tour."

Cowdrey, with startling originality: "I don't believe you."

Insole: "I mean it. He's been here for the past couple of hours. Only just left, in fact. He had terrible reactions after his bowling on Saturday. He had to see his own specialist on Sunday and then saw the surgeon down here this morning. It was hopeless. There was no chance he could go to South Africa."

The time was now roughly five minutes past four. By four-fifteen we had chosen D'Oliveira as Cartwright's replacement. There was nothing to argue about. Although we had not announced it at the time, D'Oliveira had always been first reserve. Now, on cricketing grounds, pure and simple, from which we never deviated from first till last, he automatically came into the party.

It then took us four hours to work out a press statement. We produced dozens of different versions and then tore them all up. In the end we saw there was no point. Yet again, nobody would believe us, whatever we said. We finally wrote the simple facts in a press statement and released it immediately to the news agencies.

I was home in time to see the ten p.m. television news. D'Oliveira had swept all the other world news out of the headlines.

Unhappily for all of us, and for cricket itself, we moved into further trouble. Unknown to us at Lord's, Dr. Vorster, the South African premier, was due to speak the following night at Bloemfontein, in the Orange Free State. This is the very heart of Afrikaanerdom, and if any place in the world was going to be inflamed by MCC's apparent change of heart over D'Oliveira, this was it.

Had we known of Vorster's engagement in Bloemfontein we might have held up the D'Oliveira announcement by several days, but I cannot believe this would have made any difference. We had always intended to let the South African Cricket Association have a list of our official reserves, with D'Oliveira's name included, but now it was too late. Vorster pounced. He savaged us pitilessly on that platform in Bloemfontein—and then cancelled the tour.

When I watched the television film of Vorster's speech the following day I reacted like everyone else in Britain with a deep love of sport. I was very sad. It is tragic that our world is so torn by a distrust of one another's motives. I still could not bring myself to believe that the situation was totally irreparable. My next thought was to fly to South Africa myself and through the Cricket Association request an interview with him. There were many far more skilled envoys than myself who could have gone. But I had been at the heart of things throughout and could answer every question. I knew every move that had gone on in reaching this decision. The power of my plea would be in its straightforwardness. I would not have minded being grilled by the South African Premier and his Cabinet colleagues for as long as they liked, and I backed myself to calm him down; but there was really little hope of making him retract what he had said.

D'Oliveira's strength and dignity throughout those awful days were marvellous. But the tension was demoralising. He telephoned me after Vorster had made his cancellation speech and it was typical of him that his first thoughts were for his colleagues. "I'm terribly sorry," he said, "that I should be the cause of you and the lads missing the tour." He sounded at the end of his tether and said he wanted to come and see me as soon as possible. He drove to my home in Kent the following day, arriving late in the afternoon. We had dinner around the fire and spoke from five p.m. until two o'clock the following morning.

While we were having dinner, alone, my wife rushed in to tell us that the television news had just reported that two officials of the South African Cricket Association, Arthur Coy and Jack Cheetham, had arrived in London. This was yet another dramatic development. Was there still hope, we wondered? Apart from the reports of Vorster's speech, MCC had received no official announcement from the South African Cricket Association that the tour was off, so they had cabled them and asked for the Association's position by two o'clock the following Friday, when the full MCC Committee would be meeting at Lord's. Instead of cabling an answer their response was to send their two top officials to London in person, and in such secrecy that the journey was worthy of a James Bond script. Coy and Cheetham booked their flights from Johannesburg under assumed names and maintained their fictitious identities when they booked into a London hotel. No MCC official had any idea where they were staying. They had, however, been recognised by an alert reporter at Johannesburg Airport. The news was flashed to London. So while Messrs. Coy and Cheetham were signing assumed names in the hotel some millions of Englishmen knew they were here and wondering why.

They contacted MCC the following morning and arrived at Lord's for the lunch that was to precede the committee meeting. I sat at their table. They were both distressed and it was a difficult meal. We attempted to steer the conversation away to other subjects, but it was no good. Even so, I left the table still in ignorance of the real motive of their visit.

Coy and Cheetham were given a warm welcome at the meeting. They felt they had to come in person to offer their abject apologies for a situation they could hardly believe or accept. Each man spoke briefly and emotionally. They then left the room and flew back to South Africa. This was the last move, and the saddest controversy in cricket was over.

It remains a sad point in my cricketing life that, in the end, I did not captain an England team in South Africa with Basil D'Oliveira in it. It will be the tragedy of D'Oliveira's life that he did not play on the cricket grounds of his homeland on equal terms with any man on earth. Yet, if one can stand aside from the sadness, I feel that eventual good will come out of it all—yes, at what huge price, I know—but I am not sure that we can put a price on the freedoms that we all wish to see. If it had not been D'Oliveira, it would have been some coloured cricketer born in Blackheath or Bradford in a few years' time. I suppose it might be easier for someone like this to visit than for a coloured cricketer born in Cape Town to return as a free man.

There will be no cricket between England and South Africa, as I understand it, until the South African Government makes it possible for all cricketers, of whatever colour, to play with and against one another quite freely. How long will it take to break down Afrikaaner attitudes? I believe it will come in my lifetime. As Sir Alec said: "Things are moving faster than any of us fully realise." The situation will respond more to warmth than to threats or demands from pulpit or cricket pavilion. We must do all we can to encourage this with the voice of reason.

After the MCC tour was called off, the Cricket Council made it clear that communication between South Africa and the rest of the cricketing world would be restored when there was evidence that real opportunities were being afforded to coloured and African cricketers to mix in friendly competition with white cricketers. Everyone looked forward to that day, and the situation where a team representing South Africa would be chosen from all cricketers in that land, regardless of colour.

The South African Cricket Association have worked unceasingly to this end and their distress has been hard to watch from a distance. I was flattered when Jack Cheetham and Boon Wallace, President and President-elect respectively, chose me to be the captain of a side to include a number of coloured cricketers for the first time. I was most anxious to be part of the fight-back, as long as it was planned on sensible lines. This required the goodwill of all the cricket associations, white, coloured and African. I flew to Cape Town to see Hassan Howa, the head man of the Coloured Cricketers' Association, who gave me the warmest possible welcome, respected my motives but was unyielding. I went on to Johannesburg and met a few senior members of the African Cricket Association. They were just as warm in their welcome and longed for me to bring a side. It was all most confusing. I felt that, on balance, it needed a little more time. To rush in without the blessing of Mr. Howa and his colleagues would only aggravate a delicate situation unnecessarily. Timing was all-important. I think I was right to play it slowly.

However, Derrick Robins, who has made such a significant contribution to cricket over the years, decided to move in. With Brian Close as captain he took the first of a number of teams to visit there. This was an all-white team, which broke the ice. Having established himself he was able to take West Indian John Shepherd (Kent) and Pakistani Younis Ahmed (Surrey). They were accorded the normal courtesies and were well received. I applaud his zeal in trying to maintain cricket links with South Africa. Whether the coloured cricketers feel that he has done the best by them, I am not in a position to know first hand. Only time will tell.

This problem requires great patience. In the individual sports like golf, tennis, athletics and boxing there have been clear strides made. I admire the tremendous efforts of Gary Player to give opportunities to coloured golfers and bring them in on the competitive circuit, but it is in the team games that things are not quite so easy. The most recent development involves international cricketers from every country visiting South Africa to play in commercially sponsored International Single-Wicket Tournaments. All the time, so slowly as to be almost imperceptible, there are signs that things are moving. Let us hope so. Of one thing I am certain. They have had enough of the admonishing finger; much more will be achieved by warmth and goodwill from the world outside.

# 28

The cancellation of that tour to South Africa shattered the Five-Tour-Plan I had so enthusiastically drawn up before our departure for West Indies. Part One had been successfully accomplished. Part Two, to recapture the Ashes from Australia in England in the summer of 1968, was beaten by the weather. Australia won the first Test handsomely and we won the last Test dramatically. The second Test and the Ashes would have been ours if rain had not halved the playing-time. Part Three, our expedition to South Africa, never materialised. Part Four, the South Africans' visit to England, died a retaliatory death. Part Five? Part Five I saw as my farewell to the major stage of cricket, and it would be dishonest not to say I saw it as sentimentally as an actor or an opera singer who wants to leave the stage with a memorable performance. Part Five was where I hoped to return to Australia for the fifth time, this time as England captain, and win the Ashes with a team I had built, nurtured and encouraged. I was to learn, of course, that such romantic conceptions are not only born in the minds of fiction writers, but can die there as well.

For me it died on the afternoon of Sunday, May 24th, 1969, in a league match against Glamorgan when I snapped the Achilles' tendon in my left leg. The previous summer, while scoring a century in my hundredth Test match, I had been injured but was back within a month. This time I was out for the season. England were playing three Tests against West Indies and three against New Zealand. Ray Illingworth was appointed England captain. I wrote to congratulate him and wish him well. With that I bowed out, my plans unfulfilled.

I have always had a very high regard for Illingworth as an outstanding all-round cricketer. Indeed, at one stage early in his career, when he had a dispute with Yorkshire over money, he wanted to leave for another county and wished to come to Kent. I am sure we would have invited him but before we could extend an invitation he had patched up his differences, and any plans we might have had fell through. I was disappointed for I knew his potential. He would have been a great asset to our side.

Curiously enough he achieved some of his finest county performances against Kent, which showed me his skill and temperament in the heat of battle. He played one magnificent innings on a final day at Leeds to steal a Yorkshire victory out of a match we might easily have won, and then, at Dover in 1964, he virtually beat Kent on his own. Yorkshire won the toss, batted first and, on a bad wicket, were at one juncture 41 for four. Illingworth then took charge of the match. He scored 135 out of Yorkshire's all-out total of 256, took seven for 49 in Kent's first innings and seven for 52 in our second. We were beaten by an innings and thirteen runs.

His England Test career until the start of the summer of 1969, had been a very different story. On his first overseas tour to West Indies he played in all five Tests and took only four wickets at a personal cost of 93 runs apiece. In fact he bowled better than those figures imply but, as a batsman, he literally looked as though he would never get to the other end. It was a mystery to me, as much as it was a disappointment to him. Captaining him occasionally in England I found him quiet, straightforward and well organised with regard to his own field placing requirements. We never had the luck to be successful together as a partnership; nothing establishes a bond more quickly than this. I think of my opening partnership as a batsman with Peter Richardson in 1956 and later with Geoff Pullar in 1960; David Brown, Jeff Jones, David Allen and Robin Hobbs as bowlers.

He was in my side in the first Test against Australia at Birmingham in 1961, when Australia scored 516 for nine against us in their first innings. The match was eventually drawn but not before Australia had taken almost 400 of those runs off us in a single day. Ray Illingworth emerged with two for 110. He was disappointed with himself and I was disappointed with the day. We had taken some punishment which did not bring out the best in either of us. Many times I have looked back to that day and wished he had taken seven for 110 in a long, well-controlled spell of bowling. This would have established him more quickly as a natural successor. But he had a number of rivals, Allen, Titmus, John Mortimore and later Pat Pocock. Like Brian Close, although he appeared on the scenes early, he was not seen at his best in Test cricket until he was well past thirty, after he had left Yorkshire in fact. His impact on Leicestershire has been tremendous. Just the calm, shrewd, steadying lead their many talented players required.

It was essential to get fully fit after my injury in 1969. Two short winter tours came as a gift from the gods. I went to Jamaica with the International Cavaliers during the early months of the year and confirmed only one thing: how desperately irksome it was at the age of thirty-eight, after a nine-month absence, to discipline oneself back to full match fitness, something I had always taken for granted. After that three-week tour I was able to return to West Indies for a further month before the English season opened, captaining the Duke of Norfolk's eleven. Here, at last, I started to get going and I returned to England determined to be fitter than I had ever been for Australia.

Back home, a change in the planning of the county cricket programme meant that we played less than the usual amount of cricket during May. This, together with a run of low scores, meant I lost the momentum I had just started to build up. The South African tour had been cancelled and we were playing five Tests against a Rest of the World eleven instead, but whoever the opponents had been, it was obvious that I could not be chosen for the first Test. Alec Bedser, Doug Insole's successor as chairman of the selectors, was kind enough to telephone and explain that the selectors thought it unfair to me to consider me for the opening match. But he emphasised that it was important for me to get back into the Test arena as soon as possible.

While Ray Illingworth led England in the first Test I found my touch with the bat in county cricket with centuries against Sussex and Essex. Illingworth, however, had had an excellent match, bowling extremely well and getting runs also. He was automatically named to captain the second Test at Nottingham and I was brought into the side.

The captaincy issue remained a daily topic and built up to a peak as we approached the third Test at Birmingham, during which the selectors were going to make the official announcement about who would lead in Australia. I assumed that it would be released, as usual, at the end of the match. I was wrong. They met on the Monday, the fourth day of the game, and reached their decision while I was batting in the middle. The first I knew about it was when I came off the field. Alan Smith, one of the selectors, asked me to have a word with Alec Bedser in the secretary's office.

Bedser said: "We're sorry about this. We know what an ambition it was of yours, and how much it meant to you, but we've chosen the other fellow."

I said: "Fair enough."

He replied: "We would like you to go as vice-captain."

I said: "I am honoured to go to Australia as a player but I'd like time to think about the vice-captaincy. I'm not sure that it's quite in the best interests of the side—nor am I sure that Ray Illingworth would want it."

They did not expect me to demur and it did not quite fit in with their plans, especially as they had already told the press. The selectors obviously wanted to clear up the matter there and then and to make an announcement without delay. From my point of view it was not quite so simple. I genuinely felt that Ray should have had a younger player as vice-captain. For my part I had been vice-captain in Australia three times. I would enjoy a tour without that responsibility. Yet, as it was pointed out, I had a lot to contribute, especially to David Clark, the newly appointed manager, in the matter of day-to-day details. Eventually, I fell in with their wishes.

As we left England we all knew that we were the better side—South Africa had just demolished the Australians—and that we were favourites to win the Ashes. To me only one thing mattered. Would cricket—the whole game—be richer for our visit?

# 29

There were moments in that summer of 1970 when life would have been infinitely preferable on the moon. But there was also consolation on the grand scale: Kent won the County Cricket Championship for the first time since 1913. Perhaps we were destined to do so from the night of our Centenary Dinner in the Great Danes Hotel, Maidstone, early in the year. For it was there that Edward Heath, a successful Kent sportsman himself, who took a close interest in our cricket, made an uncannily prophetic speech. It was still several weeks to the General Election and the polls were almost unanimously against him but he said: "I should have thought that until now 1906 was probably our most important year. It saw a change of Government and it saw Kent win the County Championship for the first time. Now 1970 ... well, what could be more certain?"

Three months later he was Prime Minister and Kent, half way through our championship programme, were at the bottom of the table. But we, too, made it in the end. It was a gratifying moment, for captaining Kent, like captaining England, is not something that starts to happen when you lead your team down the pavilion steps and on to the field.

For me it had been a fifteen-year commitment, even a crusade. It all began with the arrival of the cable inviting me to take over the county captaincy from Douglas Wright in 1956. I was on tour in South Africa at the time, staying at one of the famous honeymoon hotels along the Garden Route. My first thought was of the men who would be playing under me if I accepted: Arthur Fagg, who had toured Australia with the England team back in 1936; Fred Ridgway, who had toured India five years previously; Jack Pettiford, who had played wartime games for Australia; Doug Wright, thirty-four times an England Test player and the man who was handing over the reins of captaincy because he had become weighed down by the struggles and the responsibility; Godfrey Evans, already approaching ninety Test matches for England and one of the most magnetic characters in the game. All these men were established cricketers while I was still at school. Now I was being invited to lead them. It was a daunting prospect and I challenged Godfrey Evans, who was also on the tour, to ask him how men of his calibre would react to me as captain. Evans's reply typified the man. "We'll all be behind you, master. Give yourself everything you've got and we'll all give you a hand."

I accepted. After the first season *Wisden* gratuitously reported: "Even the astute captaincy of Cowdrey, who led them for the first time, failed to inspire Kent. They finished thirteenth, a rise of only three places compared with the previous year."

At that time there was little prospect of a successful run with Kent because of the fifteen players only half were fully established. Even to consider winning a championship title with unseasoned resources was a pointless dream.

Happily, the Kent Committee agreed to my request for a cricket manager and our choice could not have been better. Leslie Ames, one of the great figures of Kent cricket, had retired from the game to run a hotel in Hastings and sports-equipment businesses in Maidstone and Gillingham. He was persuaded to return as "manager", a post unknown in county cricket at that time. Here was a recent player of international repute who had the respect of my most senior players. This proved invaluable. So began a friendship and partnership that, eventually, was to bring the success that looked so unobtainable in those early days. We knew it was going to be a long haul and agreed, ironically, that it would probably be the 1970s before we would be set to become the champion county of England.

We were starting from scratch in almost every aspect of cricket management. The first priority was to find players, for unlike Yorkshire or Lancashire, who at the crook of a finger could beckon any one of two dozen very capable cricketers out of the leagues, we were not producing enough talent in our own county.

The Association of Kent Cricket Clubs, the brain-child of Bryan Valentine, had been formed in 1950, and was just beginning to bring results in the shape of promising schoolboys. Jack Overy, their devoted secretary, can now look back over two decades of service to Kent cricket and his part in unearthing some of our famous names, Alan Knott among them. Kent owes a huge debt to Claude Lewis for the hours of coaching and the influence he exerted over the young. Where would we be without the zeal of Colin Page, now happily the Kent cricket manager in succession to Leslie Ames. It meant searching behind every sight screen and roller in Kent, and the winter after my first season as captain I attended 164 social functions, not just to talk but more to listen and learn about Kent cricket in the clubs and schools. This was time well spent.

Our grounds, too, gave little indication that county cricket had reached the twentieth century. The contrast between our facilities and those of Surrey at the Oval, for example, was about as stark as that between a fourth division football club and Highbury. At the Oval the team had a spacious dressing room while Stuart Surridge and Peter May not only had a room to themselves but a steward to clean their boots, carry their suits to the cleaners and bring a gin and tonic for any guest who might call in for a chat. At Canterbury, meanwhile, Kent's players were getting splinters in their feet off a dressing room floor that had been roughed up by the studs of Frank Woolley. There were a couple of antiquated showers in each dressing room, and one bath, if you could wait long enough for the water to emerge from Harbledown—none too warm. On the historical Bat and Ball ground at Gravesend the dressing room was no bigger than a beach hut, and we took it in turns to change. An individual peg for each player was out of the question. Gillingham, Blackheath and Tunbridge Wells were not a lot better. Maidstone, Folkestone and Dover were the closest we came to having a luxury ground but they, by most other county standards, were old fashioned. Several of our players solemnly believed that Kent could never win a championship playing on nine different grounds with such variable conditions. It was as if we were always playing away.

In the year before I became captain we showed a loss of £12,000. This was soon arrested but it took us five years to create a presentable team of cricketers who had a real chance of winning matches. Confidence could only come with experience. That was precisely how it worked out. In 1963 we finished thirteenth but I felt confident enough at the next annual general meeting to tell our members: "We have now got a team of good cricketers. My biggest problem is to lead that team on to the field and convince them that they can actually *win* something. Mostly they are young, immature and inexperienced, though we have a young Test cricketer or two on the horizon. But at last we stand a chance."

In 1964 we had our first breakthrough. We finished seventh. In 1965, and again in 1966, we were fifth. The following year we were runners-up to Yorkshire for the title and won the Gillette Cup, our first major prize. In 1968 we were runners-up to Yorkshire again, winning more matches than they did but being beaten in the end on bonus points. It seemed then that 1969 could be our year. What I had not calculated for, however, was snapping my tendon in the third week of that season. We won nothing, so all our hopes were vested in 1970, our Centenary Year.

If Edward Heath had high hopes of us for that year, few others did after two months of the season had elapsed. On July 1st all was gloom. We were bottom of the Championship table with 58 points. Surrey were then leading with 126. Our mid-week crowds were dwindling away, disenchanted with our performances after promising so much. Through no fault of mine I was involved again in the public discussion on the England captaincy, which did not help. I was still only just regaining full fitness after that injury thirteen months previously. Then came the ultimate catastrophe: a disastrous exit from the Gillette Cup at Canterbury. It was one of those days that happen in the game of cricket, but to be honest there was no excuse. At Canterbury we bowled Sussex out for a reasonably low score and then, from the very start of our own innings, threw our chances away with quite spectacular determination. Our opening batsmen, Brian Luckhurst and Mike Denness, made a sound but slow start. We fell behind the clock and the pressure came on to the other batsmen. Someone had to produce the innings of a lifetime and it did not materialise. The Sussex bowling improved and the fielding was superb. They could hardly believe their luck as they ran out easy winners.

We were bitterly disappointed, particularly our two opening batsmen, both of whom were to play such huge roles later in the summer. Little did we realise that this was to be the most significant thing that had happened to Kent cricket for more than half a century.

We had two days off, and we called a team meeting to air our problems, learn from our mistakes and, maybe, start afresh. This I did at Maidstone on the evening of the first day of our next match, against Derbyshire. I began the discussion by saying: "At last we have a team as good as any in the country. Yet here we are on the floor, not getting the bonus points we are capable of and not winning matches. Everyone must make a contribution. If anyone has something to get off his chest, please speak out. I want everything aired and the decks cleared so that we can settle down to good cricket." Leslie Ames produced an old-fashioned broadside for good measure and every player had valuable points to raise. The team appeared to be at one again and we turned our attention to the tasks in hand. How were we going to get out of trouble? The first thing we agreed was to go hell-for-leather for bonus points. I may be overstating the case, but I shall always think that the spirit generated in that meeting provided the basis for our winning the Championship.

In that match against Derbyshire we scored more than a hundred runs an hour to win. I then left to play in the Test match at Birmingham and returned somewhat drained after the publicity of the captaincy saga. However, at Hove in Kent's next match it was the fun in the dressing room that cheered me. We were met with a green wicket. I won the toss and would have put Sussex in had the weather forecast not been so unpromising. Instead we batted and might easily have been all out by lunch. We lost two wickets immediately and the third ball I got from John Snow singed my hairline. Buss was swinging the ball about in circles and I gave two sharp, stinging chances. But luck was with me. Luckhurst and I somehow survived until lunch and then, in the afternoon, batted well. On the following day we played Sussex in a Sunday league match and won. On Monday we resumed the Championship match and almost bowled Sussex out twice in the day. We won by an innings and were beginning the long climb up the Championship table. I was gratified that my innings on a difficult wicket had played a part.

The real climax started with exactly a month to go in the season. After an overnight drive in torrential floods we arrived at Weston-super-Mare at two forty-five in the morning to play Somerset. Later that day I lost a toss I was most anxious to win and we had to go into the field. Somerset made a fine start. The lunch score was ominous. Then Bob Woolmer bowled them out brilliantly. By now we were bonus points crazy, with batsmen streaking between the wickets in pursuit of an extra batting point and bowlers going after tail-end batsmen as if they were openers, in search of an extra fielding point. It was in this frenzied atmosphere during our victory over Somerset that I pulled a muscle. This presented a personal problem as the final Test at the Oval was about to start. I was certainly not a hundred per cent fit to play there, but I played and got away with it. In my absence and without Luckhurst, Knott and Shepherd, Kent played Gloucestershire at Cheltenham and achieved another superb win. Seemingly out of the game for the best part of two days, Kent needed 340 to win on the final day and got them on a wicket-taking spin. Underwood had taken eleven wickets in the match. Denness set up the victory with a fine captain's innings of 97 and Asif produced a glorious hundred.

In the space of a month, therefore, the pressures on every Kent player turned full circle. After the despair of worrying about survival we were now serious contenders in the Championship race. It was during that month, while batting with Asif against Middlesex at Canterbury, I happened to say to him: "What a tragedy the season isn't a week longer. We would win the title the way we are playing now." Asif looked at me in astonishment. "No, no skipper," he said. "You've got it wrong. We've got enough time. If it was any longer we would get stale. I've already told Mike Denness. We shall win it in our last match at the Oval. Nothing could be more certain than that. You'll see." I enjoyed his enthusiasm but I must confess that my belief in the power of Oriental mysticism did not quite extend to sharing Asif's confidence. But nothing would shake him. Not a day passed without his sharing his joy with the entire team: "There's nothing to worry about. We'll all be drinking champagne at the Oval."

Happily Asif's prophetic ability was matched, at this time, by his cricketing talent. He batted superbly well against Middlesex, Somerset and Gloucestershire, scoring his runs at a devastating pace. Then against Surrey at Blackheath, he not only played an innings of a lifetime with a whole galaxy of astounding shots in his 106, but won the match in the closing minutes with nerve-racking aplomb. We had picked up a large harvest of points but that was not enough. We had to win the match as well. This had been a very promising match for our young all-round cricketer Graham Johnson, who had taken six wickets for 35 with his off-spinners. He had a long spell in the second innings and when the last pair of Surrey batsmen looked to be winning the match, he trapped the final wicket to finish with match figures of twelve for 151—his first major contribution as a bowler. With only seven balls to go Surrey needed twelve to win with the last pair in. Off the fifth ball of the last-but-one over Pat Pocock opened out to hit Graham Johnson for six. He connected beautifully. It was an interesting situation as we watched the ball in the air. If that shot went for six Surrey would require six runs off the last over to win a match that would have kept them above us in the table. So, the Championship could be decided by the fate of that shot flying out to the boundary in the now failing light. We had only one fielder out in the deep, none other than our Pakistani prophet. Asif took off from wide-mid-on like an Olympic sprinter, ran fully forty-five yards, threw up his hand and caught as remarkable a catch as I have seen in cricket. It would have been six. Now, we had won. We moved up to third place in the table above Surrey.

There were three matches to go, against Nottinghamshire and Leicestershire at Folkestone, and against Surrey at the Oval. When Leslie Ames and I examined the wickets at Folkestone our hearts sank. Here we were in sight of the title and what we were looking at were two of the most beautiful pitches ever prepared in Kent. They had "draw" written all over them. "At least we shan't have people accusing us of fiddling our wickets," said Ames. "Still, if you lose the toss twice you might just have a chance of coming in from behind on the final days." It seemed that some of Asif's prophetic genius had rubbed off on our extremely English secretary-manager.

I lost the toss against Nottinghamshire and Gary Sobers hit us from Folkestone to Boulogne. They scored 371 for three and deprived us of all but one bonus point. On the Monday we were at one stage 20 for five. But one of the survivors was Luckhurst, who not only stayed there but emerged from that crisis with 157. Alan Ealham won his county cap that day by holding out with Luckhurst, making 57 and getting us back into the game. On the final day Sobers set us a fairly tough declaration target: 282 at 93 an hour. This time it was Mike Denness who led the way. We won in the last over, and Alan Knott kept his head very well in the last few minutes.

I again lost the toss against Leicestershire. They reached 100 for two and were then all out for 150. It gave us five valuable bowling points, for at that time Lancashire were just ahead of us in the race, with Glamorgan well ahead of them. It inspired us to go after batting bonus points as we never had before. With six of our eighty-five overs still to come we were 278 for four, the launching point for one of the most blazing attacks seen anywhere that summer. We not only passed the 300 for another bonus point but, with seven balls to go, reached 328 for yet another with John Shepherd and Johnson batting together. The prospects of getting still one more were so remote that I went to take a shower. It was at this point that Shepherd flashed a shot over the slips for four which meant that we were 18 runs short of 350 and our thirteenth bonus point of the match at the start of the eighty-fifth over. My shower was interrupted by an enormous roar. Johnson had hit the first ball of that over out of the ground. He then hooked a four and took a single: 343 with three balls to go. Shepherd threw his bat at the first and missed. The second, off the back foot, he struck straight into the pavilion for six. There was now one ball to go with one run needed. Shepherd deposited it over the covers for four. Eight batting points. We won the match and took 23 points. Once again I was mindful of that team meeting at Maidstone. What a transition from our cricket earlier in the season.

That huge haul of points removed a great deal of the pressure from our final match at the Oval. I calculated that we did not even need to win. Five bonus points would be enough to win us the Championship.

If the casual reader finds this repeated reference to bonus points confusing he is not alone. On the Sunday afternoon before that final match at the Oval, Kent's league match against Hampshire at Bournemouth was being televised and one of the viewers was Edward Heath, watching the match from Chequers. A few minutes after I was out I was called to the Hampshire secretary's office to take a telephone call. The Prime Minister said: "I have been trying to work out how many bonus points we need to win at the Oval. How many do you think we need to be certain?" My answer was to invite him to the Oval to see for himself. He was good enough to say he would try to come to Friday afternoon's play.

I won the toss and it was not an easy decision. I would have liked to have batted but the wicket was grassy. I could not back Kent to score more than 200 on it which would only bring two points. On the other hand I was anxious in case Surrey, who had no reason to give us anything, might declare at a very low score to deprive us of the chance of getting bowling bonus points. In the end I took the gamble and put them in. In fact we got them to 159 for nine before Stewart declared to deprive us of a fifth point. This meant that we still needed some batting points to be certain of the championship and most gratifyingly for me, at the end of a season of at least one huge disappointment, I scored a century on a difficult wicket. It was one of the best innings I have played in England and it came at a time when we had lost three wickets for 86 and by some strange irony Asif, who had for so long been predicting this as the scene of our ultimate triumph, could hardly hit the ball off the square. But he stuck there tenaciously and, in the end, we achieved eight points from the match which I believed would put us safe.

Lancashire would have had to score 27 points from their final match of the season to catch us. Even with Clive Lloyd in their ranks I did not believe they could do it. There was nothing left in the game for the spectators except for the Kent supporters who sat blissfully happy in the knowledge that after fifty-seven years their county was again the champion county of all England.

Edward Heath, the man who had defied the public opinion polls to win his way to Downing Street, joined us to celebrate his own double forecast of many months earlier. It was only a brief respite for him in a full diary and his chauffeur had been warned that there might be a quick dash to the Oval. He arrived wearing his Kent Centenary tie, shared our champagne and extended an invitation to the players and wives to a celebration dinner at No. 10. Somehow he was able to keep an evening free and provided an occasion none of us will forget.

During that last day of the match I was asked to meet the press at the Oval to talk about what, in the end, had been a remarkable Championship recovery—bottom in July but top in September. One of the questions asked was: "When do you intend to pack up?" Most sportsmen, I suppose, would have had a pretty speech prepared for that nostalgic moment. I had nothing prepared because I had never thought about it. But I found myself saying, "I shall retire from the Kent captaincy at the end of the 1971 season." It was a reflex reply which, on reflection, has proved to be wise. It was time for a new face, a new hand and fresh ideas. There is a right time to close.

# 30

My fifth and last tour of Australia, or so I thought, under Illingworth was something of an anti-climax. Try as I did, and that probably was the trouble, I tried too hard, I just could not get going with the bat. The first two Tests I batted for several hours, time to have got well set, but I failed to dominate. On each of the four previous trips I had scored heavily and made a Test hundred each time, but now it was not to be and it was most disappointing. It was a successful tour in that we won the Ashes before large crowds. Ray Illingworth handled things on the field with his customary dexterity and he bowled particularly well when the pressure was on. He was notably well served by fast bowler John Snow, whilst Bob Willis, flying out as a replacement for injured Alan Ward made a great impression on his first major tour.

The spotlight often seemed to centre on Snow who saved himself for the big occasion and bowled with tremendous hostility and power when it really mattered. He is a beautiful athlete and his perfect rhythm gives him real speed. His success determined the fate of the series. The Australian crowds took exception to the team's demeanour on the field once or twice, finding Ray Illingworth's unprecedented walk-off at Sydney hard to understand.

My Kent colleagues, Brian Luckhurst, Derek Underwood and Alan Knott all made exciting contributions, much to the delight of our Kent manager, David Clark.

I enjoyed my last few weeks in New Zealand. No warmer hosts are there anywhere, and I derived a lot of pleasure from two good innings in the last Test match in Auckland. This seemed to set me up for the summer ahead and I got off to a wonderful start for Kent. I only played fourteen innings but scored 600 runs. Just as I had visions of clinching an England place again I was struck down with a most serious bout of pneumonia. I was rushed to hospital and was under special care for a few days. I was not to play again that year and on rather a sad note relinquished the captaincy after fifteen eventful years. I had seen the foundations well laid and it was a consolation to feel that I was handing a team over to Michael Denness the equal of any in the land.

1972 and 1973 were years of Kent superiority, with Warwickshire Lancashire and Surrey our real rivals. In the event, all four teams had their complement of international players to release and this imbalance, however good the reserves, made all the difference in the winning of prizes. The clash of Test matches with sizeable chunks of the domestic programme is inevitable in the short season of an English summer, and sides like Hampshire and Worcestershire, who provide few Test players, have been at an advantage. In fact, Hampshire have been clever enough to have Barry Richards and Andy Roberts available most of the time and both are match winners in their own right.

Kent and Lancashire have been promoters' dream sides in recent years, with so many exciting personalities. The crowds who have flocked to these matches at Old Trafford or Lord's will have memories to last a lifetime. If you were lucky enough to see Asif's innings in a Gillette Final at Lord's, or Clive Lloyd's in the World Cup Final, these were pure gold. Sobers is the greatest cricketer of my time, undoubtedly, but Barry Richards is possibly the best batsman of this last decade. Greg Chappell is now at the height of his powers and looks like being the best batsman of the next decade. It is time that England produced another Hutton, Compton or Peter May again to lead the field. How does one compare Richards and Chappell with those three champions? I don't know.

1973 holds the memory for me, of course, of my 99th and 100th hundreds and a cheeky 29 in the Benson and Hedges' Final at Lord's. In 1974 I was as fit as I have ever been, batting and catching with a sharpness that surprised myself. I hooked Andy Roberts for an exciting four on a wicket of uneven bounce at Basingstoke, and was promptly felled by his next ball. I took the ball on my chin, spreadeagled my stumps (and so was bowled) cracked a few teeth and took an involuntary count of about a hundred and ten. But I was playing really well again a few days later and was being written into the MCC team to tour Australia, as one of the best six batsmen in England. I felt in good enough form to justify that and I have to admit I was a disappointed man not to be selected in the original party. Of course I was thrilled to be called in later, but one needs three weeks to acclimatise to Australian conditions. It was infuriating to have to try to do this in three days.

This recall to the country's colours, and the last I presume, was as dramatic as any in the history of the game. I was forty-one when the MCC side, led by Kent's Mike Denness, were so struck by injuries in the face of truly fast bowling that they sent for help. It is warming to know that the players themselves sat down around their hotel room one evening and chose the man to help them out. It was a superb compliment, at least that is how I felt it.

So at the drop of a hat I left for Perth on the Saturday and arrived very early on Monday morning after a twenty-four hour break in Bombay. I went straight to bed and woke up to work out how I could get fit for early action. To my surprise it looked as if I might be called upon to play in the second Test at Perth, which was just four days away. The team went off to play against a country eleven at Geraldton when I took to the nets, on Tuesday, Wednesday and Thursday.

Tuesday was very hot indeed. I was in the net by nine-thirty but had to pack it in an hour later. I took catches with batting gloves on my hands to try to break them in again without doing damage to joints. I was out later in the coolest part of the afternoon, until the sun went down, and again retired to my room to do my sums on the injuries and possibilities. Yes, I could well play. Dennis Amiss and John Edrich were both injured. On Wednesday, obviously, I had to take some sun, so I went out early; then again at 1 p.m. just for twenty-five minutes. I showered, and retreated to the cool until five p.m. I was exceptionally fortunate in having volunteers of the highest ability to help me prepare. Tony Lock was marvellous. Graham McKenzie, too, at home to rest from his labours with Leicestershire, came to bowl, and let himself go. He pitched it up for a while and then shouted out, "Short one coming" and he whacked the ball hard into the ground. I still dared not take high catches, though I had to settle for being hit the odd time in the net. I suppose

222

it is all part of the sharpening-up process.

Now it is Friday, the first day of the Test. I *have* to play, it has been decided, and the morning paper leads with the story of how I will most likely be tucked away, down the order, at number 6. The game is not discussed much among the team. Before the start I stroll back from the nets, chatting to a couple of Englishmen, spared the tensions of knowing that I am going in early. The toss is ours. We are to bat, that is settled, when here comes Mike Denness to me to enquire: "How do you feel like batting number 3?" It is like a dream now.

It might have been a good thing. Brian Luckhurst and David Lloyd stayed for just over an hour, when Brian was out. So in I went to join David Lloyd. I had never batted with him before, and quite honestly did not know him at all well. The score was in the forties and I had to play Walker who was bowling into the breeze. David Lloyd then did something which I will never tire of recalling for all to know. He walked down to me and said that he would take Lillee, who was really running, bursting himself downwind, producing tremendous pace and bounce. And David did exactly that for three consecutive overs. What a generous thing to do! We had some fun out there too, as the odd one from Lillee and Thomson flew past and over our heads. "If they'd only drop one or two short I could hook 'em!" David would say. It was challenging and stimulating cricket, very much the way I learned to bat with Peter May, the game so much more fulfilling. Unfortunately, David was badly hit in that match.

That day I managed to last out 125 minutes for my 22 (Lloyd got 49) and was glad when Monday, the rest day, came so that I could get back to the nets again for a little more accclimatisation. Sadly, Luckhurst's hand, so badly bruised in the first innings, showed up on X-ray with broken bones. Who would open in the second innings?

By a process of elimination it fell to me, although I was not to know that until tea time, about half an hour before being launched into it. The Perth wicket is one of the fastest in the world and this was a torrid experience as I remember. Thanks to the "Fremantle Doctor", a still breeze which tends to blow down the wicket, the real pace and hostility can only be hurled at you from one end. This is quite a relief. Anyway, David Lloyd and I battled away, but in the end we were well and truly beaten by fast bowling.

In Melbourne, Sydney and Adelaide, the batsmen struggled to

dampen the fire of Lillee and Thomson. Walker and Mallett played vital supporting roles and they were an underrated attack. Yet their batting was suspect and I always felt that if we could make 400 somewhere we would win a match. In fact, this happened at Melbourne; we looked the superior side. But it has to be admitted that Thomson was injured, and with the series decided there is always an element of tension missing, like playing for the bye in a golf match.

Attendances were good and the interest created by these two speedsters provided a much needed fillip to the game in Australia. The crowds have always been vociferous in that part of the world. But the "tin can chorus" which used to strike up mid-afternoon, the banging together of empty beer cans at the slightest excuse, was a new and unattractive feature of a Test match day. The brewers are now considering a plastic-type container to muffle the cymbals.

If I did not have a lion's share, at least I was part of an England Test match victory against Australia in this my last Test match, on the ground, too, which with Lord's, Sabina Park and Canterbury, has always seemed to mean happy hunting for me. It was during this match that a few folk made up a banner, at considerable expense, as a farewell salute to me and, to use their words, a mark of affection. How could I show my appreciation? I was quite overcome.

Thus, my Test career began and ended in Australia. Indeed, those six tours mean that I have spent nearly three years there, more time than I spent at Oxford. Because of the distance involved, I probably know my way round Australia better than many Australians, and if ever I return I shall always feel at home.

1975 was the most glorious summer, with the most continuous sunshine and good weather of all the years I have played. The Prudential World Cup and the short Test series against Australia proved a successful replacement to the cancelled visit of South Africa, and these in addition to the four-tournament domestic season. The Championship, the Benson and Hedges, the Gillette and the John Player, made it a full season. In terms of finance it meant a share-out of £625,000 to the counties at the end of the year.

After I had announced my retirement from Kent cricket, I longed for one more good innings at Canterbury. The gods smiled. It has been the pattern of my cricketing life that my moments of success have usually come just when the signs are least auspicious. There was little atmosphere on the last day of the match against Australia. Defeat stared us in the face although the wicket was still full of runs. We got off to a poor start and at lunch time Ian Chappell told the coach driver to be ready at four p.m. to drive them across country into Hampshire. "We have ordered dinner in the hotel at Southampton."

However, it proved to be my day. Everything went right, and it was one of the best innings I have ever played. At tea time we had just the glimmer of a chance of victory, although 354 still looked a good way off. 85 in the last hour is always on if wickets are not sacrificed and we stormed home, for the first time since 1899. The Australians missed their dinner, too, arriving at Southampton nigh on midnight. We got our total for the loss of six wickets and at the end of that second innings the scoreboard read: M. C. Cowdrey 151 not out and R. A. Woolmer 71 not out.

It was an eventful week for the Cowdrey family. My eldest boy, Christopher, captain of Tonbridge, made a hundred and chose his younger brother, Jeremy, aged fifteen, to play in the Tonbridge eleven for the first time as a leg-break bowler; whilst Minimus, eleven year old Graham, at Wellesley House made 48, his top score for the first eleven, and my wife, Penny, made 18, easily her top score, for the Mothers in an adjoining pitch. Away in Bexhill, my daughter, Carolyn, who has had more than her fair share of fielding and bowling and all too little chance with the bat, was playing some gentle tennis. Very sensible, too.

# 31

Despite all the forays and hurly-burly of my involvement in the Test match scene, my heart and roots have always been firmly in the County of Kent. It is hardly surprising that having played twenty-five full seasons for Kent, fifteen of them as their captain, I feel that part of me will always be on the St. Lawrence Ground at Canterbury.

I sat next to Frank Woolley in his eighty-sixth year, on the players' balcony, watching Kent bat. A wicket fell and halted our conversation mid-sentence. "How would you like to be going in now, Frank?" I asked. With a broad smile and a little chuckle, his head erect and commanding, his clear blue eyes lit up and he looked forty years younger. In his expression I could see why he put the fear of God into all bowlers.

58,969 runs, 2,068 wickets, 913 catches, 145 first-class hundreds— so much success came his way, yet we must not think of him in figures alone. It was the aura of his personality, like a magnet, which drew people out of the villages and along the country lanes to see him on Kent grounds.

Having survived a number of years in the grey of the tunnel, before the light of the sixties started to open up and bring us all so much fun, my experiences are something of a contrast to his. Yes, I have scaled the peaks occasionally; I have a number of high spots to remember and savour, but the memories of our tough days, building, faltering and setting out afresh have left their mark. Every morning, whenever Kent are playing, I shall have a tremor of anticipation about the day ahead. And as I sit on the players' balcony and watch a Kent wicket fall I expect my heart will beat a little faster and I will find my hand reaching out in one involuntary movement for my cap, bat and gloves. It has been my life.

Kent, with Surrey, Sussex and Hampshire saw the early beginnings of cricket, the country squire entertaining on his estate and the village cricket scene at the weekends. When the County Championship was under way, Kent were always acknowledged as one of the Big Six with Lancashire, Yorkshire, Surrey, Nottinghamshire and Gloucestershire. Cricket seems to have been as strong in the villages of Kent as anywhere in England, and eventually the dominating figure of Lord Harris focussed attention upon us. Cricket was his first love and he lived for the county of Kent. Later, as Treasurer of MCC, he ruled English cricket with a warm heart, if an iron hand. He could not tolerate second best and inevitably Kent cricketers were to have considerable influence in the early part of this century. He was very much the central figure in the traditional Canterbury Week, renowned throughout the cricket world, which became one of the social occasions of an English summer.

It was into this background that I had the privilege of being put through my paces as a young Tonbridge schoolboy. The Yorkshiremen try to convince me how tough a school theirs is, but nothing could have been more primitive than the facilities at Canterbury when I started, nor more severe and unyielding than the discipline imposed under secretary Gerald Hough and professional coach Punter Humphreys, a fine cricketer in his day. Neither would take any nonsense from pip-squeaks. I was there to listen and learn and to do what I was told. In every sense of the word the game was bigger than the player. I hope it will still be so a hundred years from now.

We have always had the philosophy of taking county cricket around the county of Kent and, in consequence, we play on more grounds than anybody else, with traditional Weeks in the main centres. Gone, alas, is the Angel ground at Tonbridge, the home and headquarters of Kent cricket before we moved to Canterbury after the First World War. Tonbridge Week was quite something but was not to survive after 1946. The Nevill at Tunbridge Wells, a picturesque ground completely enclosed by foliage with its colourful bank of rhododendrons in the spring, gave me my first view of Kent cricket at home. As a schoolboy I sneaked away on two half-holiday afternoons and in my excitement to miss as little of the play as possible the bus seemed as if it would never get there. I purred with pleasure when Bryan Valentine recognised me in my "barge", my Tonbridge straw hat, as he led the team on to the field after tea. Bryan Valentine was more than just a gifted sportsman; he was a lovable personality; he was an England cricketer in his own right, a fine soccer player, and as a schoolboy at Repton a better tennis player than Bunny Austin. He went with the England side to South Africa in 1938–39 and just as his England career was about to blossom, the outbreak of war brought it all to an end. Happily for him, and more so for Kent cricket, his influence was brought to bear as captain for three seasons, 1946–48. Whenever Bryan Valentine was playing there was gaiety and laughter, coupled with the right balance of tough cricket on the field, and it is to my regret that I never had the fun of playing with him for Kent.

Canterbury, from the first innings I played there as a fifteen-year-old, has always been kind to me. There were several occasions in my career when I came to the Canterbury Week weary and almost despairing of my game, only to find my cup over-flowing a few days later. Today in Brian Fitch we have one of the best young groundsmen in England and he keeps the ground looking like a new pin.

Is there a more glorious ground than The Mote at Maidstone? It has something of the dignity and peace of Arundel. Year after year I looked forward to it with great anticipation—always seemed to bat well but never came away with a significant innings. Just as time was beginning to run out, and I was called on to bat in the unlikely position of number seven, Malcolm Bristow—again one of the best groundsmen in the land—must have given these two wickets an extra roll of luck for me, for in four days, I scored against Somerset my 99th and against Surrey my hundredth hundred. The picture on the scoreboard showing 99 against my name in that last innings sent my heart beating faster than the medical profession would have liked. Asif and I met for a chat in the middle of the wicket. With a typical feel for the situation he said: "Just keep your eye on the ball and push it anywhere and I will run." There was no possible chance of a single, or so it seemed, when I pushed the ball straight to cover, but before I could make a decision Asif was almost arriving in my crease. All I had to do was scramble to the other end somehow. What a magnificent partner to have at that moment.

Gillingham by contrast is less glamorous, but in the seat of the Medway towns it is wonderfully supported, especially in those early years when we were building up the interest again. It holds a fine memory for me because I was to score two hundreds in the same match against Essex and some important championship victories, albeit on poor quality wickets. Alas, the wicket is adjudged not good enough for us to play there now; we badly need a venue in that part of the county and I hope we shall be able to return there one day.

The Bat and Ball at Gravesend is full of tradition and rich in memories, mainly of Frank Woolley's prodigious six-hitting. If at times our crowds found the seating primitive and slightly un-comfortable, there was a cosiness about this little ground as they basked in the run-feasts, for it really was a fast-scoring ground. I scored my first fifty for Kent at Gravesend and played well enough to set the tongues wagging. A few years later I was to score 198 against Lancashire before Brian Statham, who was staying with me throughout the match, knocked my stumps flying. However, I invited him again! As at Gillingham, county cricket is suspended here for the time being.

Traditionally, Blackheath has become known as the Surrey grave-yard, but in my time Surrey were a magnificent side and there was not much cricket expected on the third day as they demolished us so easily. Happily, we were to put that right once or twice before the end of my days as captain, and there against Essex I made 250, my highest score for Kent. Blackheath, like Gillingham and Gravesend is under suspension for the time being because it was adjudged that the wickets were not good enough for first-class cricket. However, a lot of work is being done with all three grounds and I look forward to the day when they come under consideration again.

It was at the Crabble Ground, Dover, that I played my first match for Kent on a home ground. It has a unique setting, with balconies on different levels and the Kent dressing room providing an aerial view down the line of the ball. I can never look across the ground at the ring of pine trees without trying to re-live the day in 1937 when Kent were set to score 217 in 95 minutes, and made them in 71 minutes. In recent years, Sobers for Nottinghamshire and young Bernard Julien, Kent's Trinidadian all-rounder, have played innings there to make the gods smile. I have made a pair there, been left 99 not out, but can also boast two good hundreds. I would like to see bigger crowds at Dover, for it is a ground worth preserving and I associate it with cricket in August and holiday time.

Everyone enjoys Folkestone Week and one day we must revive the Folkestone Festival again. Here is another fast-scoring ground, with good light, a good view of the game for spectators, and plenty of car parking space. How was Leslie Ames so careless as to get out for 295 there? One of the reasons I still hope to keep playing first-class cricket is that Folkestone is the only ground in Kent where I have not made a hundred, much to the dismay of the second most famous set of twins in cricket, Len and Jack Godden, who are so well known in Folkestone.

There have been a lot of good matches at Dartford, at present the nearest ground to London. I recall some notable bowling performances, and Fred Ridgway's fifteen wickets in a match stands out like a beacon. I have scored 140 there twice, one of those innings brought to an abrupt halt by my vice-captain, Alan Dixon. A wicket had fallen and as he walked in past me in his usual cheerful way, he exhorted me to keep going and not to throw my wicket away. First ball, in his anxiety to get off the mark, he misjudged his call and ran me out by the length of the pitch. We are still good friends.

In fact, Alan Dixon, Colin Page, Derek Ufton, Stuart Leary and I all started together. Alan Dixon played for Kent as a sixteen-year-old and then took some while to settle into county cricket. I recall the day I gave him his county cap after he scored his maiden hundred at Worcester. He was a most useful dual-purpose bowler, a slow off-spinner and a medium-pace seamer whose eight for 15 against Surrey at the Oval still stands as the best bowling performance in the Gillette Cup. He was a tireless cover-point and a most loyal vice-captain. With the premature death of Ray Dovey who had managed the school shop and been cricket coach at Tonbridge for fifteen years, Alan now follows him, and all Tonbridgians will wish him a long, happy stay.

No one has worked harder for Kent cricket than Colin Page. He began as an opening bowler who moved the ball appreciably in the air. He had prodigious powers of spin in his fingers and he became a good off-spinner in later years. He has captained the second eleven with great energy and as Leslie Ames's successor he has an important role to play in our future.

The two ex-Charlton footballers, Derek Ufton and Stuart Leary, had rather frustrated cricket seasons, arriving late and leaving early. Derek was an able reserve to Godfrey Evans when he was on Test duty and was good enough to play for Kent as a batsman. There was something of George Best in Stuart Leary's football and he was a gifted cricketer, too. He was one of the best close-fielders of my time and a useful leg-spinner. Most of all I am grateful to him for the fund of humour which lay behind a dead-pan face. This was worth its weight in gold.

In my first years as captain Arthur Phebey and Bob Wilson, right-hander and left-hander, forged a really good opening partnership together. Bob Wilson was a magnificent out-fielder; in fact, Phebey, Wilson and Dixon were three genuine county cricketers whom one would love to have seen enjoying some representative cricket.

Alan Brown and David Sayer were good attacking fast bowlers in their day, whilst David Halfyard came to us from Surrey, travelled round England on a scooter and managed to take a hundred wickets most years.

In my formative years with the county I was helped a great deal in different ways by the four England players, Douglas Wright, Godfrey Evans, Arthur Fagg and Fred Ridgway. To stand at slip while Doug Wright was bowling was an education. He was an easy-going companion, always charitable, yet the hardest possible task-master with himself. No one in my experience has practised or trained harder in the nets. Godfrey Evans was at his peak and was just one long, continuous ball of fire, on and off the field. As he came towards the end of his career I spent time studying him, for I never thought we would see his like again. I do not see how anyone could be better than Godfrey Evans was on his day and I can pay no higher compliment to Alan Knott when I say there are many days when he is clearly as good.

Naturally I learned a lot batting with Arthur Fagg. He was shrewd in his assessment of a situation and he has become one of our finest umpires. Fred Ridgway was an under-rated fast bowler. Short and stocky, he got a surprising amount of lift out of the wicket. It was a tragedy from his point of view that we were short of class bowling during his time and he tended to be bowled for rather over-long spells.

There were a number of others, good cricketers too, who made occasional appearances and it was fun to have played alongside them. I think of Tony Pawson and Jack Davies, both magnificent fielders, Tony Mallett, Alan Shireff and Geoff Smith, three opening bowlers who shared the load with Ridgway. I think of Peter Hearn, Dickie Mayes, Ted Witherden and John Prodger, all good batsmen. There were two University players, John Pretlove and Jimmy Allan from Oxford and our first Scotsman. He had the distinction of scoring two hundreds in a match against Northamptonshire.

Behind all this was the warm and genial figure of Claude Lewis, capped by Kent in the early thirties as a good little slow left-arm bowler, now our scorer, but in my early days captain of the second eleven and coach. It was he who met me at the barrier of Liverpool Street Station on our way to Norwich for my first second eleven match and took me under his wing. He has done so much for the young players in Kent for twenty years and more.

The years of triumph became possible only with the development of a host of good players together. I do not need to elaborate on the opening batting partnership of Denness and Luckhurst, and they both went on to become distinguished Test cricketers in their own right; Underwood and Knott are household names and match winners. We could not have achieved so much without the all-round skill of Graham Johnson or the yeoman service that Norman Graham has given us. Catches and run-outs win matches, and Alan Ealham has produced these in abundance. With Alan Knott away so much on Test duties, his deputy had to be rather a special person, ideally someone who could bat as well. David Nicholls has accepted this peculiar role and has become a very good cricketer. When Peter Richardson came to leave Worcestershire and moved south, he chose Kent as a place to farm and to play cricket, and naturally his skill and gaiety have brought colour to the scene. We were disappointed to lose John Dye just as he was growing in stature, but I have high hopes of our most recent contribution to the England side. Bob Woolmer has been improving every year, a true all-rounder. If he can fill out a little, build stamina and retain fitness he should have a lot to give us and England as we look ahead.

I speak with the greatest possible warmth of our three friends from overseas, John Shepherd, Asif Iqbal and Bernard Julien. Leslie Ames and I were struck by the immense promise of young John Shepherd when we were touring Barbados in the early sixties. He served an apprenticeship with our second eleven and has become part and parcel of everything we have won. I am only sorry that he has not played more in Test cricket for he was clearly good enough to do so. Those who have travelled with him in South Africa recently speak in glowing terms of John Shepherd the ambassador, and it is in this field that he has a contribution to make when his competitive cricket days are over.

I could say all the same things, too, about Asif Iqbal. I do not think we could have won the Championship without him and John. We in Kent will follow Asif's time as captain of Pakistan with great pride.

Our latest acquisition from Trinidad, Bernard Julien, has been cruelly thwarted by quite serious injury. Much to his dismay, and the disappointment of us all in Kent, he has not yet been able to give us the full range of his powers. We admired his hundred for West Indies against England at Lord's, a show of astonishing maturity in one so young. For Kent, as yet, he keeps whetting our appetites with little cameos of brilliance, and for his sake we hope that he will have an injury-free period ahead so that West Indies, Trinidad and Kent share his genius.

In Kent, we are fortunate to have a number of distinguished cricket names, old players, to lean upon, always prepared to provide a wise word or helping hand. In my case there seem to be a host of people wishing me well, wanting it all to go right, whether it be Bryan Valentine, David Clark, Leslie Ames, "Hopper" Levett, Claude Lewis—and so I could go on. In the background, because he is such a busy man, are the warm interest and wonderful enthusiasm of the senior Kent captain, Lord Cornwallis. So often he would appear suddenly on the end of a telephone or convey a letter of great charm, never critical, often making a helpful suggestion or two, and always encouraging.

We have also been fortunate to have good treasurers in these times when solvency is elusive; first Leslie Gremer, and now Oliver Grace (now Band of Brothers Chief) have worked manfully behind the scenes. Happily another Tonbridge schoolboy, a fine cricketer in his younger day, is this year's excellent chairman of Kent cricket— Walter Brice.

This has been my life in the service of Kent cricket. Very humbling, never dull, truly rewarding.

# 32

Over the years the magic password of cricket has brought me some fascinating experiences and taken me to some unexpected places. After all, it is not every day of the week that one is invited to be the late Graham Hill's passenger, hurtling round the Brands Hatch track, swivelling round S-bends. Graham's death was a stunning blow to sportsmen everywhere and an irreparable loss to his family. He was a very special character.

It had become an annual event for the worthy sportsmen's charity Sparks that a number of sportsmen compete in a personality race as hors d'oeuvre to the Race of Champions. The prerequisite for competing was participation in two practice days beforehand with some official tuition from the Master himself. Thus, Richard Meade, Freddie Titmus and myself were to be seen clinging on to anything we could catch hold of as Graham Hill talked us round a dozen laps, travelling a little faster each time. Richard Meade was used to courses and circuits and acquitted himself well. But for several of us, Henry Cooper and myself in particular, our performance on the day in front of an enormous sea of faces was as sedately dignified as the London to Brighton.

All my life I have had a flirtation with the game of golf, devoted to cricket but always on the look-out for the chance of a few holes. As a young Tonbridge schoolboy I spent many hours of my winter holidays in Harry Weetman's shop at Croham Hurst, Croydon. At that time I lived on the side of the course and some days I would be there from dawn to dusk. I spent hours on the practice ground with him and remember special occasions when he would say, "Come on

I must get my irons going, we must play a few holes together." He could never understand why I spent so much time on the cricket field. "You want to leave school," he used to say, "forget all this bookwork and I will take you on as my assistant; I will have you in the Ryder Cup team by the time you are twenty-five." I used to laugh and was surprised that he was serious. I have often wondered what would have happened if I had taken him up on his offer. He became a good friend whom I followed very closely, and his premature death was an awful shock.

In my early days with Kent there was no Sunday cricket and Sunday afternoon was the time for golf, especially when we were away from home. On tour there are more days off from cricket than in England and I regarded golf as a healthy outlet, though I was wary of getting my swing too grooved. The games, technically speaking, are not complementary.

In South Africa in 1956 we spent some happy hours playing with Bobby Locke who adored cricket. One of his pupils was Gary Player just setting out on his career. It was fun to see master and protégé together in contrasting stages of their lives.

It is fascinating how cricketers catch the golf bug and vice versa. Sam King, doyen of Knole Park and Ryder Cup veteran, adores watching Kent cricket, provided he can sit behind the bowler's arm, incognito and in total silence. Nothing must disturb his concentration as he feasts on every move. When I want to illustrate the true professional sportsman, I always refer to Sam, superlative match player, always the gentleman, with his soft, quiet manner.

Another golfer-cricketer, a left-handed batsman, is Australian Peter Thomson, five times British Open champion. He turned his back on cricket at the age of fifteen and chose golf. He knows as much about cricket as most cricketers. He came down to Chislehurst to play in a charity match for me one day and I guaranteed him half an hour at the wicket and at least double figures. I was batting with him when his half hour was up and he had had a fair share of fun. The opposition captain signalled to his bowlers that it was time to bowl him out. This they proceeded to do but not before he had got a very good hundred!

The three best cricketer-golfers are probably Arthur Milton, Tom Graveney and Ted Dexter. I was Ted's caddy when Australian Norman von Nida invited Jack Nicklaus and Gary Player to have a look at Ted. This took place at the Kooyonga Golf Club at Adelaide on the day before the Australian Open. Ted was somewhat erratic but he produced enough brilliant strokes to send the distinguished champions into a huddle. We all dined together that evening, and a fascinating exchange of sports gossip preceded a quite serious invitation to Ted to give up cricket, settle in the United States and make a concentrated bid to become a tournament golfer. This little triumvirate would be his sponsor and tutor. Just as my imagination was running away with me with visions of being Ted's permanent travelling caddy, with homes in various parts of the world, Ted dismissed the idea with the disdain with which he usually dismissed fast bowling.

In 1968 two sportsmen moved house, quite independently, to arrive in Limpsfield as neighbours, and Brian Huggett and I have forged a real friendship. This was strengthened when he was kind enough to invite me to partner him in a Foursome Pro-Am at Turnberry Golf Course in the autumn of 1969. I was recovering from my ruptured achilles tendon and walking on the golf course was the best therapy. After six dramatic rounds in torrential rain and gale force wind we ran out winners. I could write a small book on some of the problems I set my partner, but as he is still of sound mind they are probably best left forgotten. It was a great experience and, moreover, it has given me a closer insight into a fine British sportsman with a perfect temperament.

Golf at Oxford was enormous fun. I did not get a Blue but I played a number of times for the University. Prince R. K. Pitamber from Nepal, captain one year, gave me every encouragement. I had the fun of visiting many well-known golf courses for the first time, of playing with Henry Cotton and Leonard Crawley, and sitting next to Bernard Darwin for dinner at Rye. Leonard Crawley was a fine cricketer, opening the innings for Cambridge and Essex. He was invited to go on tour with MCC to Australia and with the British Walker Cup team round about the same time. I cannot think of a more difficult decision. Cricket's loss became golf's gain.

In Dayton, Ohio, I was invited to address 500 executives after lunch on the English mystique that is cricket. Fifteen minutes was allowed but my discomfiture, as I wriggled with complicated answers, caused such merriment that they were half an hour late back to their offices. They presented me with a baseball bat for good measure and left me with the promise that they would produce a team to beat us by the year 2000.

I have been on short cricket forays to Scotland, to Ireland, to Cornwall and to Guernsey and Jersey, each one of them with a hard core of cricket lovers. At Swansea, for my last match in Wales, I was presented with a miner's lamp, touchingly engraved, as a mark of appreciation. I was very moved by this.

As a member of an Old Tonbridgian cricket eleven which won the Cricketer Cup, our reward was a two-day visit to the champagne country, as guest of our sponsor, Moët and Chandon. The Common Market, it may be, but MCC have a big missionary job on their hands here. But it will come.

I flew for a week to India to play in a match and on another occasion to Pakistan for two big matches in aid of the Flood Relief Fund. Here I was under the captaincy of Rohan Kanhai and we enjoyed a hundred partnership together. For both of us it was a pleasant change to be batting alongside as friends when we had been enemies in Test matches for so many years.

E. W. (Jim) Swanton was the first to introduce me to West Indies when he invited me to captain his three-week tour to Barbados and Trinidad in 1956, and I have had a special affection for these sun-lit, happy isles ever since. There were to be other short tours to the Caribbean. Bagenal Harvey, whose organisation of the Rothman International Cavaliers was responsible for introducing us to one-day limited over cricket, invited me to captain their team to Jamaica. On my major MCC tours to West Indies we spent most of our time in Kingston and this short tour with Rothmans introduced us to the beauties of the North coast in a number of little townships, mostly by the sea, except for the Tate and Lyle ground at Mandeville and the Alcan Bauxite ground at Monimusk. I was to see some of this area again when I captained the Kent team on a three-week whistle-stop tour of the Caribbean, our prize for winning the John Player Sunday League in 1972.

I was on the small committee set up to raise money for the Frank Worrell Memorial Fund with the late Duke of Norfolk in the chair. At the end of one of these meetings he took me aside and said: "I would like to take a cricket team to West Indies after Christmas. After your triumph there, I imagine you may be invited to take the side to Australia. I would love you to captain my side and collect a number

237

of the most promising young cricketers in England, all of whom might have a chance of going to Australia with you." Naturally, I was thrilled to accept and we had the happiest possible month. It is interesting to look back on the names, most of them still making their way at that time. Denness and Greig is not a bad start, two men who were to captain England. Ward, Old, Birkenshaw, Underwood and Hobbs, Sharpe and myself—nine of us who were to play for England again.

It was on this tour that I saw the young Bernard Julien. He looked like Gary Sobers in embryo, caught a good slip catch, threw well from the boundary, opened with the new ball, bowled two varieties of spinners and could bat. It was a delight to meet his family in Port of Spain and as we discussed Bernard's future they put their trust in me when I said that if he came to Kent we would take good care of him. He has won a Test place and made a memorable Test hundred against England at Lord's. As I have said, his progress has been cruelly thwarted by injury, but here is a young man with talent in abundance, a heart as expansive as his smile; he could really make a great impact on the game.

It was typical of the Duke that he thought of including Charlie Elliott, our leading Test umpire of the day. It was on that tour that we visited Tobago, an enchanting island situated off Trinidad, with superb beaches, two townships, three cricket grounds and a lovely hotel and golf course complex belonging to a Sussex family, Pat and Ken Coghlan, cricket devotees. Tobago is charmingly unsophisticated, a place to relax in, and the Duke fell in love with it. He was not a man for holidays or being away from England, but on medical advice, as a result of his illness, he spent a few weeks each February in the sunshine, and Mount Irvine brought him many happy hours. Gordon Cunningham, the Scottish professional golfer, played with him most days.

He was very poorly when I left for Australia in December 1974 and it was no real surprise when the news of his death was relayed to the MCC team at Adelaide in January. "What was he like?" one of the players asked Alec Bedser. "He took a great interest in everyone. He was the kindest man I ever met. He really was a gentleman." It warmed my heart to hear Alec's reply.

Lavinia, Duchess of Norfolk, a fine sportswoman in her own right, is most anxious to see that cricket continues at Arundel and that the lovely ground is maintained. It is not going to be easy. But all those who enjoyed cricket there over the years, watching or playing, will feel moved to help in various ways, I am quite certain. Bernard, sixteenth Duke of Norfolk, was a man of many parts. But he was never happier than when playing host to cricketers on his ground in Arundel Park.

As my cricket-playing days recede I hope to make contributions to Barclays Bank International, with particular interest in those countries which, through cricket, I have come to know, and the House of Whitbread Fremlins the Brewers. If you play cricket for twenty-five years for the premier Hop County, it goes without saying that there is a close link between cricket and the brew that is essentially England.

For outside interests, I am indebted to Lord De L'Isle for inviting me to become a Member of the Council of the Winston Churchill Memorial Trust. The idea behind the memorial to the great man is to send about eighty Fellows a year on Travelling Fellowships to visit countries of their choice, a journey which will assist them to further their particular aspiration when they return to this country. There is a huge demand, and selection from the high quality short lists is both a fascinating and taxing responsibility. Lord De L'Isle takes great pride in his lovely private ground at Penshurst Place which can boast a cricket match against Dartford in 1724. It was a particularly happy day when we celebrated the 250th anniversary of this event in 1974 with the Kent eleven challenging an International Side in front of a huge crowd.

I am proud, too, to have become a Member of the Council of the Australia Society, based in London and formed to foster Anglo-Australian links.

In seeking to unearth more about spiritual things, a quest which was helped and encouraged by my family, I have been fortunate to have met and have come to know a number of saintly folk. Lawrence Waddy, Headmaster of Tonbridge; David Sheppard, Bishop of Liverpool; Cuthbert Bardsley, now retiring after fifteen years as Bishop of Coventry, have all influenced me a great deal in their various ways.

It was extraordinary that in my first University cricket match, the opposing captain on the one side, Sheppard, and Peter Blake on mine were to enter the Ministry. Moreover, Brian Boobbyer, playing in the match, has given his life to Moral Rearmament.

One of my close friends at Oxford, Ron Welldon, who was to die so young, introduced me to the work of Christian healing and went on to work at St. Christopher's Hospice, in south-east London. In 1973 I was to be introduced to, and greatly helped by, one of our most inspired healers, Mary Rogers, who lives and works in Sussex. Her visit to Australia coincided with the MCC tour in 1975 and it was rewarding to be a witness to her quite remarkable powers. I am convinced that this is a facet of the work of the Church, shrouded too long in mystery, which is becoming more widely accepted all the time.

As I set out into the cricket season of 1951, there was no certainty of how long I would last and what lay in store. We lived in uncertain times. The same applies today.

I am not expecting to play for Kent in the first half of the 1976 season, but in July and August they know that there is a loyal old 'un in the wings if it is that sort of reserve they are looking for at any particular time. In the years ahead there may be a call to some post, however humble, in the game's administration, but I shall play life slowly, a season at a time.

For the moment I am content to pause and savour the special favours this game has showered upon me: so much travel, so many people, such a long period close to the hub of the game. Happily, I have never grown tired of it and have managed to keep the cynics at arm's length.

Yes, I suppose the highs and the lows come through when I reflect now on the years in the game. Yet in retrospect even the bad times had their lighter side. When I gave up the Kent captaincy, having led them to the County Championship in 1970, I was tempted to stop. What more was there? But I was still the young schoolboy at heart and I had to keep playing. To be honest, I would love to have played for England for years as a batsman pure and simple without the encumbrance or the controversial wrangle of the captaincy. My conclusion was that I relished the camaraderie, day after day, in the dressing rooms and members' enclosures; the fresh challenge in the middle; new techniques; wrestling with old faults. Then off the field came the invitations to new places to meet new people. The last days were so different from the first. Is it nostalgia for the past, or is it true, that under Peter May my cricket days were happiest?

What else comes back to me? Gubby Allen was such a formidable figure in the game as chairman of the Selectors in those days. He and Peter May were the best combination in English cricket in my time. Gubby would go to such lengths to get things right. His critics chided him for being too long-winded but he was thorough and the players respected that.

There is an element of luck in team selection as to whether you are proved right or not. You may pick the logically right side for the match and the players may not come off on the day. But Peter May and Gubby Allen had a remarkable hat-trick in 1956. They picked David Sheppard out of Islington for the third Test match at Old Trafford and he scored a hundred. They picked Cyril Washbrook, aged forty-two, to strengthen the middle order batting for the fourth Test at Headingley and he made 98, and they recalled Denis Compton for the fifth Test at the Oval and he made 93. There was a trio of remarkable comebacks. If I had been chairman of the Selectors, after that, I would have felt like retiring and putting my feet up!

On the subject of comebacks, nothing gave me more pleasure than the restoring of Tom Graveney to the England side in the '60s, after a long break. Whilst he was a very fine strokemaker as a Gloucestershire man, he became a much more complete player with Worcestershire. I cannot help feeling that a mistake was made somewhere along the line when Tom Graveney slipped out of the England side for about five years. It was the happiest possible day when he made 96 at Lord's against Australia, the full house rising to him and giving him the reception he deserved. He was such a loyal friend to me on my tour of West Indies. By happy coincidence he was batting with me when I scored my 307 in Australia (I would never have done it without his cajoling) and again when I scored 100 in my 100th Test at Edgbaston. After a spell in Queensland and in Essex, it is now good to see him the benevolent and prosperous landlord of The Oak, near Cheltenham racecourse, happily secure in his native Cotswolds.

I have talked about Peter May before in this book, but I cannot speak too highly of him if I am to do him justice. He was a dedicated leader. He was able to get people to play for him. Failure meant that you had let him down, as much as the side. This is how it ought to be. I used to be his chauffeur at Test match time, picking him up in London so giving him time to prepare himself. We have talked over the tactics on the way to Trent Bridge, Old Trafford, Edgbaston and Headingley. At times my task was to commiserate and console—

above all to listen, to be ready to find something to smile over.

That is the time in a career, the early bustling days, when good friendships are formed, and these are so important to the esprit of a team. For instance, Peter Richardson and I became close friends. It was a friendship born of pressure because we opened the England batting together in his first five Tests. I had been thrown into the job without any experience at all of going in first, even ahead of good players like Don Kenyon, who was Peter's partner in Worcestershire, and Reg Simpson. When I returned to the Kent side between Tests I was able to sit back and watch a demonstration of opening an innings by Arthur Fagg, This was in 1956, and I was still trying to make the grade in the public gaze. From my first appearance in Tests with Len Hutton I was still learning, but in the England side, not just with Kent. Often I would go to the wicket with the same great apprehensions as the little boy who played for Tonbridge, and ask for guard from the umpire with a bold voice so that my trepidation would not be detected. However, in that 1956 series Peter Richardson and I put on two important partnerships, 151 at Trent Bridge and 174 at Old Trafford. Richardson was a romantic figure. His blond hair and relish for scampering the quick single caught the public imagination. He had a rare bubbling humour which led him into trouble from time to time, but it certainly enlivened grey days.

There was still a question mark surrounding my England place when 1957 came around. There was that disappointing tour in South Africa during the winter and now, in the new summer, the intricacies of Ramadhin and Valentine had to be sorted out as well as coping with the menace of Roy Gilchrist. It was a memorable period in English cricket when the talent was plain to see and I was fascinated to study each individual under pressure in a Test match situation, Tyson, Statham, Trueman, Wardle, Lock, Laker, Appleyard, Bailey, Graveney, Evans, Loader. Quite a thrill for a young player!

What else stood out in that favourite part of my career? Freddie Brown I think was a magnificent personality. He led MCC superbly in Australia in 1951. "Lettuces, lettuces, hearts as big as Freddie Brown," they shouted in the Sydney Market. He travelled as a journalist with Hutton's side and finally went as manager in 1958–9. He would bowl as long as you wanted him to in the nets in 1954, a lovely, lumbering action, full of slow rhythm, a classical shoulder action to create the dangerous loop in the flight of his leg-breaks. I admired his approach to cricket and it is one of my regrets that I did not play more with him. As manager he was, behind the bluff mask, the kindest, gentlest man, unselfish to a degree and always wishing the best for you.

I have always had an affection and admiration for Denis Compton. What young cricketer-footballer fan of my young schooldays was not entranced by the picture of Compton moving down the wicket to the slow bowlers or flitting down the left wing for Arsenal. Denis, more than anyone else I ever played with, was born to play games. I could not imagine him doing anything else. He was born, too, to give pleasure and radiate fun. As a batsman he was very correct in defence, highly unorthodox and adventurous in the destruction of bowlers. I only played with him, unfortunately, in the years after his celebrated knee injury, but Compton on one leg gave me more to enthuse about than most players on two.

Those who played in the Test match at Old Trafford in 1955 will surely never forget his two innings there against South Africa, 155 and 79 not out. His car had broken down *en route* and he had been brought to Manchester by a friend in a tiny plane. It was his only way of getting there on time and his kit had to be baled out, save for a pair of boots. On the morning of the match he wandered round the dressing room collecting odd pieces, rather like a star who has just opened the Christmas Fayre. When one considers how important the putter is to Jack Nicklaus as he sets out to win the British Open championship, one can imagine that the type of bat is rather important to a batsman's success. When I get a good one I am reluctant to let it out of my sight, but on this day Compton unearthed from the bottom of Freddie Titmus's bag a grubby and well-seasoned object, which might well have been on exhibition at Lord's as used by W.G., and he took it to the match. "What do you think of it?" said Godfrey Evans with a chuckle. "Nothing special," replied Denis who seemed, much to my astonishment, not the least concerned. We won the toss and he proceeded to play two of the greatest innings I have ever seen. The strokes poured out of this old bat with a mellow ring, it might have been Yehudi Menuhin at his special best.

I have a special affection for two Lancastrians, Geoff Pullar and David Lloyd. Geoff opened the batting with me throughout the tour of West Indies in 1959–60. Hall, Watson and Griffith were hostile, the bouncers common diet. Nothing would deter Geoff or ruffle his benign composure. We never had the slightest disagreement over running between the wickets, or anything else. We would both offer to take the worst of the bowling, if one of us was in more difficulty than the other. That is how I remember him, phlegmatic and generous even under that sort of pressure. What can I say of David Lloyd who took three consecutive overs of Lillee at Perth whilst I was able to break into things in that match? There is no more humorous cricketer than David.

In the bright West Indian sunshine I can picture David Brown and Robin Hobbs. I can see David after a day's bowling for MCC not having the strength to get a pen out of his pocket to sign an autograph. When we have been in a jam, and a couple of batsmen really going well, he has come to me and said: "A couple of overs before tea, skip?" You know he is whacked, but he is also prepared to run in and give you everything. He did just that in Trinidad and took three wickets in an over.

It would be impossible to spend a few hours on a cricket field with Robin Hobbs without feeling younger and the load lighter. He is a brilliant fielder and has the knack of being able to combine attacking, combative cricket with a twinkle in his eye.


On announcing my retirement in 1975, Tony Greig and the Sussex Committee paid me the huge compliment of inviting me to give three years to them in the hope of providing a source of encouragement and counsel to their young players. It came so unexpectedly. It swept me off my feet. The young schoolboy within ached to go on playing. Twenty-six seasons with Kent ... now forty-three, can I still play well enough to give a lead? ... in a poor economic climate in the country, can one afford to go on playing?—even W.G. kept a medical practice going, even if his confinements had to await the close of play.

Alas, it was time to go.

I have to go now with a first-class career coming to a close. It has been like tackling a vast jig-saw with a number of vital pieces missing. It has always been a search for the undiscoverable, getting warmer all the time but with never the slightest chance of mastery. May it be the same a hundred years from now, the game always bigger than the player.

# Index

# Index

248

249

Hill, Graham, 234
Hitler, Adolf, 20
Hobbs, Sir J. B., 13, 28, 30, 82
Hobbs, R. N. S., 178, 184, 188, 208, 238, 244
Hole, G. B., 68
Holford, D. A. J., 168, 182
Homefield Preparatory School, 24, 27 et seq., 36, 37
Hope, Bob, 59
Hough, G., 227
Howa, Hassan, 205–6
Howard, G. (team manager), 60, 80
Huddleston, Trevor (now Bishop of Stepney), 194
Huggett, B., 15, 236
Humphreys, E., 227
Hutton, Sir Leonard, 15, 24, 47, 51, 52, 57–65, 63–72, 82, 85, 100, 104, 105, 110, 119, 145, 221, 242
Hutton, Lady (Dorothy), 59

Iqbal, Asif, 97, 216, 217, 221, 228, 232, 233
Illingworth, R., 119, 122, 191, 197, 207–10, 220
India, 38, 115–17, 128, 151–3, 154, 169, 170, 171
Insole, D. R., 173–5, 198, 202, 209

Jackson, H. L., 44, 45, 89
Jamaica, 41, 101–2, 106–7, 112, 113, 136, 143, 145, 179–83, 185, 209, 237
Jardine, D. R., 68, 82, 115, 165
John Player Sunday League, 98, 224, 237
Johnson, G. W., 95, 217, 218, 232
Johnston, Brian (BBC correspondent), 201
Johnston, W., 67, 68
Jones, Jeff, 179, 192, 201, 202, 208
Julien, B. D., 229, 232, 233, 238

Kanhai, Rohan, 97, 107, 178, 189, 237
Kanpur, 117
Karachi, 186
Kaye, Danny, 59
Kent, 13, 14, 18, 42, 43 et seq., 47, 48, 52, 53, 54, 74, 75, 76, 78, 81, 82, 83, 86, 87, 88, 89, 91–2, 94, 95, 97, 112, 117, 122, 124, 125, 127, 144, 153, 159, 160, 169–71, 172, 197, 201, 206, 208, 211–

19, 220, 221–2, 223, 226–33, 237, 238, 239, 240, 242, 244
Kenyon, D., 175, 201, 242
King, Sam (golfer), 235
Kingston see Jamaica
Kipling, Rudyard, 115
Knight, B. R., 119, 196, 198, 200
Knott, A. P. E., 187, 190, 191–2, 213, 216, 217, 220, 231, 232
Knott, John, 43
Krishnan, 23

Laker, J. C., 54, 55, 60, 87, 100, 101, 145, 146, 242
Lancashire, 81, 97, 101, 144, 159, 169, 193, 212, 218, 219, 227, 229, 243
Langridge, J., 82
Larwood, H., 68, 82, 165
Laver, Rod (tennis player), 34
Lawry, W. M., 158, 200
Leary, Stuart (footballer), 230–1
Leeds, 24, 75, 80, 127, 157, 158, 168, 197, 208, 241
Leicester, 18, 86, 125, 200
Leicestershire, 33, 36, 38, 42, 191, 197, 198, 209, 217–18, 222
Levett, W. H. V. (President of Kent), 233
Lewis, Claude, 213, 232, 233
Leyton, 198
Lillee, D. K., 144, 224, 244
Lindwall, R. H., 60, 63, 72, 75, 105, 137, 144, 146
Lloyd, C. H., 81, 97, 159, 185, 219, 221
Lloyd, D., 223, 244
Loader, P. J., 100, 101, 146
Lock, G. A. R., 54, 55, 60, 87, 100, 144–5, 190–1, 222, 242
Locke, Bobby (golfer), 235
Lord, Thomas, 79
Lords, 14, 18, 24, 32, 37, 40, 41, 43, 44, 52, 54, 71, 74, 75, 79–80, 81, 88, 126, 127, 130, 131, 132, 138, 151, 158, 159, 162, 164, 166, 168, 172, 182, 196, 201, 202, 204, 221, 222, 224, 233, 238, 241, 243
Luckhurst, B. W., 214, 215, 216, 217, 220, 223, 232

McConnon, J. E., 55
McGilvray, Alan (Test commentator), 110

McGinnis, J. (writer), 128
McGlew, J. D., 123-4
McKenzie, G. D., 156, 222
Macmillan, Rt. Hon. Harold, 167
McMorris, E. D., 143
McNeill, J. (Tonbridge housemaster), 40
Maidstone, 213, 215, 218, 228
Malan, 'Sailor', 114
Mallett, A. A., 199, 224, 232
Manchester, 75, 80, 127, 136, 138, 154, 167, 193, 195, 196, 243
Marley, R. C. (Hon. Member of MCC), 181
Marsh, R. W., 14
Marshall, Howard (commentator), 51
Marylebone Cricket Club (MCC), 13, 14, 15, 22, 23, 34, 38, 51, 52, 54, 57, 59, 62, 64-5, 74, 75, 79 *et seq.*, 99, 110, 111, 115, 116, 119, 132, 133, 151, 153, 165, 172, 175, 181, 185, 195, 201, 202, 204, 205, 222, 227, 236, 237, 238, 240, 242, 244
May, P. B. H., 34, 36, 58, 59, 60, 67, 70, 72, 77, 84, 99, 102, 107, 119, 122 *et seq.*, 128, 167, 175, 180, 201, 213, 221, 223, 241
May, Virginia, 100
Mayes, R., 232
Meade, R., 234
Meckiff, I., 146, 147
Melbourne, 14, 34, 68-9, 111, 135, 138, 149, 223, 224
Menuhin, Yehudi (violinist), 243
Menzies, Sir Robert (Australian Prime Minister), 163
Middlesex, 42, 81, 82, 88, 99, 185, 201, 216, 240
Milburn, C. A., 168, 185-6, 196, 199
Miller, K. R., 71, 72, 75, 144
Milton, C. A., 49, 235
Muhammad Ali (boxer), 75
Mold, A., 144
Morris, A. R., 60, 64, 67, 70
Morris, Norman, 48
Moss, A. E., 123-4
Motz, R. C., 157
Murray, D. L., 178

Nabarro, Sir Gerald, 74
Nash, J. E., 80, 170
Nayudu, C. K., 115

Nepal, 236
New Delhi, 152
New Zealand, 57, 59, 73, 85, 114-15, 157-8, 190, 207, 220
Nicholls, D. K., 232
Nicklaus, Jack (golfer), 235, 243
Nida, Norman von (golfer), 235
Nixon, Richard M. (U.S. President), 128
Norfolk, 44
Norfolk, 16th Duke of, 17, 132-4, 209, 237-9
Norfolk, Lavinia, Duchess of, 238-9
Norrie, Sir Willoughby (Governor of New Zealand), 59
Norwich, 44
Northampton, 55
Northamptonshire, 49, 55, 74, 89, 232
Nottingham, 158, 168, 171, 209
Nottinghamshire, 44, 217, 227, 229

Oakman, A. S. M., 43, 114
Old, C. M., 238
Old Trafford, 80, 81, 136, 145, 193, 195, 221, 241, 242, 243 *see also* Manchester
Oppenheimer, Harry, 114
O'Reilly, W. J., 51, 87
Oval, 24, 42, 43, 44, 51, 52, 55, 56, 75, 80, 92, 110, 124, 125, 130, 154, 156, 157, 158, 168-9, 170, 172, 173, 174, 185, 190, 197, 198, 199, 200, 201, 213, 216, 217, 218-19, 230, 241
Overy, J., 213
Oxford University, 47-50, 51, 52, 53, 54, 73, 74, 76, 130, 166, 224, 236

Page, J. C. T., 213, 230
Pakistan, 55, 78, 97, 115, 116-17, 128, 169, 170, 171, 172, 186, 206, 217, 233, 237
Palmer, Arnold (golfer), 150
Parks, J. M., 43, 102, 159, 179
Pataudi, Nawab of, 186
Pawson, H. A., 232
Perth (Australia), 109, 111, 190, 191, 222
Pettiford, J., 212
Phebey, A., 231
Philip, Prince (Duke of Edinburgh), 15
Pitamber, Prince R. K., 236
Player, Gary (golfer), 150, 161, 206, 235
Pocock, P. T., 185, 190, 192, 209, 217
Pollock, Graeme, 53

Trinidad, 97, 101, 105–6, 112, 113, 178, 180, 185, 187, 189, 229, 233, 244
Trueman, F. S., 85, 88, 100, 119, 120, 126, 154–7, 242
Tucker, W. (surgeon), 201
Tunbridge Wells, 213, 227
Turner, F. M., 191
Tyson, C., 54
Tyson, F. H., 55, 60, 63, 66, 67–8, 69, 89, 100, 101, 144, 242

Ufton, Derek (footballer), 230–1
umpires, 124, 146, 147–8
Underwood, D. L., 78, 197, 216, 220, 232, 238

Valentine, B. H. (Captain of Kent), 14, 91, 213, 228, 233, 242
Voce, W., 165
Vorster, Dr. B. J. (South African Prime Minister), 195, 202–4

Waddy, Canon Lawrence (Headmaster of Tonbridge), 16–17, 239
Walford, Charles (Headmaster of Homefield), 27–32, 33, 35, 36
Walford, M. M., 82
Walker, M. H., 14, 227
Wallace, Boon, 205
Wandsworth Gaol, 15
Ward, A., 220, 238
Wardle, J. H., 52, 55, 68, 69, 100, 101, 242
Warr, John, 88
Warwickshire, 82, 85, 89, 91, 97, 171, 172, 198, 202, 221
Washbrook, C., 81, 82, 85, 241
Watson, Chester, 104, 105, 106, 244
Watson, W., 54

Weekes, E. D., 189
Weetman, Harry, 234–5
Welldon, R., 240
Wellings, E. M. (journalist), 117, 128–9
West Indies, 14, 41, 44, 52, 79, 97, 99, 101–3, 104–8, 112–13, 122, 123, 126, 135–42, 145, 146, 153, 159, 167, 168–9, 171, 172, 173–5, 176–92, 193, 195, 206, 207, 208, 209, 233, 237, 244
Wethered, Roger (golfer), 16
Whitbread-Fremlins (C.C. as Director of), 16, 239
White, J. C., 190
Willis, R. G. D., 220
Wilson, R., 231
Wilson, V., 70
Wiltshire, 44
*Wisden Cricketers' Almanack*, 63, 123, 136, 172, 212
Witherden, E., 232
wives, position of, 118–19
Wood, Jack, 80
Wooller, W., 55
Woolley, Sir Frank, 88, 139–40, 213, 226, 229
Woolmer, R. A., 216, 225, 232
Worcester, 197, 198, 230
Worcestershire, 49, 93, 193, 198, 221, 232, 241, 242
Worrell, Sir Frank M., 107–8, 135–6, 139, 141–2, 237
Wright, D. V. P., 45, 52, 81, 83, 87, 89, 111, 144, 211, 212, 231
Wyatt, R. E. S., 82

Yardley, N. W. D., 82
Yorkshire, 52, 54, 83, 92, 154, 169–70, 171, 172, 198, 208, 209, 212, 214, 227
Younis, Ahmed, 206